KU-176-205

Imogen Edwards-Jones is the co-author of the *Sunday Times* non-fiction bestsellers *Hotel Babylon*, *Air Babylon* and *Fashion Babylon* as well as author of the novels *My Canapé Hell*, *Shagpile*, *The Wendy House* and *Tuscany for Beginners*. She lives in west London.

Anonymous is the manager of an exclusive five-star island resort.

BEACH
BABYLON

IMOGEN EDWARDS-JONES
& Anonymous

CORGI BOOKS

TRANSWORLD PUBLISHERS
61-63 Uxbridge Road, London W5 5SA
A Random House Group Company
www.rbooks.co.uk

BEACH BABYLON
A CORGI BOOK: 9780552156868

First published in Great Britain in 2007 by Bantam Press
a division of Transworld Publishers
Corgi edition published 2008

Addresses for Random House Group Ltd companies outside the UK
can be found at: www.randomhouse.co.uk
The Random House Group Ltd Reg. No. 954009

The Random House Group Limited supports The Forest Stewardship
Council (FSC), the leading international forest certification organisation.
All our titles that are printed on Greenpeace approved FSC certified paper
carry the FSC logo. Our paper procurement policy can be found at
www.rbooks.co.uk/environment

Typeset in Sabon by
Falcon Oast Graphic Art Ltd.

Printed in the UK by CPI Cox & Wyman, Reading, RG1 8EX.

2 4 6 8 10 9 7 5 3 1

Mixed Sources
Product group from well-managed
forests and other controlled sources
www.fsc.org Cert no. TT-COC-2139
© 1996 Forest Stewardship Council

FSC

For KA

Acknowledgements

With very grateful thanks to Anonymous for his humour, generosity, trust and patience, to the wonderful Eugenie Furniss, the handsome Doug Young, the fabulous Laura Sherlock, the dashing Larry Finlay and all at Transworld for their fabulousness.

Prologue

All of the following is true. Only the names have been changed to protect the guilty. All the anecdotes, the situations, the highs, the lows, the scams, the drugs, the excesses, the mark-ups and the insanity are as told to me by Anonymous – someone who has spent the last twenty years in the business managing some of the very best resorts in the world. Although the incidents are real and the celebrities play themselves, the resort itself has been fictionalized and the stories, narrated by Anonymous, have been condensed into one busy week in the resort. But everything else is as it should be. The rich drink the cocktails, the poor make them, and everyone else tries to make sure there's enough caviar and pink champagne to go around. It's just another week in one of the world's top resorts.

Monday a.m.

It is six o'clock in the bloody morning and I'm already hot. I am always bloody hot. Tropical-island paradises are all very well if you can lie back, half-naked, on a lounger and sip a long, cool drink while someone else buffs your sunglasses. But try and do anything else, like wear clothes and manage one of the top-ten luxury resorts in the world, and you sweat. My freshly laundered linen shirt is already sticking to my back and my linen trousers are creasing around my balls. I'm also not feeling that bright. I drank a whole bottle of Dom last night in an attempt to de-stress after the hell of last week and I have one of those dry-mouthed champagne headaches that sits like a sharp needle behind my right eye. What I really need is a lie-down in a cool room, followed by a full English. Instead I am standing here at the end of the jetty, looking out to sea, waiting for one of our eighteen boats to arrive.

Fortunately I am only meeting our new deputy manager, Ben, and I have known him for a while, ever since we worked on reception together in a posh hotel in Kensington some five years ago. I've come a long way since then. I have climbed the greasy service-industry pole with speed and aplomb and landed myself one of the best jobs in the hotel industry. And now my mate's on board.

Dawn is blushing pink over the horizon, there's a smell of salt and hot spices in the air and I can see the white hull of the *Hummingbird* cutting through the water. The crew are manning their stations, dressed in their white shorts and polo shirts; they look impressive even at this distance. I have to say I've been a bit naughty and blown $600 by sending one of our two fifty-five-foot Sunseeker yachts to the mainland to collect Ben. Normally these only collect VIP guests; staff usually have to hang around at the airport and wait to come across on our daily gas-guzzling ferry, but I wanted to impress the pants off him and bring him over in some sort of style. I can see him standing on deck, waving. He looks a little incongruous in his dark suit and leather shoes. He's wearing a token pair of *Miami Vice* reflector shades.

The boat glides into the man-made harbour and moors up. The crew, like a well-oiled and well-drilled machine, throw down the ropes and help the tired-looking Ben down the gangplank.

'Ahoy!' he says as he lumbers towards me, getting back his land legs.

'Welcome to Alcatraz,' I smile, walking over to shake his clammy hand.

'Look at this fucking place,' he says, throwing his arms in the air. 'It's like fucking paradise!'

'It is, mate, it is,' I agree, smiling away as two of the crew walk past, carrying Ben's luggage. One of my front-of-house staff approaches with a small tray on which there's a cool, damp, tightly rolled hand towel and a chilled fruit-juice cocktail complete with straw and lotus flower.

Not that a drink and a quick rub-down are going to make much of a difference, because the bloke looks shit. But then again, most people look shit when they arrive here. It is something to do with the whole day they lose getting here. One of the problems of holidaying in the middle of nowhere and getting the true Robinson Crusoe experience is that it takes so bloody long to arrive you need a holiday to get over the flight. Even if you do fly First Class, or come on your own jet, which I have to say most of our guests do.

But poor Ben has come steerage and he has the bloated face and creased suit to prove it. At least this will be his last time travelling with the hoi polloi – one of the perks of being a manager here is a Club Class ticket home. It wouldn't be good for the image of the hotel if one of the guests were to bust us travelling Economy Class. And this place is all about image. Image and artifice. Christ, half the island wasn't even here ten years ago. It's been added to and enlarged by brute force and concrete so many times that no one can quite remember where nature left off and man began.

I can tell Ben's impressed because he is quiet, trying to take it all in. We walk along the jetty and through reception. Unlike the fairly shitty desk-and-phone set-up we used to man together a few years ago, this place is an open Balinese pagoda with huge pillars, stone statues, bubbling water features and white marble floors. There are fat comfortable sofas, low tables laid with fans of meet-and-greet booklets, huge tropical floral displays in five-foot-high vases and ocean views whichever way you turn. We have a couple of stunning Thai girls on reception at the moment, plus three buggy drivers hanging around outside to take you wherever you want to go. Ben can't quite believe it. He walks very slowly behind me, gently muttering 'Wow' to himself at every new thing he encounters. Finally he finishes his drink, hands back his used towel and joins me on the other side of reception.

'I can't believe this place,' he says, shaking his head.

'How long have you been the manager here again?'

'Eighteen months.'

'But it's like you're running a small country,' he says.

'I know,' I say, nodding at one of the buggy drivers, who leaps into his golf cart and accelerates towards us.

'And you're the despot.'

'I'm not a despot,' I say, thinking I am more of the benevolent-dictator type.

'But you've changed the time here on the island,' he says, looking at his watch and comparing it with the large clock on the wall. 'You're an hour behind the mainland. What's that about?'

'Making a statement,' I say. The driver travels the three yards to the front of reception and gets out of the buggy, vacating the driving seat for me. I sit down and indicate for Ben to sit next to me.

'What sort of statement?'

'That this is our own place and we can do what we want. Although,' I smile, 'ever since our head office has moved to the UK it has slightly buggered things up. It means we have to stay late in the office to make conference calls to London, which is a little pissing-off. We did think about having summer and winter times on the island and then about taking the clocks back two hours to make it easier for ourselves. But then I realized that the sun would set at about four thirty, which is not the best time for a cocktail.'

'No,' he agrees. 'I imagine that there might have been a few complaints from the guests.'

'So,' I say, rubbing my hands together. 'A tour of the island? The morning meeting and then I'll show you where you're living?'

'Sounds perfect to me.'

I floor the buggy accelerator and set off down one of the numerous white-sand tracks that zigzag across the island. With 120 acres of lush tropical forest, the island has a ten-kilometre coastline, fifteen sandy beaches and some 20,000 coconut trees. Each of the guest suites is a minimum of 900 square feet of freestanding luxury villa. They have plasmas, surround sound, double beds, sitting areas, terraces, sunken baths and a shower both indoor and out, plus direct access to the beach and stunning sea views. Some have their own swimming pools. Others are built on stilts over the ocean. And some have their own swimming pools as well as being built over the ocean. Each villa has at least one host who is on call 24/7 to cater to the guests' every whim and command. This is extreme luxury for the extremely discerning and comes at an exclusive price tag. We have six categories of room and prices range from $1,500 to $6,000 a night – and that's before you've had a glass of wine and cracked open a packet of Pringles, which despite being three dollars a half-tube in the minibar are always very popular. We have 140 villas, numbered from 100 to 240, and over 800 staff, which means the employee-to-guest grovel ratio is very high. So not only do we attract the rich and famous to our little tropical island, we also cater for the extremely high maintenance indeed.

I'm cutting through the undergrowth as quickly as I can. Part of me – OK, all of me – is showing off to Ben, proving I know this place like the back of my hand and that these shitty buggies can shift over 20mph with a good wind behind them and a Schumacher-in-waiting at the wheel. We speed past various groundsmen clearing up fallen leaves and cutting back the rapacious undergrowth; they all pause and nod as the managerial cart goes by. I feel a bit like a feudal landlord; the effect is not lost on Ben.

'This is like a fantasy island,' he grins, a sheen of old-alcohol sweat breaking out across his cheeks.

I smile back at him, noting my infinitely more soigné reflection in his shades. 'On your left,' I say, 'is the gym.'

Ben looks over at the fabulously designed pavilion of fitness. Set right at the water's edge so you can jog off all that expense-account fat while staring at the ocean. Equipped with all the latest gadgets, Pilates and medicine balls, it is staffed by various international gym nuts, including Keith, a sixteen-stone brick-shit-house from South Africa. He is one of those rippling silent types who drink protein shakes and chug back the amino acids. He also cures his own biltong in the staff village.

'It looks empty in there,' says Ben, peering over the top of his shades.

'It's a bit early for guests,' I say. 'They tend not to surface until at least eight o'clock and don't go to the gym until after breakfast.'

We carry on winding our way through the lush forest. The sun is up now and you can already feel its heat as it penetrates the undergrowth to gently grill your skin. Spending all this time out here has made me very weary of exposing myself to its rays. I have lost count of the number of times I have seen grown men so scarlet and burnt they've been incapable of walking in to breakfast, having fallen asleep after a liquid lunch the day before. They end up with skin so red raw and hot you could sizzle a rasher of Danish on their nuked thighs.

'There's the spa,' I add, pointing through the palms. 'It doesn't look anything from the outside but inside it's fucking fantastic.'

'It looks pretty fucking fantastic from here,' says Ben, eyeing up the gaggle of Filipino and Thai women dressed in white uniforms walking into reception.

'We've got eighteen therapists, each doing six treatments a day, seven days a week, with one hour for lunch.

The place is open twelve hours a day and still we get complaints that it is too difficult to get an appointment.'

'It must make money, then?' asks Ben.

'Sadly it's a franchise with some French company that trains the girls and sends them here. We only get 10 per cent of the profits, about $120,000 a month. But the girls in there get the best tips.'

'I bet they do,' he says, licking his dry lips.

'About $1,500 each, over and above their $600 basic.'

'Shit. Really?'

'Who would have thought that a few creams, a rub and a lie-down could generate so much money?'

'Yeah,' agrees Ben, running his hands through his lank dark hair. 'I suppose it's all those high-maintenance Russian mafia birds.'

'Weirdly, we have almost as many blokes as women.'

'That's metrosexual millionaires for you.' He shrugs. 'It was nearly all birds, bitches and concubines where I was in Mexico. I thought the place I was managing there was swish, but this is something else.'

I have to say it's good to have Ben here. Not only is it great to have someone who has the same language and sense of humour, someone from the old days, but it is also nice to have someone to show how far you've got. To share the spoils of all your hard work, to see what you've made of yourself. My girlfriend Kate is appreciative. But she didn't know me when I was full of caffeine and half-inched bottles of vodka, pulling double shifts to pay the rent. We met in the Four Seasons in Bali and fell in love over mohitos and shadow puppets in Ubud. We've been together two years; she followed me here, and after one week of unemployment she ended up running the island boutique.

'Here we are, then,' I say to Ben, pulling up outside a rather unprepossessing line of wooden buildings. 'Here's where it all happens.'

'Oh, right,' says Ben, getting out of the buggy and stretching in the sun. He has managed to sweat right the way through his suit and already has salt stains under his arms. 'You would have thought with all the profit you lot are making they might have given you a nice set of offices.'

'Profit? Who said anything about profit?'

'What?' he says, looking a little stunned. 'You mean you don't make a profit here?'

'We have a $55-million turnover and we still don't make a profit.' I smile. 'Welcome to the wonderful world of luxury resorts, mate. Shall we?' I pull open the heavy glass door and a cold blast of air-conditioning escapes. 'We've got some introductions to make.'

I usually call the morning meeting between eight and eight thirty, but today it is slightly earlier than usual so that everyone can have the opportunity to meet Ben and get to know him a little before the shit hits the collective fan. We walk past my office – through the glass I can see that my desk is already loaded with the endless amounts of paper I have to sign off – and make our way down the corridor towards the meeting room. Inside is a long polished table surrounded by high-backed chairs. In front of each chair is a green blotter, a pad of paper, some freshly sharpened pencils and a bottle of imported mineral water. Looking around the table, taking in the slightly tanned faces, I can see that almost everyone is here already. It is a long list – the front-office manager, the financial controller, the resident manager, the director of human resources, the training manager, the head of housekeeping, the senior villa host, the IT manager, the purchasing manager, the sales manager, the spa manager, the bar manager, the chief engineer, the security manager, the reservations manager and, finally, the recreation manager. In fact, more managers than you can shake a fucking clipboard at.

Hilariously this is not some overzealous display of unity put on for Ben's benefit. All these people turn up to the morning meeting every day. The size and infrastructure of the island dictate that we all need to meet once a day, otherwise we'd be frantically driving around on our buggies, hoping to bump into each other

 Beach Babylon

in order to sort out what the hell was happening. This way at least we have so-called face-time before we all piss off to our various little empires.

The last person to arrive is Geri, the rather rotund spa manager who came to us from Liverpool via Soneva Fushi, or was it Gili? I can never remember. Anyway, she was poached by Dave, our recently departed deputy manager who flew to the Maldives on a minibreak for some R&R and a little industrial espionage, only to come back with Geri and a very good pastry chef. She walks into the room and immediately starts with some long-winded story that involves early-morning tears and tantrums and a fallout between the Shiatsu masseuse and a Thai manicurist in the spa.

'They're a breed apart, those girls,' she huffs, plonking herself down next to me. 'They're all so bloody sensitive.'

With everyone sitting down, I launch into a bit of a welcome speech for Ben. I tell them how we met in Kensington. How he always used to try and sleep his way through his shifts. And how, against all the odds, he became a big swinging dick in the Gulf of Mexico, turning some piece-of-shit loser resort around into a five-star destination-holiday hangout. I add that I hope he will be another steady hand at the tiller of this glittering six-star establishment. There is a polite ripple

22

of applause as everyone welcomes him to the island. However, looking around the table, I can see that Bernard's long Gallic nose is already out of joint. He was rather hoping to be promoted after Dave was unceremoniously sacked for having his hand in the till and copies of the keys to the cellar, which contains over 9,000 bottles of rare and vintage wines, in his room. But head office and I had other plans.

Ben's welcome out of the way, we get down to business. Bernard goes through the logbook of yesterday's events. Sunday is my day off and as I am a bit of a control freak I tend to be a little nervous about Monday's logbook. Who knows what might have happened while my back was turned and I was swilling down some bubbles?

'So,' says Bernard, clearing his throat. 'We've got the German industrialist in villa 130 under house arrest.'

'What the fuck?' I say, leaping out of my chair.

'It was the only option,' insists Bernard, shifting in his seat. 'Mohammed? Back me up on this . . .' He looks around the table for support.

'How? Why?' I am looking from surly Bernard to surlier Mohammed, head of security. 'What the fuck happened?'

Bernard launches into a story about how this German got so pissed last night that he forced the lock on one of the buggies parked outside the main restaurant and drunk-drove it at great speed the length of the island. He was chased by security, crashed the buggy, then tried to run away from the scene of the crime. He didn't get very far as he was too drunk to run in a straight line and was detained by two guards. He fought with the guards, hit one and was eventually overcome by another two. He was escorted back to his villa and told to sleep off the $650 bottle of 1998 Philip Togni Cabernet Sauvignon he had consumed. This morning, while I was on the jetty meeting Ben, they had apparently approached the man and asked him to leave. At which point his wife had cried like a baby and asked to stay. The husband practically went down on his knees and begged, so they suggested that he wrote a letter binding him over to keep the peace.

'And here it is,' says Bernard, waving it in the air. 'He has signed it and sworn that he will not leave his villa for the whole of his stay here.'

'So let me get this right,' I say, looking at the scrawled note. 'He is paying $2,500 a night to sit in his villa all day and not come out?'

'That was the only way,' says Bernard.

'I know we have a no-violence policy,' I nod. 'But I can't believe he agreed to it.'

'His wife made him sign – she was desperate to stay. I don't think she could cope with the embarrassment of going back early to Hamburg.'

'Yeah,' agrees Geri. 'I mean, what would she say to the neighbours?'

'I don't think she is the sort of woman to have neighbours,' says Bernard rather sniffily.

'Anything else?' I ask.

'No, that's it from last night,' he replies.

'Not too bad.' I smile and rub my hands together. 'Not too bad at all. So,' I turn to our reservations manager, Garry, a handsome blond queen, appropriately from Queensland. 'How's occupancy and who's coming?'

'Right,' he says, sitting up and smiling. Garry's all eyes and teeth – and ears. He always has the best gossip. Give him a beer and he'll tell you exactly who is doing what and to whom on the island. So he is the perfect person to be in charge of VIPs and finding out who might be VIPs. 'Occupancy is running at 97 per cent, which is up 8 per cent on last year, and what we would normally expect around this time of year.'

Unlike a city hotel with a steady flow of businessmen, our occupancy rates vary enormously; and also, unlike city hotels, we can't cover our arses by double-booking rooms and overbooking suites, because we have nowhere to put extra guests and nowhere to bump them on to. We're an island in the middle of fucking nowhere, and when people finally get here, the least we can do is give them a cold towel and a bed. Having said that, our client list is also very seasonal. The rich, famous and connected tend to come here in the winter. High season is November until the end of March – with a fistfight for villas over the Christmas and New Year period and a gentle brawl for Easter and half-term. Low season is June to October, when the high-spend, high-end market gravitates towards their villas in the Med and their yachts in the south of France. Leaving us to cope with mainly Brits, who think they have made it but haven't quite. The room rates halve and so does the spending power of the clientele. They don't have money for the extras and complain at every turn. Thankfully, it is November and the lowlife has gone home. It's only high spenders from now on.

He continues, 'I've checked the list and Googled everyone. We've got three VIPs, two returnees and Liz Hurley's here to do a bikini shoot.'

'Liz Hurley?' sniffs Ben from the corner of the room. 'She's fucking hot.'

There's a general murmur of male approval around the table, followed by a five-minute discussion about just how hot La Hurley actually is. All the blokes are enthusiastic, it's just the women who dissent and I suspect that's sour grapes. I look across at Ben, who still looks uncomfortable in his suit but seems to have perked up no end. I have to say I am a little less impressed by the prospect of Liz Hurley. I have seen so many beautiful women in various states of undress and total nakedness that it is going to take more than the million-dollar face of Estée Lauder to put lead in this hungover, jaded pencil. However, Garry's mention of Mr McCann, the owner of a TV channel in the States, is enough to get my juices flowing.

'He's got a Grand Villa and a couple of Water Villas,' lists Garry, running his finger down his occupancy page. 'And he's coming in on his own jet this afternoon. He's expected at four on the mainland and has booked a private transfer. As he is a returning guest, he's said you don't have to meet him on the mainland.'

'Oh,' I say. 'How much was his bill last time?'

'Just under half a million US,' says Garry. 'His requests are simple. Duck-down pillows, Cristal in the minibar, and – oh,' he adds, looking up, 'he's bringing his own girls.'

'Girls?' asks Ben.

'Girls,' I nod.

'Oh, girls.' Ben nods back, finally twigging. 'Girls, girls.'

'Jesus Christ.' I roll my eyes and look at him. 'It must have been a very long flight.'

Monday p.m.

Ben was forced to sit in his stiff suit for another half-hour or so while I went through the rest of Garry's Googlings. I know it sounds mad to check out the guests at a resort that purports to be a get-away-from-it-all haven, where we don't expect people to dress for dinner, but you would be surprised how many times even the most incognito person resorts to the 'Do you know who I am?' line, just as soon as they can't get the wine they want, or a six p.m. massage. So instead of the staff simply shrugging and saying, 'No idea, Mr Gates,' everyone gets the once-over before they come here, so we don't miss a trick, or indeed the world's richest man. We also check to see if they have stayed with us before and go through their records, noting their little whims and foibles and marking down any problems and difficulties we had with them last time they were here. And nine times out of ten, the potentially difficult guest's name crops up again in the morning meeting. Leopards don't change their spots, no matter how loaded they are.

And neither, it appears, has Ben. Way back when we were louche boys on reception, he used to be doing the girl from housekeeping in various rooms at various slack times of day in the hotel. Any room that was vacant and inspected was fair game for a quick one. He's only been here a few hours and he is already flirting with Ingrid, the new, relatively sexy Danish girl in public relations. She is laughing and flicking her blonde hair and he is giving her the best smile a jet-lagged bloke can muster. She's impressed. I feel a sharp frisson of irritation, rapidly followed by dread. Maybe hiring Ben wasn't the best decision after all. I direct him to get on my buggy and tell him we're off to the staff village to show him his accommodation. He gives Ingrid's arm a squeeze and I can tell it is only a matter of a few drinks down the staff bar before they're something for Garry to gossip about.

We drive along the sandy path that snakes past the main dining room and pool area, which, I have to say, is the pièce de résistance of the hotel. Linked by wooden slatted walkways, the main restaurant is perched on pillars and juts out into a bay of turquoise sea. Open to the elements, there are stunning views on the three sides. Next to it is the beach and three separate swimming pools. The first is a horizon lap-pool. Made of smooth black slate, it has fresh-water showers by the steps with two sunken granite sun decks at the other end. Another is a whirling, swirling mass of small pools and fountains and bubbling jacuzzi areas, while the third is a small shallow splashing area for children. There is a beach bar that pumps out rum and reggae, hundreds of white-towel-covered loungers and hot and cold running service to keep even the most demanding guests satisfied. Books and magazines are laid out on a few tables. There are iPods for general use, plus jugs of iced lemon water, circulating trays of sliced fruit and little china tasting spoons of ice cream. There are cold towels for your comfort and convenience and, of course, the bloke to buff your sunglasses. Little wonder, then, that once a guest has plonked himself in the sun here, it is hard for him to move.

Ben looks slightly overawed.

'No wonder this place has got six stars,' he says, pushing his *Miami Vice* shades up his sweaty nose. 'I have never seen anything like it.'

'Amazing, isn't it?' I reply, as I make a sharp left through the undergrowth into the staff village. 'And here is where everyone lives.'

When I say everyone, I obviously mean the staff, because the village itself is actually so well hidden in the middle of the island that I'm sure most of the guests don't even know it exists.

I park the buggy next to the giant sewage works that occupies the middle of the staff village, along with the generators and the reverse-osmosis plant that takes thousands of gallons of seawater and converts them into drinking water. As I turn I see the look on Ben's face. To say that he appears disappointed is an understatement.

'Is this it?' he asks.

'What do you mean?' I say, looking around the place. I am so used to it I suppose I have ceased to notice quite what it looks like.

'Where are the sea views?' he asks.

'Sea views?' I start to laugh. 'You don't think we're going to waste a sea view on staff, do you?'

'Do you mean I have come all this way and escaped the noise of the city to sleep next to a generator and inhale the gentle aroma of other people's shit?'

'It doesn't smell of shit,' I say, breathing in. Actually, come to think about it, it does a bit. 'It's only the direction of the wind. You'll get used to it.'

'Yeah, right,' he says. 'I'll look forward to that.'

'Honestly, mate.' I slap him on the back. 'Things aren't that bad. It's only because you are tired. Look,' I say, trying to sound optimistic, 'your room isn't bad.'

Truth is, he has the best accommodation in the place.

As the highest-ranking manager after me, he has a small wooden house complete with sitting room, kitchen, bedroom and veranda. He has a TV and I have pinched him a DVD player from the stockroom, just to make him feel a little more at home. Granted the place is tiny and the view is of the carpentry area, where they are currently refurbing twenty of our nine hundred sunbeds; but if he only knew what the rest of the staff accommodation was like he'd be thanking his promotional stars.

Everyone else has to share and it depends on how low down the pecking order you are as to how many you share with. Kitchen cleaners, gardeners and villa cleaners are housed six to a room. The village was not originally built to cope with this many staff, but we found after we opened some ten years ago that we needed around eight hundred staff to keep the show on the road. So we put bunk beds in the rooms and hoped for the best. Next up are the waiters, who are four to a room. The villa hosts are in twins, sharing their bathroom with another twin. Supervisors have single bedrooms, sharing their bathroom with one other person. Department heads, such as the guys at the morning meetings, are in single accommodation with a small patio and their own bathroom, and only executives like Ben have the sitting room, the kitchen, the veranda and the bathroom to themselves. Anyway, staff accommodation has always been shit. I am not sure exactly what he was expecting.

'It's like a fucking kibbutz,' says Ben, watching a buggy pull up outside his villa with his suitcases. 'I mean, look at all the washing hanging out and the vague attempts people have made to personalize their space with a few plants. It's like a South American slum, and let me tell you,' he mutters, 'I have seen plenty of them.'

'It's only because you need to get used to it,' I say. 'There's the team bar down there.' I point to an area with a pool table, a large TV for football and various tables and chairs gathered around a wooden bar covered in flags of all the twenty-seven different nationalities that we have in the village. 'That's a riot in the evening. The drinks are cheap and there is different food every night for a dollar. Monday night is pizza night, Tuesday is burgers, Wednesday is hot dogs, and so on. Every couple of weeks or so everyone gets fresh crab from the mainland.'

Ben just looks at me. His white face is puffy and sweaty; his mouth is curling with sarcasm. 'Fuck me sideways,' he says. 'It sounds fantastic.'

'The staff restaurant is nice,' I say. 'There are salads and things like that. There's a shop for toothpaste and chocolate . . .'

'Right,' he says.

'And you can have mates to stay and they can eat in the canteen for around eight dollars a meal.'

'Why would I want to do that?' he asks.

'I don't know,' I reply. 'I am only saying.'

We walk along together, making a tour of the village. Ben kicks bits of rubbish with his leather-soled shoes. Perhaps I should have warned him. I am feeling racked with guilt now. It is such a responsibility employing a mate. You want them to have a good time, and enjoy working here, and at the same time you want them to be the best person at their job. Judging by the way Ben's reacting I don't think he is going to do either.

There's a wailing noise coming from the loudspeaker attached to the side of one of the buildings.

'Jesus!' Ben jumps. 'What the fuck is that?'

'It's the imam calling the staff to prayer in the mosque,' I say.

'What? You've got a mosque?'

'That's right. Fully functioning. It's behind you.'

'That'll come in handy,' he says, not bothering to look up, kicking an empty Diet Sprite can across the track, 'when I fucking convert. Honestly,' he adds, putting his hands in his suit pocket and sighing loudly, 'it's no wonder you have problems recruiting and keeping staff.'

Well, he's not wrong there. People are always pissing off halfway through their contracts. It usually happens at around ten months. It's almost as if they reach some sort of tipping point where they can't stand living in paradise any more. There's too much sun, sea and bloody sand; they just have to make a run for it. If you last two years here you should get given a medal. I'm only eighteen months in and I have to say I'm feeling it.

You can't go to the movies. You can't go to a restaurant, apart from the three that are on the island. You can't drive a car. God, do I miss driving. The speed, the smell, the sound of the engine. You can't go to the pub. You can't get a pint. You can't eat anything that doesn't come presented in a fucking gourmet tower. All I want is a Guinness and a packet of pork scratch-ings. I want to go somewhere where I'm anonymous, where no one wants to ask my opinion on something, somewhere where I can sit quietly, gently sipping my pint, watching West Ham get relegated. It's not much to ask, is it?

All you can do here is work, go to your room or get shit-faced in the team bar. Everyone does it. They get pissed almost every night. Hans, the six-foot-three German dive instructor, refers to the team bar as his sitting room and is in there every night until either it closes at eleven or he falls over. Whichever happens first. Mind you, he is the only member of staff here to have broken the five-year barrier so he is a little bit strange.

They either drink or they shag. There is a huge amount of sex going on. And for some reason the Japanese sushi chef seems to be getting most of it. I don't know whether it is the long hair or the knives, but Yoshiji seems to get the girls going no matter where they're from. I have lost count of the number of weeping females I have had in my office, complaining how he's broken their heart. Another thing I have noticed is that everyone who turns up here with a steady boyfriend back home always seems to ditch him within the first month of being here. Relationships don't seem to last the long distance and the weird time zones.

But strangely, when it comes to sex in the staff village, there's an international divide as well. The Indians and the Sri Lankans stick together. The Thai girls hang out with the Filipinos, exchanging giggles and manicures and pedicures under the trees. The locals are not allowed to drink with or be in the same room as a member of the opposite sex, unless they are married, which kind of limits their fun. Meanwhile, the Westerners all sleep with each other. So in fact the only person who has truly international relations is Yoshiji.

It's no wonder then that we have a drug problem in the village. You would've thought because we are an island in the middle of nowhere that we would be immune to the vagaries of modern-day living. But apparently not. I know that some guests choose to bring cocaine in on their private jets or have supplies of the stuff in their super yachts that we moor offshore. However, none of this filters down to the staff, so we turn a blind eye. Just so long as we don't see the mirrors and notes, there is nothing much we can do about it. But it's not coke in the staff village. It's smack. Or brown sugar as they call it here.

There's always been a bit of a heroin problem on the mainland, in the very poor areas in and around the capital, just like any other metropolitan city, I suppose. But we have only just recently started to get it here. We've always had hash hanging around and I am of the opinion that there is nothing wrong with a few spliffs after a hard day at the coalface of the hospitality industry. It only ever makes you want to snooze and eat a bit more. But one of the gardeners reported a drug deal going on on one of the beaches the other day. It was three thirty p.m., which I thought was a little extreme. At first I didn't believe it, however when the culprits came into my office and claimed that they were simply buying and selling a CD, but couldn't agree on the band, I knew something was up. The guy from the watersports centre said it was Robbie Williams. *The waiter couldn't think of any music he might like* to listen to, and just stared at me like a moron when I asked him. It turned out that the boat boys were bringing the stuff across in the resort catamarans and flogging it in the village.

I don't know why I was surprised. It is always the boat boys who have the drugs. Go to any resort anywhere in the world and they're the ones with the hash and the pills and, as it turns out here, the smack. Perhaps it's the sort of job that attracts those types of people. Beach bums who like a smoke need to earn a living somewhere. Or maybe it is the job that makes them that way. It's not exactly taxing, shoving fat businessmen into Lasers and rescuing them half an hour later from the house reef. Anyway, wherever I have been working all over the world, the rule of thumb is, if you want to score go to the boatsheds.

So the boat boy was terminated and escorted off the island on the staff ferry, and I presume half of my silver-service staff went cold turkey over the weekend. Still, most of them turned up for work on Monday, which is more than I could have hoped for. But then I suppose they need the money. As does everyone who works here.

Not that we get paid a huge amount. The gardeners are on $50 a month, the villa hosts on $350. The pedicurists in the spa are on $1,000 and I'm on $10,000. But you have to remember that not only do we eat, drink and live for free while we are on the island, we get tips and service charge on top of that. So the guys in the spa take home about $2,000 gross a month, including their tips, and the villa hosts can double their salary as well. So none of us are doing too badly in the end. Except the gardeners, poor sods, who don't get tipped at all.

I am about to launch into some sort of motivational speech with Ben, telling him about his prospects within the group, about how prestigious this resort is and how bloody brilliant it is going to look on his CV, when my mobile goes.

'Hi, *merde*, where are you?' It is Bernard.

'In the staff village,' I say. 'Why?'

'Because you are supposed to be with me at Palm Sands beach doing a wedding.' He is whispering loudly down the phone.

'Fuck.'

'Yeah, double fuck,' he says.

'Stall them,' I say.

'How am I supposed to do that?' he says. 'They are standing right in front of me.'

'I don't know,' I say. 'Take some photos.'

'I have done that already.'

'Take some more!'

I make my excuses to Ben, who petulantly makes his way over to his villa. He'll feel much better once he's had a sleep, I think as I leap into my buggy and floor the accelerator. God, what I would give for a real car.

I turn right outside the village and head towards Palm Sands beach in the north of the island where we do most of our weddings. There's a nice view with some swaying palms and usually a boat or two in the background. I have lost count of how many times I have stood under the flowered pagoda, sweating my bollocks off in my linen trousers, grinning for the camera with my arm around the bride and groom, giving it my best general-manager face for the in-house photographer who also doubles as a pastry chef. We have so many weddings on the island you can't blame me for forgetting.

We've got eleven this month and they're almost all Japanese. We have a special package for $2,600 per couple where they get married on the beach and have one candlelit dinner as part of the deal. The bride also gets her hair and make-up done by girls from the mainland, as well as a manicure and floral headdress and bouquet – though I have to say the ceremony is not legal. It is more or less a blessing on the beach, performed by either Bernard or myself or, if we are both busy, then anyone else who happens to be around at the time. Not that the bride or groom really know what the hell is going on anyway. They almost never speak English, which doesn't matter per se, but is somewhat problematic when it comes to repeating the vows. You could say 'I hereby declare you are divorced' and they would simply mutter 'High, high' and be none the wiser.

I also can't help thinking, as I park up my buggy and walk briskly through the palms, that it is not that romantic. Kate and I are going to have the biggest piss-up known to mankind when we get married – we're going to fly people in from all over the world to this small beach town on the east coast of Australia where she is from. When I finally get around to popping the question, that is. But these guys just fly in on their own. They get married on the Monday and then spend the rest of the week snorkelling. I don't call that a send-off, but then, you know, each to their own.

'Good afternoon!' My smile is broad but if you look closely the eyes are not exuding sincerity. But my hand is outstretched and the fingernails were trimmed and buffed yesterday afternoon in the spa. The bride and groom smile and bob their heads. They are both short and slim and so very young-looking. The girl is rather cute in her floor-length white silk dress. The skinny straps are almost the same colour as her skinny white shoulders. But the groom looks a little stiff in his black suit jacket and open-neck white shirt. His shiny black shoes are slipping into the sand. He is not the most uncomfortably dressed young man I have seen. We do get quite a few who do it in full black tie. But not usually in the middle of the afternoon.

Bernard pisses off almost as soon as I arrive. He's going to make sure Mr McCann's villa collection is up to scratch. The bloke and his 'girls' are supposed to be arriving some time this evening. But seeing as he is coming in a private jet, it could be any time.

The wedding goes without a hitch. They are married before you can say 'I do' – which of course neither of them can. I have to admit I speed things along a bit. I skip a few of the boring bits about people objecting. The beach is empty, bar a couple of horizontal guests and the photographer, so I can't imagine that being a problem. I cut straight to the snog and the ring, which, let's face it, is the best bit. As I am standing there, my arms in the air, presiding over the marital kiss, this vision of bikini-clad loveliness comes towards me. She is wheeling one of the 280 resort bikes and is followed by a photographer and an assistant carrying a large silver reflecting circle.

'Jesus Christ,' I mutter. 'Is that Liz Hurley? I think I'd better check in on her beach barbecue this evening.'

'High, high,' agree the newly-weds, looking up at me.

Monday Sunset

Just over half an hour of photographing later and the Japanese newly-weds are firmly ensconced in the back of their buggy, doing the scenic tour of the island, stopping off at more photogenic spots on the way. The route includes the swimming-pool area, the main restaurant, the dive-boat jetty and the main reception. The photographs are then mounted into a special book and presented to the happy couple as a gift when they leave the hotel. You see, it is not all take, take, take in this business, sometimes we like to give a little something back as well.

Meanwhile, with the newly-weds out of the way, I go and introduce myself to Miss Hurley. Since she arrived during my day off and I've been tied up with meetings and Ben all morning, this is the first time that I have had a chance to meet her. And she is really rather stunning and delightfully plummy. She is also apparently rather low-maintenance. She is loving the hotel, and can't find a thing wrong. Which must be a first.

Celebrities tend to be the bane of our lives in this business. Unlike the Russians or Arabs or City-rich businessmen, the famous swan in here, waft around, flop into the pool and expect us to comp their stay, along with all their wine and their grub. Most of them are so tight-fisted they won't even shell out for the numerous mani-pedi-fanicures they treat themselves to in the spa. They are extremely useful from a PR point of view, and Ingrid is all over them like a cheap suit, but in terms of meeting budgets and targets they are a nightmare. They always end up costing us money, so I try to ration them. I know it's important to keep them coming, to keep the name of the resort up there in lights, but as far as I am concerned most of them can pack their dental-floss bikinis and head off to the Maldives or the Seychelles, where I'm sure they'd be terribly welcome.

That said, we're delighted to have Liz. We haven't had a bikini shoot done here for a while, so I am thrilled, Ingrid is turning cartwheels and Bernard has offered Liz a free beach barbecue that I am intent on gatecrashing this evening.

Just as I am confirming my presence, laughing a little too loudly at one of her jokes, my mobile goes.

'OK, *merde* . . .' It's Bernard. 'Monsieur McCann landed at the airport half an hour ago and he should be here any second.'

'Fuck me, that's quick,' I say, striding away from Miss Hurley.

'I know,' agrees Bernard. 'He chartered a seaplane.'

VIPs are always doing that. They arrive on the mainland in their private jets and then decide that they can't be bothered to take one of the beautiful fifty-five-foot Sunseeker yachts that we've sent for them at the cost of $600. Instead they opt to charter a seaplane at $3,500 for a ten-minute flight, saying the fifty-minute boat journey takes too long. I don't know why they can't enjoy the boat trip and have a drink while watching the sunset, giving us another half-hour to make sure their Grand Water Villa has been turned down properly. Now we've been caught on the hop and I'm really in the shit. I am at the wrong end of the fucking island with only a bloody golf buggy to get me to the main reception before Mr US TV turns up with his extensive collection of long-legged prostitutes.

I tear down the main track, overtaking all the villa hosts on their way to check and turn-down their rooms. Their buggies are loaded with fruit for the complimentary baskets, bottles of water for the minibars, fresh towels, incense for the burners in the rooms and finally bags of flower petals for the luxury turn-down, where we pleat and fold the top sheets into intricate patterns and cover the beds with petals on the night before they leave.

I am speeding past the beach bar when my phone goes again.

'Hello? Is that the general manager?' comes this clipped Brit voice so bristling with efficiency it is enough to make your blood run cold. I slow the buggy down and pull over. We are not allowed to drive while using our mobiles on the island and as the GM I have to set an example. Sometimes I obviously don't give a shit, but I am about to be overtaken by a line of villa hosts who I have just burnt up, so now is a good time to be seen to be obeying the rules.

'Yes it is, madam. How may I help you?'

Turns out that the cold cow on the line is none other than Mrs Thompson, a very rich woman from London who, if I remember correctly, has been to stay here three times in the last eighteen months. I need to concentrate.

'What's the problem?'

'The thing is,' she starts, 'last time I was here we had a duplex where I could keep an eye on my two children and the nanny, and this time we don't.'

'Oh, I am terribly sorry, madam.'

I can tell this woman means business, otherwise she would not have got through to me. She must either have chewed the ear off everyone else in order to get through to the top, or I must have given her my card with my mobile number on it the last time she was here, in which case I must have deemed her important. I am a little wrong-footed by not being in my office, otherwise I would have pulled out her file and seen how much she spent last time, in order to work out how much arse I might have to kiss. At the moment I am relying on instinct and it's telling me to go for the full backside.

'Anyway, so now I have two villas side by side and I can't see my children. I want a duplex. I booked a duplex and I want it now.'

I explain to her that we don't have one, otherwise she would most certainly be in it. It is not in our interest to split up families. But she doesn't seem appeased. In fact she is sounding increasingly aggressive.

'I want to see my children, I want to be able to hear them,' she continues.

'Right,' I say. Time for the big gesture, I think. 'I know what we will do, madam. I'll get the gardeners to come over right now and remove the hedge and all the plants between your villa and your children's villa. That way you'll be able to see them and hear them.'

'What?' She sounds stunned. 'You'll take the garden out?'

'The whole thing,' I say. 'Right away.'

47

'Now?'

'Right now.'

'Oh,' she says. 'Um, make sure you do it quickly.'

'Right away,' I say. 'Good evening.'

She hangs up and I am straight on to the chief gardener, who is a lovely Sri Lankan chap called Jiwan. I tell him to haul some gardeners out of the staff dining room and get them to pull the hedge out. I tell him I want lots of gardeners. Even if he thinks he can do it with two or three, I want eight or even ten, so this woman thinks she has caused an almighty stir. He says he understands and will sort it out within the next fifteen minutes. So I get back behind the wheel and head off down to reception.

I just make it down to the jetty to see Mr McCann's seaplane land. It's not the sort of seaplane we're used to – this one is larger and shinier and a model I haven't seen before. I tell one of the yacht crew to go and talk to the pilot and get his card, after Mr McCann lands. A sexy seaplane and pilot are always useful in this sort of business.

Bernard and I are standing side by side like a couple of goons waiting for the plane to taxi up to the jetty and for Mr McCann to disembark. Finally the door opens and out he pops.

Why is it that rich men are always so short? Maybe that's what makes them rich in the first place, a pushy desire to overcompensate. All I know is that they invariably compound this problem by hooking up with unfeasibly tall, glamorous women, who only serve to highlight their diminutive stature and fading bad looks.

Dressed from head to foot in white linen, with a heavy gold watch and chomping on a cigar, all five-foot-two of Mr McCann walks towards me with a great grin on his face. He stops before he greets me and pretends to shoot me in the stomach with a pair of fore-finger pistols and then rapidly punches the air like a championship boxer, while growling like a tiger. We are clearly very old friends.

'Good ta see ya, good ta see ya,' he says, giving me a tight hug. 'It's been too long!'

'Good evening, Mr McCann,' I smile. 'It is very nice to have you back.'

In fact it is bloody marvellous to have him back. He is just the sort of VIP this place was built for. And by the looks of it, he seems to have brought one, two, three . . . six of his daughters' friends along for the ride. You have to admire the energy and foresight of a man who thinks that he is going to need this much entertaining.

'Ladies,' I say, nodding and smiling, knowing they are anything but. 'Welcome.'

'Thank you,' says the tallest and darkest in a thick Russian accent. Her long honey-coloured legs disappear into a pair of well-cut Ralph Lauren shorts.

49

These girls are the cream of the crop. They must be setting Mr McCann back almost as much as the rooms themselves. 'Darling,' she says to Mr McCann, 'shall we go?'

The sun sets on the horizon as the absurdly glamorous party weaves its way along the jetty towards reception. Headed by the diminutive Mr McCann, the line of languid women is preceded by a line of some ten men in white polo shirts and crisp shorts, each carrying aloft one Louis Vuitton suitcase. The party ignores the trays of cool hand towels and cold drinks (when you arrive on a Falcon 900 you don't really need refreshing), and they head off to the line of buggies that we have waiting for them.

'One thing,' says Mr McCann as he pauses, one leg on a buggy, the other on the ground. 'I've got the same villas as last time, right?'

'Ah,' I say, walking rapidly towards him, rubbing my hands, with my best service-industry smile in place. 'Not exactly the same. But very much the same.'

'But I want the same,' he says. 'Exactly the same.'

The truth is that we have rented out the Grand Beach two-bed with private pool ($6,200 a night, including complimentary American breakfast) near Palm Sands beach to a Russian aluminium billionaire who is staying here with his wife and two children. He's got it for two weeks and booked it last year, so I could hardly bump him for Mr McCann, no matter how pleased we are to see him.

'The thing is,' I say, slotting my arm over his shoulder, 'we've had a terrible wind problem on the island, it's been blowing a gale for weeks now.' He looks around him and takes in the gentle evening breeze. 'Not here,' I hasten to add. 'But up in the north of the island it has been terrible. So I have bumped someone else out of the Silver Sands Grand Beach and put you in there. You've got the two-bed Grand Beach and the next-door one-bed,' ($4,770 a night), 'which I have to say is my favourite on the island.'

'Your favourite?' he says.

'Absolutely,' I say. 'Much quieter.'

'But further from the pool?' he asks.

'It is only a matter of minutes,' I say, and then I pause and try to look like I am thinking. 'I tell you what,' I add. 'I'll give you your own buggy plus driver 24/7 if that makes things easier for you.'

'Done,' he says, shaking my hand. His gold watch flashes in the dying sunlight. 'A one- and two-bed Grand Beach.' He smiles. 'Sounds perfect. Doesn't it, girls?'

They all giggle with delight. I watch the party as they get into the buggies and load up the luggage. He has six prostitutes plus two male assistants, which leaves rather a deficit of beds. Oh well, I shrug, I don't suppose many of them will be sleeping.

'That went OK,' sighs Bernard. 'Well done on the villa problem.'

'Thanks. The old excuses are always the best.'

'I don't know why all these returning VIPs always want the same villas as before,' he says, kicking the sand off his loafers. 'It seems a little childish to me.'

Bernard's right. VIPs have many foibles. There's the Italian woman who always wears two dressing gowns, the French guy who runs naked along the beach every morning and the Russian who wants to throw beer around in the spa sauna. But the most consistent thing they ask for is to return to the same villa each and every time they come. And they always book to come back when they are still here, and they always book to come back with friends. I have one fabulous oligarch who keeps coming back and keeps bringing more and more people each time. He is booked to return in the New Year and I have to say this time he has gone a little overboard. He has asked for twenty-five villas, but so far we have only managed to secure him eighteen. He wants to fly a whole load of his school friends over for some party, so as soon as a villa becomes available, as soon as anyone cancels, he is in there like a shot. His accommodation bill is currently running somewhere around $650,000 and he has yet to set foot on the island. He's also booked up most of our boats, paying some $130,000 in advance. I'm expecting a bill of over a million that week if the bookings are anything to go by. I think he'd buy up the island for himself if I'd let him, and kick all the other guests out. I'm going to have to be a little careful that week that all the other guests don't feel like gatecrashers at someone else's party.

But it is very hard to say no to these people. Just the other day I had some guy on the phone calling up on behalf of McLaren boss Ron Dennis. He asked me for the best villa in the place and I told him that it was full. He asked me if I knew who I was dealing with. Mr Ron Dennis, one of the richest men in the world. And I said that I was terribly sorry but there was nothing I could do, that all the Grand Villas were full. I offered something smaller, but he was having none of it and hung up. A few minutes later he called back and asked how much it would cost to have the other guests removed.

And he was by no means the worst, or the most persistent. Last year I had one bloke who was so goddamn high-maintenance, I had to move the bastard five times during his stay. The rooms weren't right. The views weren't nice. There was too much wind. He was such a contrary fucker I was convinced I would never hear from him again, he'd clearly had such a miserable time in this shit-heap. But as he was checking out, he tried to book for Christmas, saying that he wanted a duplex with a pool. Christmas is obviously our busiest time and duplexes are popular, so I told him they were already booked. So then he asked for a normal duplex and told me to build him a pool. I said they were about $200,000 to build and he told me to go ahead. All he asked was that he could have it every year for Christmas. Sadly, head office deemed his plan too disruptive to the other guests on the island, and the idea was shelved. Which is a little annoying as it would be very useful to have another duplex with pool to flog.

He is not the only one who fancies upgrading his suite for future visits. A couple of weeks ago I had another Russian staying here. He was some Siberian who was big in oil and all he wanted was a squash court. In fact he was quite insistent. He got his people to fax our people with plans and budgets. He said he would build it and pay for it himself and anyone could use it. He just wanted priority bookings, whenever he was here, for ten days a year. He was not happy when the big cheese turned him down. He stamped and said that he would take his custom elsewhere. There really is no pleasing some people.

My mobile goes.

'Hello? Is that the manager?' It's Mrs Thompson. I sigh and try to put a smile in my voice. She is clearly one of those 'no-pleasing' people.

'How can I help you, madam?'

'I have another problem. Can you come over right away.' It is more of a command than a question. It looks as though popping into Liz Hurley's beach barbecue is going to have to wait.

I arrive at Mrs Thompson's Beach Villa to find the gardeners just clearing up. They have ripped out all the plants between the two villas, which now appear very much more connected. The gardeners look hot, sweaty and exhausted as they rake the sand smooth. The poor sods are going to have to put all this back once the old cow has gone.

'Good evening,' I say. 'What seems to be the problem?'

'Ah, there you are!' says Mrs Thompson.

A large woman in her late forties, Mrs Thompson has poured herself into a pink silk kaftan that catches rather unforgivingly over the rolls of her stomach. Her sweaty white jet-lagged feet are slipping over the edge of her jaunty flip-flops. Her husband appears to be asleep/pissed/exhausted on the bed, while her two blond sons, both under the age of five, tear around the villa, slamming doors and screaming. No wonder the woman is a little irate.

'So,' she continues, 'my other problem is that my nanny here –' She points to a cowering woman in the corner, who is keeping such a low profile I didn't notice her at first. 'She only speaks Spanish.'

'*Hola*,' I say, nodding and smiling. She nods back.

'So now that she is looking after the children on her

own, because we don't have the villa I'd booked, I need a translator for her. I mean she can't order their food, she can't call for a buggy, she can't sort out their swimming, take them to the kids' clubs. She won't be able to do anything. And I didn't come all this way to babysit my nanny. I didn't come all this way to make phone calls and things. I didn't come here to look after my own children! I came to relax!' She is working herself into such a fit at the idea that she might have to look after her own children that she breaks into a sweat. Her long nose shines and dark pink pools appear at her armpits.

'OK, darling?' slurs her husband from the bed. Pissed, then.

'Fine,' she announces stiffly. 'Just sorting things again – as usual.'

'I'll tell you what we'll do,' I say, stepping forward and touching her elbow. 'I speak some Spanish, so if ever she needs anything then all she need do is call me and I'll organize it. Day or night. How about that?'

'Day or night?' she confirms.

'Absolutely, day or night,' I repeat. That shuts her up. Anything to extricate myself from this tense, sweaty environment and sink a flute with the fragrant Miss Hurley.

* * *

I leave Mr and Mrs Thompson to their screaming children and monoglot nanny. It's already nine p.m. and I am starving and keen to have a drink. I have usually had at least one or the other by now, as I have to entertain most nights. If I am not meeting a guest for a drink, I am taking a few out to dinner in one of the restaurants, or I am hosting a beach barbecue outside my villa for some VIP and their entourage.

Beach barbecues are regarded as something special. For $1,000 a couple, we will cover the sand in stunning carpets, create a fantastic seating area with silk cushions, light the place with flaming flares and feed you a four-course barbecue with cooking stations, dessert stand, lobster and wagyu beef.

But quite frankly, I have had enough of them. I don't taste the food any more. I mean, what is lobster and what does it taste of? Prawns? Squid? Little bits of goujoned something or other. Really, it's like eating chicken. When entertaining guests, I just make sure we get plenty of booze on the table. Especially when I'm in the Japanese restaurant. I get them to bring over bottles and bottles of saki. It's the only way to go. How else can you make small talk chewing on cold rice and raw fish? What I wouldn't give for some roast beef and Yorkshire pudding. A proper light fluffy one.

A phone call from Kate interrupts my dreams of Sunday lunch.

'What are you doing?' she asks.

'I'm on my way to have a drink with Liz Hurley and then I'm home,' I say.

'Cool,' she says. 'How's your day been?'

'The usual. Problems. Millionaires. That sort of thing. You?'

'Shit.'

'Anything I can do?'

'No. Just the usual. Shall I order room service?'

'Go on then.'

'Six and Fourteen?'

'No, d'you know what, I'm going to branch out and have Twelve.'

'What, prawn Pud Thai?'

'I know, controversial,' I laugh.

'No, greasy,' she says. 'See you in a bit.'

Poor Kate, I can't help but feel sorry for her. She was quite high-powered in her last job in Bali. She was guest relations manager and used to deal with the likes of Kate Moss and Meg Matthews and every other glam star who was slumming it in a five-star retreat. And now, because of me, she is stuck behind a shop counter flogging Havaianas flip-flops and Melissa Odabash bikinis to working girls for a living. She always sounds tired and it is not because she is exhausted but because she is so goddamn bored. And it's all my fault. I'm the one who made her move. I'm the one whose career is taking off and she's the one telling yawning bankers' wives that pink is the new green. I hope to God that she doesn't leave me.

I am passing the beach bar and on my way up to Palm Sands beach and Miss Hurley's for a quick drink, when the music kicks in. The bass is not quite strong enough to kick you in the kidneys, but it's not far off. It is accompanied by the tish, tish, tish of bloody rave beats. The Monday-night party has kicked off early on Fantasy Island.

Fantasy Island is a three-star piece-of-shithole just across the water from us. By day it is a charming place to look at, in a sort of downtrodden backpacker way. It's somehow nice for the guests here to be able to relax on their loungers, downing their mohitos, safe in the knowledge that they have arrived. But by night, more specifically Monday and occasionally Thursday night, they have an all-you-can-drink beach party/rave and the German guests – weirdly, they are mainly German – go crazy. They are supposed to turn their sound system off at around one a.m. but sometimes they push through till two. I call up almost every week and complain. But they now know my mobile number so their switchboard refuses to take my call, so I have to go to some lengths to get through. I borrow Kate's phone or anyone else's who is at hand. The thing is I can't be that rude, because we sometimes accommodate staff there when we are very busy. Occasionally we put people like the band there on New Year's Eve.

I have had a word with the Minister for Tourism, who we sometimes entertain on a complimentary weekend minibreak basis, and he always promises to do something. But in the meantime I call the front desk, warning them to brace themselves for the deluge of aggressive telephone calls from guests who can't sleep.

It's ten o'clock by the time I've finished chatting and I think perhaps a little too late to roll up at Liz's. She will either be in bed or enjoying herself – the last thing she needs is me putting my head over the outside shower wall and to feel that she needs to entertain me. I'll just send her a card and a bottle of pink Dom to say sorry. I call through to room service and ask them to send a chilled bottle down to her villa.

'I am very sorry,' comes the voice down the line, 'but it won't be possible to send a Dom Pérignon rosé.'

'Why not?'

'We've run out, sir.'

'What do you mean, run out?'

'We have no more Dom Pérignon rosé.'

'Well, send her another rosé.'

'We can't.'

'What do you mean, can't?'

'There is no more pink champagne on the whole

island and there won't be another shipment through until Thursday.'

'But we have the owner of a TV station here, with a large party of ladies to entertain.'

'I know, sir.'

My head lolls forward and I hit my forehead on the buggy horn. Fuck! This is all I bloody need.

Tuesday a.m.

Shit. It is three in the morning and I am wide awake. There is something wrong. I know there is. I can feel it in my bones. Kate rolls over in bed.

'What's the matter?' she mumbles into her pillow.

'I don't know,' I reply. I am sitting bolt upright in bed. 'But something is. I can sense it.'

'I can't hear anything. Go back to sleep.'

'Shit. That's it!' I leap out of bed, grabbing my clothes off the back of the chair. 'There's no noise. There are no lights. The air-con's not working. The fridge is quiet. The bloody electricity has gone off.' I look out of the window. 'The whole island is dark.' I try and ring the switchboard and can't get through. 'Shit, shit, shit. This is serious,' I say as I run out the door. 'This is a bloody crisis.'

In the buggy on the way to the staff village I try to

raise Hori, our chief engineer. With six foot four of Maori muscle, he is the life and soul of the team bar and an extremely affable bloke. Normally we get on very well indeed, but right now I am very pissed off with him because the bastard hasn't got his mobile phone switched on. Fortunately the headlamps on the buggy light the familiar route; even so it is still bloody dark. It is three twenty by the time I reach Hori's door, which I practically kick in, waking up Garry in reservations who has the villa next door to him. I have to say Hori is not a pretty sight in the middle of the night. His black hair is all over the place, his boxer shorts are huge and gaping and he smells of sweat and stale beer.

'All right there, mate?' he sniffs, running his hands through his thick straight hair.

'What's the crisis?' asks Garry, leaning over the edge of his veranda. Already dressed in a tight white T-shirt and jogging pants, Garry looks like something straight out of an Abercrombie and Fitch advert. 'Can I help?'

'The electricity's out,' I say.

'Shit,' says Hori.

'Shit,' agrees Garry.

'You can say that again.'

It's at times like this that you realize quite how isolated we are. This place really is in the middle of nowhere, which is wonderful if everything is working.

But as soon as anything goes wrong, we're fucked. We can't just ring someone up and ask them to pop over and fix it. We can't call up the electricity board, stay on hold for a while and wait for the lights to come on again. Anything that blows up, falls apart or gives up the ghost, we're the ones who have to sort it out. And one thing's certain – I didn't learn to re-boot a generator on a desert island at three o'clock in the morning at catering school.

But we can't do without it. The fallout is huge. In a matter of hours the villas will heat up, the guests will wake up and we'll have a mass of militant millionaires on our hands. And that doesn't take into account powering the kitchens for breakfast, the buggies, the TVs, the showers and the water plant.

The water plant is vital to the running of the resort. It broke down a month ago and it was a bloody nightmare. We hadn't been maintaining the thing properly and that's half the battle here. The humidity, the heat and the salt mean that things rot and biodegrade at an alarming rate. We had to replace all the large wooden umbrellas the other day at vast expense. Some bright spark had set them straight into the sand, so all it took were a few high tides for the bottoms to rot and a couple of blasts of strong wind for them to snap off at the base and fly down the beach.

But in the water plant the lack of loving care was a

little bit more expensive. It cost the hotel $97,000 just to replace the seventy-two membranes in the filter system that should have been backwashed once a week. But no one had looked after them and as a result the things leaked, and we had no water for two days. We stopped all water in the staff village; no one who worked here could shower or wash, which was a little disconcerting and unpleasant, to say the least. We asked the guests not to flush their toilets too often, and bought up all the bottled water in the neighbouring capital. We used Evian in the kettles and Volvic in the kitchens. We were about to pipe seawater into the system to fill up the showers and lavatories when the filters finally arrived. I swear I have never smiled and comp-ed so many pool-side cocktails in my life.

Hori's finally got his shorts on and we are both standing by the generators holding a couple of torches, staring into the black abyss.

'What d'you think?' I ask, squinting into the dark.

'I don't know, mate,' he says, squatting down. He grabs a handful of what appears to be white mousse off the floor. 'Look at this shit,' he says, rubbing the foam between his fingers. 'It's bloody everywhere.' Hori flashes his torch all over the vast generator system. The whole thing is covered in white stuff.

'It looks like foam,' I say.

'It *is* foam,' he says. I can practically hear his addled brain cranking into gear. 'Oh, fuck!' It's dawned on him. 'I tell you what, mate?'

'What?'

'It's only gone and overheated. The fire-suppression system has been sparked and it's covered the whole thing in foam.'

'Right.'

'It's what happens, you know, when things get too hot, to stop a fire.'

'OK.' I nod. 'So what happens now? It's broken?'

'Shouldn't be.'

'Can you fix it?'

'It shouldn't be too difficult,' he says. 'We just need to take it apart and clean all this shit off. Meanwhile the thing will cool down and we can re-boot it.'

'How long will that take?'

'Um,' he scratches his head and inhales through his back teeth like some cowboy builder. 'Eight, nine hours?'

'You've got six,' I say. 'Take as many people as you need.'

'We're going to need lights,' he says. 'We can't clean this place with torches.'

'You can rig up some emergency lights with one of the little generators we use for parties.'

'Righto,' he says.

'And the clock's ticking.'

We come out of the building to find that a small crowd has gathered. There are some twenty to thirty pairs of eyes staring at us in the dark. Crowds in the village are always rather dangerous. With so many different nationalities all living on top of each other in hot cramped conditions, things are liable to kick off at any stage. Especially at night. So I always try and avoid crowds at all costs.

'There's nothing to see here. Move on – move,' I say, clapping my hands together, trying to exude authority. 'Move on, move on.'

'What's going on?' comes Ben's voice through the dark. I can see his white torso glowing luminous in the dark. He is standing barefoot in a pair of un-characteristically demure blue-and-white-striped pyjama bottoms.

'The generator's gone,' I say.

'What d'you mean, gone?' he asks, yawning and rubbing his eyes.

'Broken down. The whole island is without electricity.'

'Jesus Christ.' He stretches. 'I thought this was supposed to be a six-star resort. It's more like a fucking banana republic.'

'Thanks,' I say, as I watch him turn and amble back to bed. 'Very helpful indeed.'

I am far too wired by the time I get to the villa to go back to sleep. It's four thirty a.m. and there doesn't really seem much point. I'm up at five thirty anyway. I am always in the gym by six every morning. It is the only moment I have during the day to call my own and I relish it. There are no guests about, there's no one bending my ear about something, banging on about something else. It's just me and the running machine.

I usually let myself in with my own master key and jog eight kilometres with my iPod on, watching the sun rise over the sea through the floor-to-ceiling glass windows. It is magical and it is my moment in the day when I remember why I am here and how absolutely stunning this place is. It is a precious forty-five minutes in an otherwise packed programme. I think one of the real sadnesses about running a hugely complicated resort like this is that after a while you cease to notice the beauty of the island and all you see are problems.

But there's no chance of a jog this morning. Quite apart from the fact that the running machine won't be working, the lack of air-con would make jogging eight kilometres in this heat insanity. I have also got to try and work out a way of organizing a resortful of hugely demanding guests without any power whatsoever. I sit out on the terrace with my torch, a pad of paper and a large glass of increasingly less cold water.

It takes me about an hour and a half to crack it. I get

on my mobile and start directing the restaurant manager to get the breakfast chefs and sous chefs to bring a few of the beach barbecues over to the kitchen just in case they are needed. He informs me that the hobs are working, it's just the electric ovens that aren't – so there will be no freshly made croissants and Danish for the breakfast bread baskets, as the pastry chefs were halfway through their shift when the generator went down. So we have bread but no pastries. Another half an hour and we might have had the lot.

All the villa hosts are on standby, waiting for their guests to wake up so they can inform them immediately of the problem. All the consumer studies that we have done here on the island tell us that if we keep people abreast of problems and keep giving them up-to-date information they are much more forgiving. People only go ape-shit when you keep them in the dark. I think it is a control thing. Give people the information and they can make an informed decision, or at least that's the theory.

I look up from my lounger on the terrace. Dawn is breaking over the horizon. The pale-pink light is turning yellow and the sea glows a pale turquoise. It is another beautiful day. I stretch, take off my J P Tod shoes and walk across the squeaking white sand towards the gently lapping waves. The gardeners are already out on the beach so it must be six thirty. I smile at one of them as he rakes the sand. Nearly all of our ten kilometres of coastline is hand raked into a herringbone pattern every morning. It takes our team of thirty gardeners most of the morning to do, but it is an important job. You don't pay a couple of thousand dollars a night in a place and expect to see footprints in the sand in the morning. The whole point of the Robinson Crusoe experience is that you step on to a virgin beach every morning. In other resorts where the villas are further from the beach you would whip along the shoreline on a tractor, trailing a rake and a bit of old carpet to smooth the sand down after you. But here, because the villas are so close to the sea, it all has to be done by hand.

In fact, most things are done by hand here. The steps of the Water Villas are cleaned every day by a team of twenty. They scrub the steps all day every day, removing any algae in order to prevent our esteemed guests from slipping into the sea and, of course, potentially suing the arse off us.

Christ! Which reminds me. We have the coconut harvesters coming today. One of the by-products of having 20,000 coconut trees on the island is that we have a hell of a lot of coconuts. Each tree produces between eight and sixteen coconuts a year, which means we have something like a quarter of a million coconuts that need harvesting. We can't leave them, of course, in case a nut falls off a tree and finishes off an international banker. From an insurance point of view we have to maintain the trees to an extremely high standard and that means harvests four times a year, and regular trimming and felling of fronds. So we get some guys over from the mainland who shimmy up and down the trunks with their bare feet with a machete strapped to their backs. It is incredible to watch. They are so fast and efficient. Although we did have one guy hack off his thumb the other day, which is not something I would like to see again. There was quite a lot of shouting and an awful lot of blood. Let's hope nothing like that happens today.

I walk along the water's edge, letting the large waves wash over my feet. A school of fish leap out of the water, hurling themselves into the air in fright. Some larger hungry bastard is after them. I stare into the water just ahead of me and try to work out what is chasing them. A baby shark with a black-tipped fin zigzags its way towards the shore. Perhaps it's the shark, or another hungry predator that's got them in its sight. They leap again, splashing back into the water like falling rain. It's not the baby shark, because it is nosing the sand right at my feet. There is something else in the water.

'Everything all right?' Kate calls me from the villa. I turn around to see her standing in a T-shirt and pants by the large sliding door.

'Not really,' I shout back. 'But we're fixing it.'

'D'you fancy some breakfast?'

Kate and I don't have a kitchen in our villa – in fact we live in a villa that is not dissimilar to one of the standard-size Beach Villas that are rented out to guests. There are a couple of modifications. We have a large terrace for entertaining guests and a substantial barbecue area for those endless flame-grilled lobster dinners that VIPs love so much. But the rest of our accommodation, from the indoor and outside showers to the sunken baths, the wall-mounted plasma TVs, the total-villa sound system and limited wardrobe space, is the same as everyone else's. We do have an additional sitting area as well, where we can have cocktails if it is raining or the wind is blowing too much. But mostly it is your standard $2,500-a-night Beach Villa with pool. Not that the pool is much to write home about – I hardly ever go in it. Kate says that she has to do about 150 lengths each time she goes in there to feel any different. It's a three-strokes-and-turn pool, but the guests seem to like it. We float candles and flowers in it in the evening when we are having guests' drinks.

But the lack of a kitchen really does affect our lives. It means I can't even make a piece of toast or boil an egg. There are times when I want to cook myself a fry-up on a Sunday morning so much that it actually hurts. Instead we live off room service. I can see the menu in my sleep. I have tried every dish a thousand and one times and for some reason they all seem to taste the same. Not that the food is bad, because it is not. It is six-star delicious. But it is that sort of international-style cuisine where Italian, Spanish, Thai and Japanese food all sit next to each other on the same page. You can have gazpacho and sashimi served at the same time, which Kate does, most nights. Our only alternative is to eat in one of the three restaurants. There's the Jap, the international and the other is Thai/Chinese. All three of them are very good, but even if you were only staying here for ten days you might get a little bored. Imagine what it is like to have only these places to choose from, and then imagine what it is like to have had to look at a menu every day for the last eighteen months.

Kate and I sit in our usual place, side by side, gazing out to sea. She is crunching a bowl of granola with yogurt and I have given up on breakfast altogether and am having my protein shake. One of the problems with entertaining all the time is the ever-expanding waistline, so if I don't have to eat with guests then I tend not to have any food at all. Coffee, on the other hand, is a necessity. I am on my second double espresso when my phone goes.

'*Hola*,' says a voice. It is Mrs Thompson's nanny. She may not be able to speak English but she is clever enough to bypass the defunct telephone system and call me on my mobile. She mutters something about wanting a buggy to take the children to breakfast and I promise her I am on to it. I walk out to the front of the restaurant and find some guy half asleep on his buggy and send him off in the direction of 162. He seems a little annoyed that I've disturbed him.

Buggies and buggy drivers are one of my annoyances on the island. Buggy drivers are essentially bellboys, but because we've given them transport and a driving licence, they appear to have promoted themselves to a bunch of cab drivers. It is extraordinary to watch. They hang around in front of the restaurant in their shades, like some sort of cartel. I never see them cleaning the buggies. They are supposed to charge them whenever they are not driving as it takes six hours to top them up. But they never do. They mooch around, playing with their radios, trying to look cool. There is even some sort of hierarchy within the fraternity. The guys who drive the eight-seaters are the least cool – the buggies are slow and difficult to manoeuvre. The six-seater drivers are better and the guys who drive the four-seaters are practically in a convertible. And they drive them so badly. They are always crashing into trees or colliding with bicycles. It drives me mad. We spend between $10,000 and $25,000 a month on repairs. These things are expensive. Landed on the island, a buggy costs $24,000, because they are taxed like cars. So we make everyone who drives one have a licence, with points taken off for drink-driving, talking on the mobile and speeding, as well as for driving without due care and attention. Offences are actually taken seriously. In the case of accidents, I have to fill out forms and get statements taken. In fact sometimes the whole thing seems so goddamn draconian that all we need are a few traffic wardens and it would be just like any metropolitan city.

On the way back to the villa to finish up my last shot of coffee before the morning meeting, I check in with Hori just to hear how he is doing.

'Not far off, mate,' he huffs down the phone. He is sounding a little tired. 'Looks like someone piled some wood up against the airing vents, which is why the whole thing overheated in the first place.'

He apologizes for missing the morning meeting, but promises that the system should be up and running within the hour. Which is just as well, as the hour between nine and ten a.m. is when most of the guests wake up and want their shower and their eggs Benedict.

The morning meeting is hot and humid and generally bad-tempered. No one has been able to wash properly, there has been no hot water for the blokes to shave with and only a few people have managed to get through the queues for some tepid breakfast in the dark staff canteen. There is a flurry of complaints from everyone as I walk in, but the most pissed off of all is Ben. He looks white and waxy and there's practically steam pouring out of his ears. I am about to sit down when he takes me to one side.

'I can't believe you persuaded me to come here,' he hisses into my ear. He is holding on to the front of my shirt like it is a pair of coat lapels. 'D'you know I had a very nice offer to run a country-house hotel in the bloody Cotswolds?'

'Honestly,' I smile over his shoulder at everyone else in the room, 'it does get better.'

'Well, it can't get much worse,' he whispers. 'I'm hot, hungry, tired. My digs are a shit hole and I am sweating like a bloody rapist.'

'It's the jetlag,' I say. 'You'll feel a lot better after a couple of days.'

'I'd better.' He releases my shirt and sits down at the table.

'OK everyone,' I say, clapping my hands and attempting a team leader sort of smile. 'Not long now. Hori's sorting out our lack of power and we should be fully operational within the hour. Any complaints from the guests, any appointments missed –' I turn to Geri, 'like in the spa – just comp the lot.'

'What, all the massages and that?' queries Geri.

'The lot,' I repeat. 'Hopefully most of the guests

won't know that it has happened. They will just notice their BlackBerrys aren't charged and the ice in the fridge has melted, but that's it. So . . .' I rub my hands. My phone goes. 'I am sorry,' I say to the meeting. 'Let me just take this. Hello?'

'*Hola*,' comes the reply. It is Thompson's nanny again, wanting to know where her buggy is. I tell her it is on its way and that if it doesn't arrive in the next ten minutes she should call me back.

'Sorry,' I apologize again. 'So apart from the lack of power, is there anything else?'

'Just *quelque chose*,' says Bernard, slowly opening the duty log. 'It seems there was an incident in the pool.'

'Oh God, really?' I sigh. I hate pool incidents because they are always bloody complicated.

'Mr Firth was teaching his son to swim in the pool . . .'

'Don't tell me, after dinner?' I ask.

Bernard nods. '*Bien sûr*.'

'Why is it that people always want to play with their kids when they're a little bit pissed?' asks Garry.

'I think it's the only time they play with them, isn't it?' asks Geri.

'It certainly seems that way,' I say.

'So anyway, he hit his leg,' continues Bernard. 'We got the doctor because he'd had some knee operation ten years ago and this was a very big deal. The doctor said it was OK, so that was that. He went diving this morning.'

'Good,' I say. I love a happy ending.

'But Keith has just called me,' says Bernard. 'And he says that it is hurting again.'

'So the tosser has sobered up,' sniffs Ben.

'Um . . .' Bernard frowns at Ben. He is not used to guests being called tossers. '*Oui?*'

'We should make a huge fuss,' I suggest. 'Get him to hospital on the mainland, get it X-rayed and then we can't be accused of slacking. Anything else?'

Bernard runs through a couple of buggy crashes and the fact that the Russian in villa 210 was found asleep in the bushes in front of his villa. Garry then runs through some of the more odd requests from arriving guests, including a special request from the couple in villa 135.

'They want to renew their wedding vows,' says Garry.

'Aaah,' says Geri.

'Jesus Christ!' says Ben. 'You would have thought once would have been enough.'

'Anyway,' continues Garry, 'Mr Forrest has asked for twenty-seven long-stemmed Dolce Vita roses and a wedding ring.'

'OK,' I nod, noting it down in my little black book.

'What?' asks Ben. 'You can do that out here?'

'For sure,' I reply. 'There is no such word as "no" in this place. Just that we haven't tried hard enough. Anything else?'

'Oh yeah,' adds Garry. 'They need the roses and the ring by Friday.'

Tuesday p.m.

I spend most of the early afternoon on the phone to Singapore, trying to sort out the Dolce Vita roses and the ring. Having bragged to Ben that nothing is impossible in the high-end-resort business, I kind of have to pull this one off and with some sort of style. For this type of occasion, we have a system of forwarding agents in place around the world. They are a bit like an extended concierge service: we pay them a retainer of a couple of thousand dollars every few months, so that we can call on them in any emergency. And so far they haven't let us down.

We've sourced anniversary music, a wedding dress, some Jimmy Choo shoes, a specific Napoleon brandy, even a couple of Russian hookers that we managed to track down in Bangkok. It was a bit like trawling Newcastle for coal, but the guest was very specific. He wanted white and blonde and Russian. Our usual whore-fixer at the airport drew a blank. Well, there's not much call around here for high-class prostitution. Most of the locals don't have two fishing boats to rub together, let alone a couple of thousand dollars for some horizontal relaxation. So we called further afield. We spread the net across a few continents. We telephoned Nairobi, Colombo, Sydney and Singapore. Eventually we found a couple of ladies in Bangkok and got them on the next flight over here. And I have to say, it struck me as they slunk off the boat and shimmied through reception that prostitution really is one of those businesses where you get what you pay for. Our Saudi chap wanted two gorgeous pouting babes and that's exactly what he got. They didn't leave the villa for the whole weekend.

But the most difficult thing I have had to sort so far was not actually for a guest but for the hotel. Last year we had some rather spectacular fireworks for New Year's Eve. It was my first year as general manager and I had a bit of a point to prove. Apparently the last guy in charge couldn't organize a piss-up at a celebrity aftershow party, so I wanted to show them all how it should be done. Anyway I got this call from the guys in Singapore who were organizing it, asking me how I planned to get the fireworks on to the island. I suggested they just whacked them on a plane. But it wasn't until halfway through the conversation that I realized they were talking about 300 kilos of gunpowder and that no commercial flight would carry that in the hold. All it would have taken was a couple of hosties having a sneaky fag in the loos for the whole thing to blow up. So we were stuck. The boat would take too long. We had three weeks to get the fireworks on to the island; otherwise my party début would be as glamorous as a dank weekend in Skegness.

There was the briefest glimmer of light at the end of my dark tunnel when one of our high-spending regulars, a real player on the Singapore Stock Exchange, called up and asked for a Grand Water Villa with pool for a long weekend with his mistress. I knew he would be coming in his private jet so begged him to bring our gunpowder with him. I promised to comp his stay and give him all sorts of extras. Amazingly he agreed. But sadly he changed his mind at the last minute, so we were back to square one with time firmly against us. In the end, I couldn't lose face. There would have been nothing worse than having the dramatic countdown only for all the guests to look out over the bay and see six rockets fly up in the air. That's not what they pay their $1,000 festive supplement for. So I called up our fixer and got him to shell out $44,000 on a private jet to get the stuff here. Never has gunpowder been on such a glamorous trip. The Lear was totally bloody empty except for 150 boxes of explosives in the hold. But the end result was worth it. We had a sixteen-minute firework display that was as grand as Millennium night in Sydney Harbour. A few of the staff thought it was a little extravagant – I think their noses were out of joint. My only problem now is trying to lose the $44,000 jet bill in the end-of-year audit.

Still, this wretched wedding ring is proving a little problematic. They need to know the design and the size of the finger and no one in Singapore is sure they can get it back to us by Friday. But I persevere. I get Kate to measure the finger of the 'bride' in the boutique and am planning to email over a digital photo of the design she has chosen from our extensive jewellery collection in the shop, just as soon as we get some bloody power. I have long since realized that if you want something done in this business, shouting and screaming and stamping your foot is not the way to do it. Calm persuasion is where it's at, except of course when you're dealing with your own staff.

'Listen,' I say, calling up Hori on his mobile. 'Where the fuck is my electricity? I am sweating my bollocks off in the office. All the fucking ice is melting in the storage rooms. We've got the fucking supply boat arriving any minute with tens of thousands of dollars of food on it and YOU have still not fixed the generator.'

'Mate, mate, mate . . .' starts Hori.

'I am not your fucking mate,' I reply. 'I am your fucking boss.'

'It's OK, mate,' he continues, ignoring me. 'I am nearly there.'

'Nearly is not good enough! The switchboard would be glowing red-hot by now if the fucking thing was working.'

'Five minutes,' he says.

'Three!' I shout.

'OK, mate.'

'I am not—'

He hangs up.

'Bastard,' I mutter and run my hands through my sweaty hair. Christ, I am hot.

I am just about to shoot myself and Hori when there is a knock on my door.

'Come in,' I say, then there's a gentle click as the lights come on in my office and the air-con moans into action. Thank God for that.

My phone goes. 'Hello?'

'It is Mr Antonov in villa 220,' comes a heavily accented Russian voice.

'Good morning, sir!'

'Is it?' he asks.

My hearts sinks. I've got myself a philosopher.

'Well, apart from a few technical glitches . . .'

'If I wanted technical glitches I would have stayed in

my own country,' he states. 'We are very good at problems of a technical nature.'

'I am sure.' I laugh, trying to make light of the heavy attitude I am getting down the phone. 'Anyway it won't be happening again, sir. The situation is sorted. It was something beyond our control.'

'Nothing is ever beyond our control,' he opines.

'No, sir.'

'Anyway,' he clears his throat, 'I am not interested in the problems you have running your little island. I want to rent a boat.'

'Rent a boat?' I exhale and look up. Yoshiji the sushi chef and Angela, the young German windsurfing and sailing instructor, are standing in front of me. I motion for them to sit down. 'What sort of boat, sir?'

'The largest you have,' he says.

'What would you like it for? Deep-sea fishing? Touring? Sunbathing?'

'My family and I would like to sail around the islands.'

'OK,' I say. 'Is that for you, your wife and your two daughters?'

'That is correct.'

'We've got a fifty-five-foot Sunseeker you can have, or an Azimut 68S?'

'Do you have anything larger?'

'Of course, we can get you anything you want. What sort of price range were you thinking of?'

'$10,000 a day?'

'Absolutely, sir. When would you like it?'

'Whenever I want it,' he says. 'Have it on standby for us to use when we like.'

'It will be ready for you later on this afternoon.'

'Excellent,' he says. 'And no more problems.'

'No more problems.'

He hangs up and I smile at Yoshiji and Angela. 'Yes? What I can I do for you?'

'We would like to resign,' they say together.

'And we want to leave at the end of the week,' says Angela. 'We are in love.'

'Oh good,' I say. Oh God, I think. Why is it always Yoshiji? What has this man got that all the girls find so irresistible? And Angela hasn't even been here for very long. She was hired to replace some bloke called Ian who was head of windsurfing and sailing. He was in his mid-forties with a bit of a gut, so we got rid of him. Quite frankly he didn't look the part. You don't want to travel halfway across the world to see someone un-attractive on the water. It doesn't exactly sell the lifestyle or indeed the lessons. So we hired Angela and the takings are up. She looks good in a bikini. She's got a nice tan and long blonde hair. She looks wonderful on the water. Like a proper water babe, if you don't look too closely. Because quite frankly, standing here in the unforgiving striplight of my office, it would take more than her pimpled faced and smoker's smile to get me into the water.

'Well that's not terribly convenient,' I say.

'You can't stop us,' she replies, with a defiant flick of her thin straight hair.

'I didn't say that. I just said it wasn't very convenient.'

'Well that's your problem,' she says. 'We are going to live in Japan together.' She leans over and grabs Yoshiji's hand.

'Oh right.' I smile. 'Have you ever been there?'

'No.'

'Yoshiji, you're being very quiet.'

'Well, sir,' he shrugs. 'What can I say?'

'We've got it all worked out,' she interrupts. 'We're going to run a restaurant on the beach.'

'It sounds great,' I say. 'I wish I could join you.'

'What?' Yoshiji looks a little stunned. 'You're resigning too?'

'No, I was just saying.' I sigh. 'Is there any way I can persuade you to re-think your plan? Any incentives that we can come up with here? A promotion? A change of quarters, maybe? To keep you together?'

Yoshiji looks a little hesitant. The change-of-quarters idea has clearly piqued his interest. 'Well . . .' he starts.

'No,' she finishes. 'We are leaving at the end of the week.'

'Well, OK then,' I say. 'If you're sure.'

'We're sure,' she says.

'I think, Angela, as you have only been here for three months you might still owe us for recruitment and training,' I suggest. 'But let me look into that.'

'Whatever,' she says, pouting like an adolescent. 'I need to get out of here.'

'I suggest you go and talk to Nina in HR and she'll go through everything with you.'

I get up and shake their hands. I contemplate making a fuss about their imminent departure, but quite frankly my three a.m. start is beginning to take its toll and neither of them is irreplaceable. Beach bunnies are two a penny in the southern hemisphere and I can go and pick up an excellent sushi chef in an afternoon in one of the international hotels in Tokyo, Kuala Lumpur or Singapore. Also, there is something about her insistence and his reticence that makes me think that this is another one of Yoshiji's special relationships that's going to end in tears and recriminations.

I get a phone call from Bernard. He is on meet-and-greet with the late lunchers in the dining room and suggests that I get my arse down there.

'I have only got Ben here to smooth ruffled plumes,'

he explains. 'And he is not the most charming of bastards. We have plenty of, how you say, pissed-off guests, who need you to pretend to give a shit.'

I get straight on my buggy and head down to the dining room. I would normally put my face around the place every morning and occasionally at lunchtime and perhaps a bit in the evening. But as GM you have to be a little careful that you keep a touch of rarity about you. The last thing you want to do is look like you are hanging around waiting to collect complaints. Nor do you want to put yourself too much in the front-line, as there is little room for manoeuvre. It is always useful for the guests to have gone through some sort of vetting procedure before they get to you, otherwise you find yourself dealing with every late breakfast or unstocked minibar. When, of course, your mind should be on higher things, like how am I going to get a plane-load of prostitutes in from Bangkok and how am I going to ship this gunpowder?

I park up and walk into the swimming-pool area to find the place is packed. It seems that the whole hotel is around the main swirling swimming pool and within seconds of my arrival I can see why. Mr McCann and his ladies have set up camp in one corner of the pool, between the jacuzzi area, the smooth manicured lawn and the beach. And they seem to be a couple of cocktail jugs in and putting on a bit of a show. Well, the girls are, anyway. Mr McCann is sitting there like a small hairy beach ball, propped up in the shade by a few cushions, watching the show as keenly as every other banker, broker and rich bastard around the pool. And his girls are doing him proud. They are dancing to the reggae coming out of the beach bar, bumping and grinding each other in a manner I haven't seen since stumbling into a titty bar the last time I was in Bangkok.

Ben's right in the thick of it, grinning away in his *Miami Vice* shades and linen shirt and trousers. He looks like he is fitting right in, laughing away with Mr McCann, making sure he is having a lovely time, while all the time keeping his reflector shades pointing in the direction of the pool. And who can blame him? The girls are stunning. There is not a spare ounce of flesh on them. Their oiled skins glisten in the sun, as do their sequinned thongs and bikinis. Most of the blokes around the pool are pretending to read, using their books or magazines to cover the rock-ons they've got going on in their Vilebrequin swimming trunks. Their wives, however, are less amused. There is much huffing and tutting and ushering of innocent children towards the beach.

'Good afternoon, Mr McCann,' I say, walking around the pool. He smiles and waves his short hairy arm at me.

'Good to see ya!' he says. 'Come and have a drink!'

'I'd love to, sir, I'd love to,' I smile. 'But sadly I'll have to wait until manager's drinks tonight to join you.'

'Cool.' He waves me on. 'See you there!'

'Ben.' I smile. 'Can I see you for a minute?'

'Absolutely,' he says, walking towards me. 'This is more like it,' he whispers in my ear. 'Much more up my street.'

'I'm glad,' I say, thinking it better to agree with him than start telling him to pull his finger out just yet. 'Will you do one side of the dining room for me?' I ask.

'Sure,' he says. His mood is certainly more buoyant and affable than before. 'D'you want me to hoover up some complaints after this morning's debacle?'

'That would be great,' I say. I knew I had hired him for a reason.

'See you around the other side,' he winks. 'Ladies!' I hear him start on a table of girls who are here for a week of detoxing and yoga. I know they've been having daily sessions with our nutritionist at the spa. 'I'm Ben, the new deputy manager. Having a lovely time?'

I walk towards the other side of the open-air dining room and approach a large white couple who have turned a pinker shade of puce in the sun.

'Good afternoon,' I say. Neither of them bothers to look up from their club sandwiches. 'Are you having a lovely lunch?' It is always better to start positive.

'Yes,' says the woman, who I seem to remember is an Elegant Resorts package booking, so I know they won't be going wild on the extras. In fact I am rather amazed to see them having lunch. These bookings tend to stuff their pockets with fruit and rolls from breakfast, hoping to squirrel enough away to avoid the expense of lunch altogether.

'Anything I can help you with?' I ask breezily, already slipping away to another table. They don't bother to reply. 'OK then . . . have a lovely day.' I turn around to the next-door table and walk slap bang into Mrs Thompson, Mr Thompson, the nanny and the two boys. Shit. 'Good afternoon.' I smile and brace myself.

'No it is not, actually,' starts Mrs Thompson.

'Oh dear,' I reply. Here we go.

'Jasper here is very burnt.' She tugs the child towards her as though he is some kind of exhibit. 'Why don't you have warnings in the villa about how hot the sun is? I mean, how do you expect us to know that factor 25 is not enough . . . ?'

And on and on she goes. I have to admit that she is not the first to complain about the strength of the sun. I remember the old manager saying to me before he left that people are on holiday here, so don't expect them to think. It is extraordinary the amount of sunburn the staff doctor treats. It is almost worth our while going around and tapping guests on the shoulder as they lie out in the sun and asking them to put some cream on. We do it on the boat on the way over, because everyone is so tired and disorientated. We offer bottles of water and sunscreen to prevent everyone – well, actually, mainly the blokes – arriving burnt to a frazzle. But for many it is still not enough. We have safety packs in the villas, warning that the sea has currents and could be dangerous, but I am thinking of putting up big sun warning signs too. However, what I do know is that whatever we do, it will never be enough for some people. For some people not even blood is enough.

And Mrs Thompson appears to be one of them. She is yapping away, chewing my ear off like a terrier on speed. Her breakfast was late. The eggs weren't hot. The butter was melted. The jam came in a pot and not on the side. She has yet to become truly abusive, but I am sure it is only a matter of time. She reminds me of the sort of clientele a mate of mine had to look after when he worked at the Four Seasons in Nevis. Apparently the New Yorkers who packed the hotel during the Christmas season were so high-maintenance and demanding, management used to get a team of psychologists down before Christmas to brief the staff on how to cope with the tirade of abuse and unpleasantness they would be getting. No wonder James didn't last long. He was last seen off the coast of Zanzibar, managing somewhere far less taxing.

I make it through the rest of the dining room relatively unscathed. Most of the guests are none too fussed about the lack of power this morning. The majority of them were still asleep, while a couple were so dozy and switched off that they completely failed to notice. I spot the bloke with the banged knee after his late-night swimming lesson. I reiterate the offer of an X-ray on the mainland and I can see immediately that he can't be bothered.

I walk past Ben, who is still smiling and chatting away to guests, making sure he is in line for some tips at the end of the week, and I decide to drop by Kate in the boutique.

The air-con is on full blast when I walk in. In fact, it is so damn cold in here I could almost use a jumper. Although I have to say I don't actually own one. Kate and I did store our winter clothes in a few suitcases in a storeroom not far from the villa when we arrived, but the whole lot had grown mouldy and rotten when we last looked, so we had to throw them all away.

'Hello, gorgeous girl.' I smile, walking towards her. 'Can I slip you a kiss while no one is looking?'

'No!' she says. 'I've got to look professional, and anyway the buggy drivers can see.'

I turn around to see three buggy drivers all lounging around, kicking sand and chatting in the shade of a palm. I am just about to go out and give them a talking to when I notice one of the coconut harvesters shimmy up the tree and hack down two coconuts. They fall to the ground with such ferocity that the drivers leap out of their skin. That'll learn them, I think, turning my attention back to Kate.

'So what sort of day have you had so far?' I ask, taking in the kaftans, the beaded bikinis, the Stetsons and the sequinned flip-flops. Who would have thought there was so much money in this tat? But apparently there is. The boutique is one of the most lucrative things on the island and brings in some $70,000 a month profit, punching well above its weight when it comes to turnover per square foot.

'Not bad.' She shrugs. 'I have had the married couple who are renewing their vows in here all morning choosing rings.'

'Oh, did you sort that out?' I ask.

'Don't worry, I got the size and the design and sent it off to the bloke in Singapore,' she says. 'Your secretary gave me a call.'

'Good.' I rub my hands together. 'Glad to hear Lynne's on the case. You coming to manager's drinks?'

'Unless I can find something better to do,' she says.

'Let's hope Lynne's remembered to send out the invitations. She forgot last week.'

Kate doesn't appear to be listening to me. She is

staring out of the plate-glass window towards the pool.
I turn around to follow her gaze.

'Oh my God,' I say. 'Here comes trouble.'

It seems that Mr McCann's good-time girls have got
bored of drinking and dancing by the pool and are all
heading for the boutique. They are laughing and
giggling and flicking their glossy hair and kicking their
slim tanned legs. One or two of them have dressed to
come to the shop, putting on hot pants or miniskirts;
others haven't bothered and are quite happily walking
topless in G-strings across the main buggy and bicycle
park. The buggy boys have never seen anything like it,
nor indeed have I. It is like some Playboy fantasy writ
large and walking towards me. All I can do is stare
along with the rest of them.

'Good afternoon, ladies.' Kate's voice brings me back
down to earth.

'Good afternoon,' I hurriedly agree. 'Come for a bit
of shopping?'

'Absolutely,' replies the tall dark one. 'We have
earned it.'

I'm afraid I don't know what to say at that point, so
I edge towards the door.

'Can I help you with anything in particular?' asks
Kate.

'Jewellery,' says one of the girls.

'Diamonds!' adds another.

'And plenty of them,' says the first.

Someone's in for a very expensive afternoon, I think as I walk out of the shop. And I bet the poor bastard doesn't even know it. I'm sure he's flat on his back with his mouth wide open, catching flies by the pool.

Tuesday Sunset

Behind the staff village, alongside the carpentry workshop and basketball hoop, we have a small harbour complete with cranes and tugs and flat-bottomed boats. It looks like a rather run-down version of any functioning port you would find in the tropics. There's rubbish floating in the water and birds dive-bombing for scraps. This is where all our supply ships offload their cargo and where our rubbish barge fills up with all the kitchen slops, restaurant waste and unmentionables from the spa. A veritable mountain of filth is shipped off on a daily basis to another less fortunate island, where it is scavenged and recycled; the remainder is either incinerated or dumped in landfill. Needless to say, this whole area is screened and is very much off limits for the guests.

I arrive as the sun is setting and the rubbish barge has

just set sail. It is leaving the harbour followed by a gathering of squawking sea birds. The hot, sweet smell of rotting leftovers still hangs in the air.

But it's not the rubbish I have come to see. The food and beverage manager, Jean-François, has called me down to have a look at some of the hams that have just arrived on the *Mary Celeste*, the huge refrigerated boat that delivers supplies to the island every afternoon. Each day it brings something different – meat, alcohol, fruit, etc. Each day it leaves empty.

Supplying the island with food and wine is a hugely expensive operation. It costs us something in the region of $20 million a year to keep our guests in the manner to which most of them have rather recently become accustomed. It is nearly half of the hotel's $55 million annual turnover and the biggest headache. Unlike city hotels, where items like fruit and vegetables, cheese, meat and fish are purchased on a daily basis directly from bespoke suppliers, we have to shop long-distance. So not only do we not have face-to-face contact with the people we are dealing with, we can't send anything back either. We can't do spot checks in our non-existent loading bay. So if the order is sub-standard and the fifty kilos of tomatoes are rotten or the ham is too fatty, we have to accept the goods otherwise we have no ham or tomatoes at all. This means we really have to trust our suppliers and establish a good relationship with them. And all this is down to Jean-François.

He is paid handsomely for this, of course – $7,000 a month – and he gets plenty of cash kickbacks and little Christmas bonuses from his mates all over the world. And I really do mean all over the world. As a luxury resort, we only use the finest ingredients and we source them in the finest places in the world. So our Parma ham is the best you can find in Parma. We buy our Patta Negra from Spain. Our cheese comes from France, as does all our bottled water, and our flour to make the croissants and baguettes for breakfast. Our sushi fish is flown in from Japan, despite the fact that there is plenty of local fish available, as is our wagyu beef and toro. Our fruit and veg mainly come from Australia, as we can't get the standard we want and need here. Our eggs come from Germany for the same reason. Our prawns are from Sri Lanka, our lobsters are from Thailand, and we bring caviar in by hand from Dubai. In fact, if any senior member of staff ever flies anywhere they are always instructed to bring back caviar and of course cigars. Last time I flew to Dubai for some hotel conference, I brought back twenty kilos of caviar in my hand luggage and 2,500 dollars' worth of cigars. We try and do the same with our foie gras, but that is one of the more difficult things to get here.

As you can imagine, our walk-in cold storage rooms are an Aladdin's cave of delights – noodles, sausage, feta, truffles, Manchego cheese. Everywhere you look there is something delicious and unexpected. Hori even sneaks pots of Vegemite on to the shopping list. My own personal favourite is the Valrhona chocolate. We bring it in to make our own chocolate ice cream. It is rich and delicious and at six dollars a scoop decadently expensive. But some would say totally worth it.

There are times when I lie in bed and worry about the enormity of the carbon footprint that we are creating here. Especially since as a small tropical island we will be the first against the wall when it comes to going under. But what can you do? We do try and cut back when it comes to staff food. Their fruit and veg are local, as is their fish. But their meat still comes from Argentina and their frozen chicken is flown in every week from Chile. We used to spend $4.70 a day on staff food, but the price has gone up to $6.80 – we are over budget by $50,000 this month alone. However, the real problem is not the expense of staff meals but the food the guests want and the fact that you can't re-invent what is considered to be a world-class menu. You can't change guests' perception of what good food is. The rich expect to eat lobster, foie gras and caviar, and it doesn't matter to them how you get it here. If you don't have the names, those headline foods on the menu, they get pissed off and they won't come again. It is as simple as that. The aim of a place like this is to keep the little luxuries coming, while the guests never trouble themselves to think how they got here.

'Ah, *bonsoir*,' says Jean-François, looking up from his clipboard. His long dark hair flops forwards. He is a handsome devil prone to knocking back stock with his Latin sommelier, Marco. 'Have you seen this piece of shit?' He kicks a whole leg of ham including the trotter across the ground. 'This is not a Patta Negra: it has not been fed on fucking acorns, it has eaten normal food, like a normal pig and will therefore taste bloody normal. We can't serve normal here.'

'Shit,' I say.

'Bloody fucking shit,' exclaims Jean-François, giving the trotter another shove. 'I am up to my neck in shit. Chef will be pissed off. This is the third time this month they have done this.'

'I think we should change suppliers,' I suggest.

'That is easy for you to say, you don't have to go to Spain to find someone else.'

'Do you have to go?'

'How else do you think I find someone?' he asks.

'Through the grapevine?'

'That's how we got this last bastard. And did you see those melons we got last week? Fucking shit. They were rotten before they put them on the fucking plane. I hate this job! I thought it was going to be sun, sea, sex and more sex and all it is are problems.'

'And sex?'

'The only person worth having sex with here is your wife,' he says.

'Girlfriend.'

'Who cares, she is bloody taken anyway,' he huffs. 'Even the fucking chambermaids are men.'

'Well, you could . . .'

'I am not that desperate.' He looks down at his list of produce. 'Anyway I don't know why that Mr McCann has to be so greedy. How can a little fatty like that fuck six girls at a time?'

'Viagra?'

'Maybe,' he shrugs.

'The gold-digger's nemesis,' I laugh. 'Before, those poor pretty girls only had to sleep with rich bastards once in a blue moon, now they must be at it all the time. It is a lot more work for a gold necklace.'

'I'd need more than a gold necklace to get anywhere near that man,' he declares. 'Anyway,' he adds, 'so we are in agreement about the Patta Negra?'

'Yup. Anything else?'

'No,' he says. 'Just the usual shitty fruit problems.'

I turn to leave and then remember the rosé crisis. 'Any pink Dom?'

'*Non*,' he says. 'Alcohol doesn't come in till Thursday.'

'Oh.' I am a little confused. 'What day is it today?'

'Tuesday,' he says. Jesus, I must be tired. 'Manager's drinks. Hadn't you better go and change?'

Shit. I look at my watch. It's six forty-five, which means I have to shower, change and be on duty in fifteen minutes at the Thai restaurant, Lotus, to meet and greet the guests. I can't believe I forgot. But then that's one of the weird things about living here: you never really know what day of the week it is. We don't have real weekends like the rest of the world. We only have one day off a week. I am really on duty the whole time. Just like the three a.m. wake-up call this morning. It is the same old shit, just a different day of the week. And now I have to go and host a drinks party.

I have to say I am not a great fan of the manager's drinks party. It is rare that it is actually a laugh. More often than not the guests just use it as an opportunity to have a moan. And the more they drink the more vociferously they complain. The staff aren't much better. We normally have about five or six managers in attendance and they always use it as an excuse to sink as many free glasses of champagne as they can lay their sweaty hands on. And the guests are just as bad. Sometimes they tuck in so much, it makes me wonder if any of them have ever had a free glass of champagne in their lives. But then again it just goes to prove that everyone likes a freebie, no matter how loaded and stinking rich they are.

I get back to the villa in time to have a quick shower and douse myself in aftershave. This job is so much about image, I have to spend time trying to look the part. I try and have my hands manicured once a week, I'll do the odd face pack and I even have the island hairdresser come to my place every other Sunday, just to give my hair a trim. You'd be amazed how quickly your hair grows in the sun here. And also you'd be amazed how much people notice. The last GM had a bit of a personal-hygiene problem and some guests actually complained. Poor bastard. He got a fax from head office telling him to shower more often and fix the B.O. problem.

Suited and sandalled and smelling sweet, I am walking out the door when Kate calls.

'They've just gone!' she sighs down the phone.

'No!'

'I know! Can you believe it? They spent $300,000.'

'That's a lot of kaftans!' I laugh.

'And quite a few diamonds,' she adds. 'I think that has to be one of the best days we've had in the shop. God bless rich Americans with more money than sense.' She laughs. 'See you in a minute,' she adds and hangs up.

Arriving at the Lotus restaurant, I am only ten minutes late. Situated between the spa, the gym and Silver Sands beach, it is in the south-east of the island. Built on a Thai theme, there are low tables on the beach with red painted benches, Chinese lanterns in the trees, giant dragons at the entry to the place and a small cocktail bar with a sort of chill-out area decked out with carpets and Balinese furniture. It is supposed to look like some sort of chic, oriental hangout. But instead it looks like a Portobello market-stall crate just washed up on the beach.

I rush past the Chinese dragons. There are only a few people mingling in the sand, sipping glasses of champagne. Before I enter the fray with my best service-industry smile in place, my secretary Lynne arrives, bringing with her the daily event sheets.

These are detailed spreadsheets with the name and villa number of every person who is staying on the island. They also tell me who they booked through, how long they are staying, how they got here – whether it was by private jet or special yacht transfer – and what their particular requests are. They are the ultimate crib sheet and something for me to refer to just in case. They basically tell me if a guest is important, and how much of their arse I need to lick once they start to complain.

Lynne takes a seat while she points out who might be tricky and who I need to have a nice chat with. The poor girl is seven months pregnant and the heat is not helping. We found her when we did a recruitment drive in Singapore. She was delighted to get the job. Sadly her last-night fling with her husband resulted in the large bulge that strains in front of her. Which is a shame for both her and me, as I've enjoyed having a secretary who is charming and efficient and good at her job, while she's enjoyed being here. She says that she will come back to work after the baby is born and leave it with her husband. But we both know she is lying.

She points out a couple of big spenders who checked in over the weekend. She reminds me of Mr Antonov with his $10,000-a-day yacht waiting for him in the harbour, should he ever need it. She adds that Mr McCann is unlikely to come as another plane-load of his special friends have arrived and he has also taken over another two villas. She heads off to put her feet up in the staff village and I help myself to a flute of fizzy water.

I normally try to keep off the alcohol at the manager's drinks, otherwise I am drinking every night of the week. I am entertaining most nights and it would be rude not to drink. When I am hosting a dinner or meeting a guest for a cocktail, it is always difficult only to have one. The guest is on holiday, they are here to relax and are in the mood for a drink and I can't get away in less than forty-five minutes. Believe you me, I have tried. I have also tried to make one drink last forty-five minutes and it is impossible. No matter how many ladylike sips I take, the longest I have managed is thirty minutes. Christ, most of the time you have to get pissed to deal with the level of conversation.

'Good evening,' I smile, walking straight up to an elderly couple who are so sweaty and pink they look like a couple of roasting kebabs.

'Awright there,' says the short man, leaning back and putting his hand into the pocket of his pistachio trousers.

'This is Mr and Mrs Bentley,' says Leila, one of the restaurant hosts. It is always useful to invite a few of these guys along to the drinks as they have much greater contact with the guests and tend to know who is who. 'This is our general manager,' she continues.

'Very pleased to meet you, I'm sure,' says Mr Bentley. 'This is the lady wife, Carol.'

'How do you do,' she says, grabbing hold of me with both of her large, hot hands. 'We're having ever such a lovely time.'

'Good, good,' I say, smiling away. 'I'm glad to hear it. Anything I can do to help?'

'Oh no,' asserts Mr Bentley. 'I have been to most of the resorts in the world and this is the best.'

'Really? How very kind of you to say so.'

'Oh yes,' his wife continues. 'We have been to nearly all the resorts in the world.'

Just my luck, I think, as I stand smiling away, drinking my water. I am shattered, I need a lie-down, and the first person I meet is bloody Resort Man. Resort Man is usually some sort of middle-aged middle-management type of bloke who takes one expensive holiday a year and never stops talking about it. He travels Club Class and makes sure his friends know exactly how much the tickets were. He's been all over the world but has never seen anything, because bar the all-inclusive transfer from the airport he doesn't leave the hotel. A creature of habit, he tends to be English or American, he loves a complimentary anything and is usually keen on golf. We tend not to get too many Resort Men staying here, mainly because we don't have a golf course, we don't ask people to wear a tie for dinner and we are reassuringly expensive.

'Have you been to the Lémuria resort?' he asks me.

'No,' I say. 'I can't say I have.'

'Oooh,' says Carol. 'It's ever such a lovely place.'

'One of the best golf courses in the world,' says Mr Bentley. 'Do you like a round? You should get a course here.'

'Yes, you should get a course here,' repeats his wife, taking a gulp of champagne. 'As I said to John just the other day, that's what you're lacking here. Didn't I, dear?'

'Yes you did, dear. It would make ever such a difference.'

'I know.' Jesus Christ, I need a drink. 'I am sorry,' I

say. 'Lovely to meet you. I'm afraid I have to circulate.'

'Of course,' says Mr Bentley. 'You're the boss.'

I walk over to the drinks tray and grab myself a glass.
I down it in one and turn around, smile in place. 'Good
evening.'

'Hi,' says the neat bloke in expensive, architecturally
designed specs. His New York accent in unmistakable.
'Marshall. James Marshall. I need to talk to you about
my upgrade.'

'Of course!' I say. Oh bugger off, I think. Don't you
know I've heard it all before and I've been up since
three in the morning? 'What seems to be the problem?'

I inhale and brace myself. I have had a few problems
with Mr Marshall already. He is what I would tech-
nically term an 'upgrade cunt' – the sort of person who
is just so bloody difficult to please that you give them
what they want just to get rid of them.

He originally booked a Water Villa with pool at
$4,000 a night. He was supposed to come via
Singapore but changed his mind. Then he couldn't get
a flight. So I booked him a private jet. Then he wanted
to come three days earlier, but I didn't have the Water
Villa with pool, so I gave him all we had, which was a
lowly Beach Villa. He ordered a private boat transfer so
he didn't have to wait for other people. But he arrived
an hour early and had to wait a full forty minutes for
his boat! He kicked up a fuss, so I upgraded him to the

best villa on the island – the Grand Beach with pool. He sits in there for three days for the same price as a normal Beach and now he is pissed off because we have asked him to move, as the place is booked.

'So let me get this right,' he says, taking a step forward and backing me up against a lantern. 'You are asking me to move for one night?'

'I am sorry, sir,' I say. 'But there is nothing we can do.'

'I can't believe you are asking me to move,' he says. 'It is so stressful and I have come here to relax and now you're giving me grief.'

I try and point out that he has been given the most expensive villa on the island for a fraction of the price, but he seems to think that it is now his right to be in the place. This sort of thing happens all the time. You're generous and kind, but your generosity is thrown right back in your face. If you upgrade someone once, they expect it every time they come here. Having now tasted the delights of the most superior set-up we have, this guy is damned if he is going back. I can't believe I never seem to learn my lesson.

Last year we had this woman who fell over and chipped a bone. The hotel wasn't grovelling enough at the time and we didn't give her enough attention, so when she complained to head office they gave her a free return trip so that she didn't sue. But all that happened is that she returned and found something else to complain about, and now she is back this week on another freebie, accompanied by her parents. I have instructed Leila and a couple of the other guys to stop them from mixing too much with the other guests, because they start to whinge and whine and they talk to someone else and tell them how they got compensated and it spreads like a cancer. Soon everyone is ringing up the spa, saying they didn't like their pedicure. Or they say their food is bad, or the room is not what they were expecting, and we find ourselves in some sort of compensation hell, where all we are doing is genuflecting and handing out free massages.

Kate appears on the other side of the beach. She is looking stunning, despite her experience at the coalface of gold-digging. I do hope all those girls on the make don't give her any ideas.

'Hi,' she says, walking over and giving my lower arm a squeeze. We tend not to do that much kissing in public; it confuses the guests. 'You've got drips all down your shirt.'

I look down. Shit. She's right. I look like a bloody toddler or an uncoordinated drunk, with half a bottle of champagne down my shirt. 'Oh God.' I roll my eyes. 'I'm going to have a word with those bloody store guys.'

Truth is, I know what has happened. Last week we

had over a thousand napkins go missing. How I don't know. Or even why. What can you do with a whole pile of pink linen? And now they are serving champagne without cocktail napkins. It may sound a little poncy, but when you're out here and trying to look like you are in charge, you need a napkin to wrap around the bottom of your glass, otherwise, as I have just demonstrated, the humidity condenses on your cold glass and dribbles down the front of your shirt, which is fine if you are not trying to sort out an upgrade cunt or sell a Russian a $10,000-a-day boat. I am about to go over and give the waiters a bollocking when Kate grabs my arm and turns her back on the Chinese dragons.

'For God's sake, talk to me,' she hisses. 'Make me look busy or something.'

'Why? What?' I ask.

'The Desperate Housewives have arrived.'

I look up to see two of our collection of four Desperates standing on the other side of the beach, each picking up a glass of champagne. My heart sinks. Poor Kate. I put my arm around her and take her over to meet Mr and Mrs Bentley. Take it from me, even a Resort Man is better company than a Desperate.

Married to a member of staff, usually a manager, the Desperate Housewives are just that. They live here on the island and do absolutely nothing. They don't cook, they occasionally clean their villas, but other than that they have sweet FA to keep them occupied.

Alison is the Chief Desperate. Married to Alan, our financial controller, she purports to be a painter but never seems to pick up a brush. The light is apparently not terribly good here. So she divides her time between the spa and the gym, but never seems to look any different. She has been on a diet since she came here fourteen months ago but doesn't seem to have lost a pound.

Deputy Desperate is Bernard's wife Monica. As the resident manager's wife, she takes her position very seriously and is always leaning on Kate to borrow jewellery from the boutique to wear for resort functions, claiming she has some sort of ambassadorial role. Worst of all she tries to get involved. She is always trying to come up with ideas on how to improve the resort. Just the other day she tried to redesign the staff uniforms.

Fortunately the other two – Maria and Lia – are married to one of the restaurant managers and the sales manager, and are a little less high profile. They tend to stay at home, boiling rice in the hope that their husbands will come home from work. They sure as hell wouldn't turn up to manager's drinks, like Alison and Monica here, looking more bouffed and coiffed than the guests.

'I have been to all the resorts in the world,' declares Mr Bentley. 'As has my lady wife here, Carol.'

'Oh really?' I hear Kate enthuse. 'Tell me, which one did you like best?'

Wednesday a.m.

Last night's drinks just went on and on. Mr Bentley talked Kate through his top-ten resorts in great detail and she grinned and nodded away like a dog on the back shelf of a minicab. Sadly it was not enough to put off the pincer manoeuvre executed by the pair of Desperates, who caught her on the way out of the loo and had her up against the basins for half an hour, while they discussed manicures and the latest polishes that have arrived in the spa. Kate told me afterwards that she would genuinely trade an hour with Mr Bentley for ten minutes with the Desperates.

Meanwhile I did the rounds. I nodded and high-ed the Japanese newly-weds, I spoke to the freebie Brits and the married media couple from west London. I spent a good half-hour talking to Mr Antonov and his wife about boats and suggested many trips that they might like. I chatted to Mr and Mrs Thompson, who turned up a little late and appeared to drink a bottle of Veuve each before loudly bickering their way to dinner on the back of a golf buggy.

Kate and I were just waving them off and contemplating room service and a quiet night when Mr McCann and his girls arrived. No one had been expecting them. VIPs of his ilk rarely turn up to manager's drinks. But I have a feeling they were in search of a party and Kate and I ended up having to give it to them.

We took them out to dinner at Samurai, the restaurant in the north of the island. Situated next to Palm Sands beach, it is supposedly the most prestigious restaurant on the island. Thankfully we got stuck into the sake and the girls put on a bit of a show, pole-dancing the black lacquer walls and dancing on top of the light bar in their high heels. Most of the guests had retired by the time the antics kicked off. After all, only the real holiday hardcore are knocking back the lychee martinis at midnight. So there wasn't too much damage done.

That said, I do feel pretty shit this morning. Lying in bed, staring up at the fan, what I really need is a litre of water and a vitamin booster drink to get me out of bed. It is five forty-five and what I feel like doing is pulling the sheets over my head and rolling over and going back to sleep.

Instead, I crawl out of bed and slide back the shutters.

'Oh fuck!' I say.

'What?' asks Kate, rolling over, her long blonde hair all knotted and tangled.

'It's raining.'

'Oh God,' she groans. 'That's all we need.'

Boy is she right. If there is one thing that is worse than the perpetual sunshine, the heat, the glare, the humidity and the bloody great bore that is good weather, it's shit weather. Shit weather is a pain in the arse. Actually, shit weather is more than that; it is the bane of our lives. There is nothing worse than waking up and hearing the pitter-patter of raindrops and looking out on a lead-grey sky.

Normal hotels in normal parts of the world are not that weather dependent. They know that if it's sunny they might have a run on the artichoke salad, or that in winter punters tend to go for the hot pot or the soup. Here, the whole bloody show collapses.

As soon as the sun goes in, the guests complain. And they complain to you, like you're bloody God and can do something about it. You get the huffs and the sighs at breakfast, you get the surly cold shoulders and you get the endless questions. How often does this happen? Is this normal? Is it global warming? Then you get the accusations – but I thought that this was the dry season? They always ask you how long it is going to last, to which my standard reply is that as this is an island the weather comes and goes very quickly. I always give them hope that it will blow over by the afternoon. The last thing you do is say that the depression is going to sit here for a week and you'll never see the sun for the whole of your very expensive trip. Otherwise all hell breaks loose and guests start trying to book flights out of here and you spend the whole day on hold for the private jet companies, as the affluent sun-seekers search for somewhere more user-friendly.

And that really is the problem in this place. It was designed for the sun, so when it pisses with rain it is not at all user-friendly. All the dining rooms are open air. So in a strong wind the glasses fly off the tables, the cloths flap, the cutlery goes into the sea and everything gets wet. We only have one room that we can seal off from the elements and that's the wine storage room, so that's where we end up putting the breakfast buffet in a force-eight gale. We did have a terrible storm recently when the wind and rain lashed the east side of the island so hard for two days that the waves tore the front off the horizon pool, cracked the pillars in the main restaurant and sent tables and chairs into the sea. We had a meeting about buying some rain blinds but we were quoted $80,000 just for the main restaurant, so they've been added to the to-do list – which means nothing will be done about them until the next time.

Sometimes I think that the big cheeses at head office don't realize that tropical islands only look this lush and green and fertile because they get so much rain. They must suppose it never rains here at all, otherwise I can't explain the consignment of paper umbrellas we received last month. Over five hundred of the bastards tipped up from China and as soon as we looked at them we knew they were useless. I knew some stupid sod had ordered them because they were a nice sandy yellow colour and looked really pretty. But firstly they blew inside out at the smallest gust of wind and secondly they weren't bloody waterproof. We had guests turning up covered in yellow paint at breakfast. They had spots or ruddy great stripes of the stuff down their shirts and dresses. So I called in maintenance and got them to collect the lot and cover the bastards in lacquer to waterproof them. The only problem was that as all five hundred of them lay in the sun drying, no one had thought they needed to be able to close. As they were folded up they cracked, got stuck together and tore holes in themselves, so we had to ditch them altogether. I am planning on a large bonfire to burn the lot of them. So at the moment we have five hundred golf brollies on order, which should see us through the rainy season and well into the end of next year.

Our other problem is that we don't have a wet-weather programme, so when the heavens open no one knows what to do. The guests can't go snorkelling, they can't take out the catamarans, they can't sunbathe, so they stay in bed and order room service. Or they stay in bed and are late for breakfast. In fact, everything becomes late. Room service is late because everyone wants it. Breakfast is late because no one wants to get up. And no one can get anywhere because the buggies are stuck.

It takes twenty minutes of rain to flood the roads. They are made of a mixture of sand and concrete so they don't drain and are easily swept away. The palms shed fronds in the wind and the main roads are blocked. But the buggies themselves are even more annoying. They are not sealed underneath so the batteries get wet in the puddles and grind to an immediate halt. The covers that are there to protect the guests from the elements rip in the wind, and the buggies take three times longer than usual to crawl through the wet sand to pick people up. And, of course, everyone now wants picking up because they don't want to walk in the pissing rain. Then the buggies get stuck. You see the guests sitting there, not getting out of their seat, thinking I am a VIP on holiday, I am not moving until someone finally brings me a yellow paper umbrella to escort me to the restaurant.

'God,' adds Kate, stretching in bed. 'I bloody hate it here when it rains.'

'I agree,' I say. 'The whole place just collapses.'

The first thing I do is call reception and get them to log on to Wind Guru to see how long the shitty weather is going to last. Wind Guru is one of those fantastically accurate websites which gives us hour-by-hour predictions of what the winds and waves are up to, how much cloud cover we can expect, and what the temperature is going to be like.

The news from reception is not good. The bad weather is here for some time. Certainly all day today and perhaps into tomorrow. Shit, I think as I sit on the edge of my bed. Time to make a few phone calls to make sure we are prepared. I ring housekeeping to make sure all the staff have their raincoats, and call up the front desk to tell them to get all the brollies we have to the main restaurant. I tell the buggy guys to put their flaps down and prepare for a lot of action. And once again I miss my morning workout and head straight to the main dining room. It is time for me to put my face about and do some smiling and a bit of morale-boosting.

As I turn the corner in my buggy and head towards the restaurant, I can't believe the damage. Jesus Christ, there must have been a storm last night and I was so full of sake that I failed to notice it. There are palm fronds everywhere, there are huge pools of water, there are buggies stuck in the sand – one is simply abandoned in the middle of the road – there's one tree down, the rain is driving against my windscreen and my shitty little wipers are not coping well. I squint out at all the mess. It's like a bloody battlefield, something out of *Black Hawk Down*.

I skid and crawl my way to the restaurant to find Hori standing in the reception area dressed in a cream-coloured rain cape and wellington boots.

'All right there, mate,' he says, looking out from underneath his hood.

'Jesus,' I say, fumbling for one of the few umbrellas. 'This is a mess.'

'Yeah,' he agrees. 'You should see the staff village. It's fucked.'

'Oh, great.'

'The showers are off again. A water pipe is broken.'

'How long will it take to fix?'

'In this weather,' he says, looking up at the slate-grey sky, 'a couple of hours.'

'What time is it now?'

'Twenty to seven,' he says.

'Make sure they're ready for after breakfast,' I say. 'That would be two days in a row that we've had no showers. The staff are going to start to smell.'

'I have to say a few are a little high already,' he grins.

123

'Anyway, what are you doing here?' I ask.

'One of the restaurant managers called me over,' he says. 'Apparently they're having a problem finding the rain blinds for the restaurant.'

'What rain blinds?'

'The ones we bought.'

'We didn't.'

'What?'

'We didn't buy them. They were too expensive.'

'No shit? You're fucking kidding me.'

'I'm not.'

'Who made that clever decision?'

'Purchasing, along with head office,' I say.

'That the same purchasing who spent a small fortune on pens from China that break as soon as you take the lid off? Or the one that bought 280 bicycles that cost more to repair than they do to buy new? The one that bought paper umbrellas?'

'That's the one,' I nod.

'Great,' he says, heaving a heavy sigh as he turns around. 'So in the meantime, what do we do about all this shit? These guys are fighting a losing battle.'

I follow him into the main dining room to discover about fifteen of the night cleaners frantically running around with buckets, cloths and mops. Some are on their hands and knees slapping the floor with wet towels, others are bent double, channelling the water with mops and brooms. And the rest of them are running backwards and forwards with buckets of water, emptying brown slops over the side into the turbulent sea. But no sooner have they cleared up the pools of water from the black slate floor than another gust of wind sends a wave lashing against the side of the swimming pool and seawater crashing up and over into the restaurant. The wooden slat blinds are slamming around in the wind. The round paper lampshades are blowing madly on the ceiling like they're possessed. Pot plants, table decorations and salt and pepper cellars have flown into the sea. And all the waiting staff are standing and staring at me, wondering what to do. There is no point in laying half the tables; as soon as anything hits them it is swept up over the side. So after a quick conversation we decide to lay as many tables as we can at the back of the dining room, inshore as it were, and pop a few more in the wine cellar area, and then basically cross our fingers and hope that the majority of the guests order room service and stay in bed.

My mobile goes.

'*Hola*,' comes the by now familiar voice of Mrs Thompson's nanny. She wants a buggy to get to breakfast and then one on to the kids' clubs. I grit my teeth and oblige. I now realize that I have become the nanny's nanny. At her beck and call 24/7, sorting out anything and everything that she can't be schlepped to do herself. I am not going to make this mistake again. From now on anyone whose staff can't speak English is going to get a little sympathetic smile and a tough-shit shrug.

No sooner do I hang up from sorting out her problems than I get a call from Bernard.

'*Mon dieu*,' he whispers down the line. 'Get yourself over here to the service villa bloody quick step smart. We have a world war on our hands.'

I can hear the shouting and screaming as I pull up outside the villa. As I am walking up the path towards the door, Bernard rushes out to meet me.

'Bloody hell fuck,' he says, stopping me in my tracks. 'We have a couple of Germans kicking off. They have hit the GSA [guest services assistant], pushed Garry against the wall and grabbed him by the shirt, and the children have now pushed the mother inside the villa and have locked the door. And all because their room is not ready.'

This happens all the time. Well, perhaps not this level of violence, but anyone who flies here on a scheduled flight always arrives in a foul mood. I think it is a sort of extension of air rage. They fly overnight, they have a few drinks, they land in a shitty airport where there is no air-con, they wait for their luggage only to have Customs go through it with a fine comb looking for

alcohol, porn and pork. They wait on the jetty, knowing they have another hour or so to go before they get
to the resort. They are in their winter clothes. It is
usually bright sunshine. They are hot and shattered and
still not here yet. Finally they set foot on the island
and find out their room is not ready and all hell breaks
loose. Or in this case they get here, find out it is raining
and then that they can't get into their room. So they
have been put into our service villa to shower and
change and relax until two p.m., when their place will
be ready. But this, sadly, has not quite hit the spot.

And now that they have resorted to violence, I have
been called in. I hang back and make a few phone calls
to neighbouring resorts Four Seasons and One and
Only to see if they will take them. The big problem,
Bernard informs me, is that even if I do get them to
apologize, half my staff are now refusing to serve them.
Finally, after much charm and persuasion, the Four
Seasons agrees to have them. So I walk into the villa
garden with my negotiating cap firmly on.

'Finally we have the manager,' says the husband
sarcastically as I cross the sand towards him. 'Pleased
to meet you at last.' He comes in for the full bear-hug
thing, smelling of stale booze, old sweat and in-flight
food.

'I gather we are having a few problems here,' I say,
patting his damp back.

'Your staff . . .' he starts.

'Have apparently been assaulted,' I finish. 'So I have found you a nice room at the Four Seasons, where you can be moved to this afternoon.'

This seems to shut him up, but only for a second. 'If you move me, I shall sue you,' he says.

'What for?'

'Um,' he thinks. 'Unfortunately for you, I am a lawyer . . . Breach of contract.'

'And he will win,' says his eldest Teutonic-looking son.

'And I will take it to the highest level,' adds the father, somewhat unconvincingly.

I look through the glass doors at his wife, lying pole-axed on the bed. She looks dead to the world and definitely the worse for in-flight refreshment. The daughter is staring at some rolling news on the TV. I have to say, I suddenly feel a little sorry for them. I know that feeling when the body is near total collapse. I get it almost every morning.

'Please don't move us today,' says the father, changing tack. 'I just don't think we can . . .' He runs out of energy.

'Listen,' I say. 'The problem is my staff are refusing to serve you because of your violent behaviour.'

'My wife's,' he corrects.

'Your wife's.' I smile. Nice lady, I think. 'So what I

am thinking is that if you write a letter of apology to the staff concerned and apologize in person, you can stay. However, any sign of trouble from you and I shall have you escorted off the island.'

'Done,' he says, sticking his hot, bloated hand out.

'OK then,' I say. 'I want that apology by this afternoon.'

'Of course,' he says, before disappearing into the villa to bollock his wife.

On my way to the morning meeting, I decide to drop into the spa to pick up Geri and check out what is going on. Normally within half an hour of waking up and finding that the weather on the island has taken a turn for the worse, the guests do one of two things. They order room-service breakfast and go back to sleep, or they book into the spa. It is as predictable as it is lame. It is almost as if their initiative disappears along with the sun. I have lost count of how many times I've been called up by bored guests asking what to do. You can hear it in their voice: their flat indecision is usually accompanied by a great fat yawn. I have my stock responses. Read a book. Watch a film. Have an afternoon bath. But then you forget that these are the sort of people who are so damn busy in their real lives, they are never bored. They work their arses off to get here, then don't know what to do once they arrive.

Geri looks flustered and sweaty when I walk in. Her white therapist's coat looks tight and uncomfortable and the phone is ringing off the hook.

'Yes I know, sir, terrible,' she says down the line. 'If we get any form of cancellation we will call you straight back. Absolutely . . . Of course, you're top of the list.' She hangs up. The phone goes straight away. 'Sorry,' she mouths. 'Good morning, how can I help you?'

Poor Geri, I have to admire her. The spa really is the frontline here. It is where the shit hits the fan and the guests kick off the most. We get more complaints about the spa than about anything else in the resort and yet it makes us the most money. The problem is that everyone's idea of a good massage is different. Some like it hard, some like it soft, some will let men do it, others, like the Arabs, kick up such a fuss about a bloke massaging them you would think you'd questioned their sexuality or something. The same goes for the sauna and the steam. The Russians like it at 115 degrees. Everyone else wants it at 85 degrees. So we have it at 95 degrees and no one is happy.

Then again, these are the sort of people who are always hard to please. They shout and scream when they don't get their appointments, and they shout and scream when you charge them for not turning up. And, bad weather aside, they all want to come at the same time. Everyone wants a massage between four and eight p.m. No one wants one in the morning. They all want a massage and then they want to go out to dinner. So the pressure for evening appointments is huge. The Russians usually book everything up in advance even before they have arrived on the island and then complain when they are charged a cancellation fee. Couple massages are very popular with honeymooners and the Swedish is what tickles the blokes.

Just as sauna temperature is dictated by nationality, so are the tips. The Arabs and the Russians are the same: they either give you $1,000 for a massage or nothing at all. The Brits are fairly standard and add between 10 and 15 per cent to everything. But the Japs are a nightmare. They leave one-dollar tips all the time, so much so that quite often straws are drawn to see who is going to bother to massage them. It's a joke.

As is the pressure that Geri is under this morning.

'Fucking hell,' she says as she hangs up. 'Get me outta here.'

Geri and I slosh through the rain to the buggy and drive off past the now packed gym to the meeting.

'Jesus,' she says, leaning back into the seat next to me. 'How long is this shit going to last?'

'All day,' I say. 'And probably tomorrow.'

'God, I hate it when it rains here,' she says, poking her head out of the side flap of the buggy. 'It's just so damn depressing. The place looks like a shit hole and those crows –' she points out a large black dank-looking bird taking cover in a palm – 'they want shooting. They remind me of *Jurassic Park*. They lower the tone of the place.'

We walk into the meeting to be greeted by a sea of miserable faces. The room smells of damp clothes and there are wet sandy footprints all over my cream carpet tiles. The windows are steamed up from all the hot coffees and there's an aroma of stale biscuits.

'All right, everyone?' I say, trying to be jolly, rallying the troops.

'Nice weather,' sniffs Ben, sitting down next to me, throwing his soaking-wet Pacamac poncho on the floor. 'If you're a fucking duck.'

'So,' I say, rubbing my hands together and ignoring the bastard. 'Anyone got any good news?'

'Um, the spa's full,' says Geri. 'To bursting and beyond.'

'Great,' I say, pointing at her with my pencil. 'We like a full spa. Anything else?' I take in the row of blank faces. 'Good . . . good . . . good,' I say, going up and down the table. 'Bernard?'

'Oh,' he says. 'The drink-driving German industrialist who is under house arrest has written asking permission to leave his villa and have dinner in the Lotus tonight.'

'He's written a letter?'

'Eh, *oui*,' says Bernard, waving it at me. 'He's been very polite. Apparently he is fifty-three today.'

'Let's send him a cake and some flowers and say yes to the dinner,' I say. 'Seeing as he asked so nicely. Good . . . So, now, the weather.' Everyone sighs. 'It will be here all day and perhaps tomorrow.'

'Oh no!' They all huff and puff and exhale, like it's my fault.

'So we need to say something to the guests.' I look up and down the table again. Everyone starts to pick fluff off their T-shirts or draw on the pads in front of them.

'Like what?' asks Ben.

'Something positive.'

The room is silent. It's like tumbleweed is blowing through the place.

'At least it's not snowing?' pipes up Hori.

'Excellent. Fucking excellent,' I say, clicking my fingers and giving him a quick finger point. 'At least it's not going to bloody snow. Perfect.'

'Maybe without the bloody?' suggests Geri.

'Of course.'

Wednesday p.m.

The meeting trailed on and on. I think the reason everyone hung around was no one fancied going back out into the pissing rain or dealing with irate and over-wrought guests. There was much banter about Mr Antonov, who has yet to set foot on his $10,000-a-day yacht. Ben suggested that one of us sail it past his villa just to remind him that he has booked the bugger. The poor crew have been sleeping below deck, waiting to pipe him aboard for a couple of days now, and quite frankly I am of half a mind to tell them to go back to the marina from whence they came.

Garry was also quite chatty. He regretfully informed me that Liz Hurley has left the resort. She flew out early this morning under a cloud of wind and rain. She apparently got my bottle of champagne and my excuses the other night and seemed pleased with her stay –

unlike most celebs of her *Hello!* magazine stature. I am just a little annoyed that I had my head so far up Mr McCann's televisual arse that I missed pressing her fragrant flesh. Oh well, what's a bloke to do? We always have to choose money before muff in this job.

Garry also told me that I am scheduled to meet a private jet this afternoon, which I have to say is the last thing I need right now. We've got nine guests with private jets parked at the airport at the moment, so it's not that big a deal for us. As part of the luxury VIP meet-and-greet service I am supposed to be the one who meets them on the tarmac as soon as they touch down. But it takes such a huge chunk out of my day I always try and delegate that to someone else. It is a three-hour round trip to the airport and back. Then there's the hanging around waiting for the jet to arrive; they are nearly always late and I obviously can't leave without them, even if I have some pressing meeting back at the resort.

I have tried doing a bit of work on the boat before, but the thing bounces around so much it is hard to keep your papers in order or your brain functioning. Also the engines are so bloody loud it is hard to make yourself audible on the mobile. So I sometimes use the cabin below deck to crash and catch up on a few zs. But to be totally honest, I then look like a crumpled wreck with my creased face and well-slept-in shirt by the time I arrive. Which is not exactly the image my bosses are after. Still, a nap can be useful if you have a bit of a hangover – though if it's a bastard there is nothing worse. Try doing three hours with room spin in a confined space; it's no wonder that the last time I ended up vomiting over the side.

But this guy, Mr Georgi, is another one of those big-cheese oligarchs who imports frozen chicken for half of Russia, or at least that's what his Wikipedia entry says. He claims to be flying incognito, but is bringing some twenty or so mates and bodyguards with him. He has taken over the whole of Golden Sands in the west of the island. He's got a Grand Beach for himself and another ten villas for his mates and hangers-on. I think it is his fortieth birthday, or maybe his forty-fifth – either way, not only is he super rich but he is also irritatingly young.

We all then talked about the size of jet he might be arriving in. One of the bizarre things about this job is that you learn a whole new language of materialism. I had never really considered the differences between private jets before I tipped up here. A jet was a jet. Some were more swish than others, but quite frankly I could not have cared less either way. Now I can tell you the difference between a Lear and a Gulfstream; I know how many people you can fit in each and how much they cost to run, how much petrol they get through, and how many dollies with drinks you need to complete the journey in total comfort.

Only last week we had this guy who was complaining about the size of his villa. He kept on saying that it was the size of the wardrobe on his plane. 'My *Flieger* [flyer] is so much bigger than this,' he said over and over. All I thought was, yeah, yeah, shut up, and my cock is enormous too. Then as I went to see him off at the airport he invites me into a bloody Boeing 747, which is the same size as *Air Force One*, President Bush's little gadabout. We go through these electric doors, where I am asked to take my shoes off, and I am met by a hostess in a dirndl with a tray of drinks. There's this thick cream carpet and mahogany everywhere. He's got these magnetized coasters so that he can put his drink down during take-off and landing. Then he opens a bottle of Dom and gives me the tour. There are big armchairs with a desk and a coffee table all on hydraulics. He has a king-size bed, a plasma, a bath, a shower, gold taps. All I could think of while he was taking me around was, why would he be bothered with our shitty little resort? I mean, I could have gone on holiday right here. No wonder he found his 1,700-square-foot villa a little poky.

Anyway, I managed to persuade Garry that it would be good for his guest relations to go and meet Mr Georgi at the airport. Ben was keen – anything for a lie-down, I suspected. I seem to remember he spent most of his shifts back in London snoozing on the desk in the back office. It's not that I don't think he deserves a little relax, it's just that he hasn't been here long enough to answer any of Mr Georgi's questions. Of which there are bound to be many, seeing as they would be stuck together on the boat for an hour on the way back.

Eventually the meeting packed up and I spent the rest of the morning staring out of the window, looking at the rain, signing stuff off. You'd be amazed how much paperwork a place like this generates. Everything has to be signed off in triplicate and I am the last person in the chain. I have a black leather book with pages and pages of contracts and expenses that need to be signed. Lynne's very efficient and puts the most important stuff at the front. But it still takes the best part of an hour, almost every day, to get through it. I also have a petty-cash float of over a quarter of a million dollars, in case the staff need to be paid in folding. And as I have become a slightly obsessive control freak, I check everything, from the staff food bills – which run into thousands – to the maintenance bills – which run into hundreds of thousands. Today I have a corker. I have to sign off on $27,000 of rocks. I mean, who would have thought that rocks would be so goddamn expensive? Christ knows where they have imported them from, but

I imagine they were collected by virgins during a rare spring dew for that sort of cash. All I know is that we need them and they are going to cost us another small fortune to shift and put in place.

Ever since we had that large storm and half the front of the pool was washed away, we have been trying to find a solution to the wave problem, and someone has come up with the not-so-cheap-rocks idea. However, now that they have arrived they're causing another headache – which is physical as well as fiscal. We've got to move 520 tonnes of rock and we have hired this pin barge to do it. It is supposed to claw its way along the sea bed to sit in front of the restaurant. And while it is ruining everyone's expensive view and buggering up the coral that surrounds the island, we are going to have to employ special divers to hand-place each boulder, so that next time the sea gets a little agitated the waves will be broken by the new barrier. We have to achieve this in between two and four days while writing a grovelling letter to every guest in the place, apologizing for ruining their view/holiday/life. However, if we don't do the rock thing, then the next time we have a large storm the pool will end up in the sea. It all seems so much simpler on paper.

As does everything in this place. It is the upkeep and the maintenance that really takes it out of me and it eats into our meagre possibility of profit. It's the little things that add up, like the roofs on the villas that all need to be re-thatched every two years, at the cost of something like $2,500 a villa. We've got eighteen boats that have to be looked after. They cost $350,000 a year in spare parts alone. Then the boilers have to be reconditioned because they keep going rusty. The water-treatment plants need all the pipes re-casing. Even the 155 plasma TVs that we supposedly have on the island (although I know some of them have already gone walkabout) need to be serviced and repaired. Guests are always losing remote controls and the sets tend to blow up in the humidity. It is no wonder, then, that I signed off on over $2 million worth of little bits and pieces last year.

Today we have a hammock issue. Actually, we are supposed to have a hammock issue, but I suspect due to the shit weather we shall be doing it all tomorrow, or indeed the day after. Jiwan, the head gardener, is supposed to be hanging double hammocks in the Grand Villas to make them appear more relaxing and laid back. But this is not as easy as it sounds. Firstly, they have to be attached to poles that are sunk into concrete, not sand – who says we haven't learnt from losing thirty parasols into the sea? Secondly, this all has to be done with diggers and drills and at no inconvenience to the other guests on the beach. We managed it last week because we sent a whole bay of guests on a free snorkelling trip. The hammocks had to be in place by two p.m. when the guests came back. It was a bit like *Challenge Anneka*, except there was no sexy backside to gawp at, just a couple of locals sweating their bollocks off in the sun. Eventually we downed tools at three thirty and we only got six complaints.

I have a quick chat with Jiwan over the phone and he confirms that he's not going to do the hammocks today. The sand is sodden and the likelihood of any of the guests taking us up on a free snorkelling trip when it is still raining and the visibility is so poor will be a total zero. He says he has plenty to be getting on with already, as we have seven trees down and more leaves blocking the roads than in any municipal town. He also says all the birds outside the villas need feeding.

'Oh God,' I sigh. 'Have the villa hosts forgotten to do them again?'

'Yes sir,' he says. 'And I have found fifteen dead birds already this morning.'

One of the more irritating affectations of this resort is that when they designed and built the villas, they thought it would be charming to have a gilded cage with a pair of lovebirds outside each of the villas. Like there weren't enough of the buggers in the trees, a mere ten feet away. But no. A twittering cage of birds hanging outside the villa is what every jaded executive wants to see when they get off a twenty-hour flight. However, what nobody thought about was who was going to look after these things? Who was going to clean out the ruddy cages and make sure that the birds didn't roast alive in the very hot sun? So now they have become another little headache for one department to pass on to another. Housekeeping say that it is maintenance's responsibility, and maintenance have passed the buck to gardening. Either way, just so long as some sod makes sure there are two birds alive and well and hopping around in each cage, I don't care.

I hang up on Jiwan, asking him to look after the birds, and stare out the window. At least the rain is easing up now. It has become the sort of low-level drizzle that you'd expect during a dreary British November. I am thinking about getting myself some sort of late lunch. On rare occasions I make it back home for lunch and order myself room service. But on a day like today, not only will they be so overstretched that my order would not be welcome, but it would also take them over an hour to get it to me, which is sadly a luxury I can't afford. And they are not the kind of guys you want to mess about. Chief Desperate Alison once kicked off at room service because they had given her six, rather than five, pieces of sushi and now her orders take more than an hour to arrive as a matter of course! So unless you want to starve, you pick your room-service moment carefully and treat them well, otherwise you'll find yourself up shit creek without so much as a bowl of tomato soup.

I walk into the staff canteen to catch the tail end of the lunchtime service. It is a large room with grilles on the windows, full of red-painted chairs and tables. There are two serving areas. One is for hot food – curries, stews and the odd vegetable bake. Next to it is a large salad bar, which is full of almost every type of salad you can think of, plus the usual carbs posing as salad, such as pasta and potato. Although the canteen is entirely mixed, with management and cleaners all eating the same food, most of the staff still self-segregate according to nationality and rank. So all the Western managers sit together, as do all the Thai masseurs. The locals, who form almost 50 per cent of the workforce, sit in packs and don't take too kindly to other people joining them.

I often use my tour of the canteen to slap some backs and single people out for some sort of VIP treatment. It can be a good opportunity for me to sit down and have a chat about how things are going, and to find out if there are any little problems or egos that need sorting or soothing.

I am piling on the rice and an unidentifiable chicken dish when I spot Ben on the other side of the room. He is sitting on his own, underneath a poster that warns against stealing from guests and the hotel, gazing into space.

'How are you?' I ask, putting my green plastic tray down opposite him. He practically leaps out of his skin. He was bloody miles away.

'Oh, hi,' he says. 'Fine, I suppose. You?'

'Oh, you know, I hate it when it's stormy here. It kind of brings out the worst in the place.'

'I know what you mean,' he says, shovelling a tomato down his throat. 'I've had nothing but big-mouthed Yanks droning on about how they've had to cancel their diving and their holiday is ruined. I honestly think that half of them actually blame us for the shit weather and think we can actually do something about it. I said to one of them, "If I had God's powers, d'you think I'd be working in the service industry?"'

'Apart from that, how are you getting on?' I ask, crunching on some dodgy bit of Chilean chicken.

'You know,' he sighs. 'It's weird. I was expecting a sort of glam Club Med and it is totally different. It is much more like someone has dumped one of London's finest hotels on a desert island and we are the tossers who somehow have to make the joke work. My accommodation is not what I was expecting and I thought we'd have a bit more of a laugh. I sat up last night drinking my bodyweight in cheap beer and I had Hans, Hori and some South African gym nut for company . . .'

'Keith.'

'That's the one. Anyway, I'm not the first person in the world to be more interested in the beer than the company, but that lot are fucking alcoholics. There was barely a grunt between them.'

'It'll get better,' I say.

'Will it?' he asks. 'Or do you just get used to it?'

'Fucking hell,' says Geri as she plonks her hefty back-side next to mine. 'Can you believe I have only just managed to get off? The spa's that bloody full you wouldn't believe it.'

'I would,' I say.

'Oh Jesus,' she says, cracking open a Diet Coke. 'We had a spa virgin in today. Amazing. They refused to put the paper knickers on and everything.'

'They must be rare,' sulks Ben. 'They are all so bloody high-maintenance you would think that most of the guests here wouldn't be able to move for pedicures and full body scrubs.'

'I know,' agrees Geri. 'But I suppose the bad weather makes them try and think of something else to do. Actually,' she says to me, pointing with her forkful of pasta, 'you've got to sort out the Desperates.'

'The who?' asks Ben.

'Desperate Housewives,' Geri and I say together.

'Anyway,' she continues, 'it all kicked off in the spa after the meeting. Alison came down and started demanding that I get an appointment for her and Monica. They wanted some sort of double girls' massage so they could have a chat and get rubbed down at the same time and I said we were full and she said don't you know who I am? And I said we are still full and she said that she would be talking to you about my attitude and I said be my guest.' She inhales. 'Honest to God, they get on my tits.'

'Right,' I say. 'I'll have a word.'

'They should know when I have guests shouting at me from all angles asking for all sorts that they are not allowed to come in like they own the place, demanding treatments.'

'I'll have a word.'

'I mean, I told them before if we don't have room for guests we can hardly accommodate them, now can we?'

'He's said he'll have a word,' says Ben.

'I know, but really . . .' She shoves a large forkful of pasta into her mouth and chomps away. We have a moment's peace. 'Oh shit,' she says. 'I forgot to tell you. We had a puker in the spa today. It was a total nightmare.'

Geri then goes on to explain in graphic detail how the chief whore (her words) in Mr McCann's entourage booked herself in for some sort of detox scrub, and while the therapist was putting on the seaweed wrap the girl rolled over on the bed and puked all over the floor. Apparently she was terribly upset and went on to explain her bulimia was so bad she found it impossible to keep food down these days. The girl says she's worried that her clients might notice if she puts on a kilo, so she can't, and that's why she vomits all the time.

'Anyway,' continues Geri, 'the therapist bursts into tears, not at the tragedy of the situation but because she is afraid that she is the one who is going to have to clear up the puke. She is so sensitive she can't face it. So guess who ends up getting on all fours with a bloody bucket of water and a cloth?'

'Who?' I ask, thinking it's not going to be Ben.

'Muggins here.' She jabs herself with her fork. 'Which is why Guerlain paid some £20,000 for my spa training, so I could clear up Russian-hooker vomit off a marble floor.'

'But everything's under control at the spa?' I ask.

'Seems to be, touch wood.' She smiles. 'Which is more than I can say for room service. I have heard people complaining about it all day.'

'Really?' I ask.

'Oh yeah,' she sniffs. 'Over an hour and a half for some breakfasts.'

'Sounds like I should give them a call.'

Youssif is almost hysterical by the time I manage to get through to him. It is four o'clock in the afternoon and he is now having to cope with afternoon tea. We don't normally serve afternoon tea. There are a couple of complimentary cakes and sandwiches that the money-saver Brits usually tuck into at about five p.m. by the pool. But usually we don't do the fancy stack of fondants that we used to serve at £25 a pop in the good old days back in London. There just isn't the call for egg and cress on a tropical island. Except, of course, today. When no one can think of anything better to do than eat. And drink.

I have to say, sometimes when the weather has been pissing it down for days, which it can do, I sort of throw in the towel and announce there is a cocktail tasting in the bar. I get Jean-François on the case and tell him to rustle up some old mixers and shitty liqueurs that we've had problems shifting and tell everyone it's Happy for Hours in the main bar. If in doubt, we get the guests totally trolleyed. Most of them crawl home to bed at about eight p.m. and give the whole hotel an early night. But it hasn't been raining long enough yet to resort to such drastic measures. In this sort of place it is a good idea to keep one's trump cards close to one's chest.

'It is a nightmare, sir,' complains Youssif down the phone. 'And the kitchen, it is running out of food.'

'I know we have no pink champagne,' I say.

'Oh, it's much more serious than that,' he says. 'Pink

champagne we can cope without. We suggest a Kir or a normal champagne, and anyway the only people ordering that are Mr McCann and Mr Antonov's wife. But it's fruit and meat. The basics.'

'Can you survive until the boat tomorrow?'

'I don't know,' he says. 'There will be no fruit for the baskets tonight.'

Wednesday night is always a terrible night for the complimentary food baskets. Normally they are piled high with tropical exotica – all from Australia, of course. However, come Wednesday, when it has been a whole week since the last fruit order arrived, we are so stuck for anything edible, we usually put a couple of Golden Delicious on a plate and hope that no one notices.

'Do you think you can manage?' I ask.

'I'll try my best, sir.'

'Well, at least it's not snowing,' I say.

'That's true,' he replies.

My other line starts to bleep.

'I'm sorry, I've got to go. Hello?' I say.

'It's me,' says Kate. 'We've got a problem. Get your arse down here.'

Wednesday Sunset

I speed down to the boutique, tearing through large puddles and sloshing rainwater over the top of the footplates in the buggy. I can't believe how much rain has fallen today; the whole bloody road system is totally waterlogged.

I corner the manicured grass roundabout next to the boutique and see that the place is packed with semi-naked ladies and one short bloke sucking on a cigar. It seems that Mr McCann and his gang of pricy diamond-diggers are back. However, Kate does not look thrilled. She comes flying out of the door to meet me as I park up. Her pretty manicured feet splash through the puddles. She is in a hurry.

'Finally,' she hisses as she pulls back the water flaps. 'Here you are.'

'I got here as quickly as I could,' I say. 'Half the

island is under water and the other half is cut off by fallen trees.'

'Don't exaggerate,' she says.

'I'm sorry,' I reply, getting out of the buggy. 'I see they're all back.' I laugh. 'What seems to be the problem?'

'What is our policy on returns?' she asks, grabbing my arm.

'What do you mean?'

'They've brought all the bloody jewellery back,' she says.

'What?' I stop in my tracks. 'But that's over quarter of a million dollars' worth of stuff!'

'I know.'

'Shit,' I say, following on behind her. There goes our holiday bonus and special backslap from the boss.

'What is the returns policy?' she asks.

'I wasn't aware we had one,' I say. 'No one really brings a sun hat or a kaftan back.'

'Good evening, Mr McCann!' says Kate. 'Here's the manager. He'll sort it *all* out.'

'Good to see ya!' he says, turning around with his cigar stuck in his mouth. He comes towards me and goes for the bear-hug/backslap combination. 'Terrible weather we're having here.'

'At least it's not going to snow,' both Kate and I say at the same time.

'Now that's true!' He laughs loudly. 'It sure as hell is not going to do that!' A couple of the girls giggle along. 'So,' he says, flicking a large chunk of ash on the floor, 'we need to talk about these bits of paper I have been asked to sign. They seem a little expensive to me.'

He hands me this wad of chits, which as I flick through them seem to add up to something fairly substantial. They are closer to knocking $400,000 than $300,000. The Russian ladies were not holding back. There are necklaces, a couple of pairs of earrings and a rather expensive bracelet, as well as a few bikinis, a kaftan and a sarong.

'The thing is,' he says, taking my elbow and leading me down the shop towards the all-in-one-swimming-costume section, 'I was fast asleep and don't really remember buying all this stuff.'

'Of course, sir,' I say.

'And also,' he continues, 'I have a dealer I buy diamonds from. If I want rocks I know where to go and this is not the sort of place where I would normally buy rocks. It's not the money!' he laughs.

I laugh too. 'Of course not!'

'I mean, I can afford it,' he emphasizes. And then some, I think. 'But it's the principle.'

Mr McCann discusses principles with me for another five minutes while his group of prostitutes wait patiently in the background. One or two of them do have the decency to look a little sheepish as he complains. Eventually it is decided that he is going to give all the jewellery back, but in an attempt not to look like a tight-wad he says that the girls can keep the clothes and bikinis. There are squeals of delight and much hugging as they all disappear off together, leaving behind a cloying smell of cigar smoke and expensive perfume.

'Oh well,' says Kate as she slumps behind the counter. 'You win some . . .'

'I know,' I reply, watching them all pile into an eight-seater buggy. 'It's just that it's a fairly expensive one to lose.'

'We couldn't exactly force him to pay,' she remarks.

'No,' I say. 'I am just wondering if he would have noticed if we'd simply shoved them on the bill.'

'I know,' she agrees. 'It was the chits, wasn't it?'

'Yeah.'

'Next time I won't get them to sign,' she says. 'We shouldn't give them the chance to think about it.'

'I think if the sun had been out he wouldn't have bothered to complain.'

'Maybe,' she says. 'I hate this place when it rains.'

'Yeah,' I agree. 'Shall we have dinner together tonight?'

'At home?' she asks.

'Well we could try,' I say. 'Or in one of the restaurants? Room service is on its last legs.'

'I don't know,' she says. 'I'm not sure if I can face sitting at a table with a menu, making a decision. Oh God.' She flops forward with exhaustion. 'I never thought I would actually long to have a kitchen.'

Kate and I agree to try and meet up later. She knows as well as I do that dinner dates are a flexible and movable feast, particularly when the weather is bad, as anything could happen.

It is growing dark as I pull up outside the spa. I know Geri has had a day from hell so I am just going to put my face round the door to show a bit of moral support. To make sure that she and the rest of her staff are coping and see that they have managed to get through the day without too many pukers and problems and hiccups.

As I walk through the large glass swinging doors of the Balinese pagoda, all seems fine. The piped world music that ranges from Enya to the panpipes and back again is playing over the sound system. The water feature – some bubbling water pouring over a tasteful black stone ball – is gurgling away. And there are a few odds and sods staring into space on the padded banquette, clad only in their soft terry dressing gowns. So far so spa, I think as I make my way past the two Thai girls on reception and through to the back office.

'But it's not right,' I hear some woman complain. 'I

mean, call yourself a five-star spa . . . and you can't even get this right. What's wrong with you lot?'

'I am sorry, madam.' Geri is using her most polite, mollifying voice.

'It's not good enough,' comes a male voice. 'My girl-friend is not used to this level of service.'

'Is there anything I can help with?' I ask, walking into the back room to find Geri looking sweaty and tired and our chief manicurist, Lai Sim, staring at the floor and trying to slip out of the room. Opposite them is a forty-something woman who has made the best of herself and a young taut, toned toy boy who appears to be along for the ride. Or indeed as the ride. Either way, they are an odd-looking couple who are proving to be rather bad-tempered.

'You the manager?' she asks in thick Estuary English.

'Yes, madam, I am.' I bow slightly.

'Yeah, well, about time,' she continues.

'This is Mrs Maddox,' says Geri helpfully. 'From villa 121.'

'Ms Maddox, if you please,' she corrects. 'And this is Dave.'

'Hello, Ms Maddox . . . Dave,' I say, smiling from one to the other, thinking that 121 is a $2,000-a-night Water Villa and not your basic Beach, so one of them has got some cash. 'What seems to be the problem?'

'Well . . .' She inhales. 'It's this nail varnish. It is not

155

my usual colour . . .' She puts her tanned hand in my face. What? I'm thinking, this is a row about the colour of someone's nail varnish?

'Really? It looks very nice to me,' I say, looking at the long bird-like claws that have been painted some form of frosted pink.

'Don't you start,' says Dave. 'We've had the Scouser tell us that the colour is fine, like she's got any taste. The thing is, my girlfriend is not happy and that's all you need to know. End of.'

'Normally,' says Geri, ignoring the Scouse thing, 'if a guest is very attached to a colour they bring it with them so that they can have the correct shade of, say, burgundy throughout their stay.'

'But it's Chanel,' says Ms Maddox. 'I thought every spa stocked that?'

'Apparently not,' says Dave. 'Call yourselves five star?' he scoffs.

'Six, actually,' says Geri.

'Whatever,' he says. 'This is the second time you've done her nails and they're still not right.'

'Second?' I query.

It transpires that as well as the deluge the spa staff have had to cope with today, Ms Maddox and her toy boy have had them running around like a neurotic bunch of therapists. Which of course they are. But this couple have been quite extraordinary in their vociferousness. Not only did Ms Maddox try on and agree a colour with poor old Lai Sim here, but she went back to her villa only for Dave to complain and bring her back to have her nails changed twice this afternoon already.

We do sometimes get the professional spa complainers. Like the villa complainers, who always wait until they have gone home to write a letter of complaint, these guys wait until they have to pay the bill before they unleash. And then it is usually for paltry petty stuff that there is little we can do about. They didn't like their massage; the room wasn't hot enough – something so annoying that it is easier to comp the treatment than argue the toss. Although I stood my ground the other day, after some woman had called on the services of our hairdresser every afternoon to sort out her cheap nylon hair extensions after she came off the beach. The poor sod stood there sifting through a whole load of man-made fibres with a pair of hot irons, until she looked less like My Little Pony. He even cut her a bloody fringe for free. The end-of-week bill came in at a very reasonable $900 and her husband/boyfriend/client refused to pay, mouthing off about how her hair had been ruined. I just ignored him and told him to pay.

But Ms Maddox, standing here complaining about the level of frosting in her pink nail varnish, is like a control freak who doesn't know how to let go. In fact,

I am beginning to feel a little sorry for Dave. No wonder he is so uptight – he's just spent the last week trying to sate the woman. I imagine she is just as exacting when it comes to sex.

Geri comps the manicure, but before we manage to congratulate ourselves on a row well avoided, there is a large ruckus in reception. Even above the clang of Indian bells it is easy to hear what the bloke is shouting.

'No, I am not paying! And I am not putting this cigar out!'

I walk out into reception to find a semi-naked Saudi gentleman striding around the place in his boxer shorts and open dressing gown. He is waving a cigar and stinks of whisky. A rather young-looking Eastern European girl is standing next to him. I recognize him immediately. He is one of our Gulf regulars who books in for a week's R&R with a different nubile lovely every time, only to return a few weeks later with his wife and three children in tow. He spends a lot and tips well, so it is in our interest to be nice to him.

'Good evening, Mr Fahad! How are you?'

'What?' he says, turning to face me. His dark eyes are glazed. The man is properly plastered. Funny how he always makes a great show of emptying the minibar when he comes with his wife, but when he's here to relax it is a very different story.

'Hello, Mr Fahad,' I try again. 'How are you?'

'I will not put this cigar out and I will not be charged for missing my massage. I am going to charge *you* for this!' He grabs at his dressing gown. 'There was not one in my locker. So I had to take this from someone else's. You have made me into a thief.' He jabs at the air in front of him with his cigar. 'A thief!'

He then walks past me, totally ignoring my over-tures, and starts shouting in Hindi at the Thai girl on the desk, his logic presumably being that she looks a bit foreign and most of the foreigners in Saudi speak Hindi. He is getting nowhere fast and I can see that this situation could get out of control very quickly. I walk over to Geri and whisper for her to get hold of Mohammed, our head of security, should matters get out of hand, and I get the Thai girl on reception to order up a buggy. I then pull the young girl to one side.

'Now listen,' I say quietly. 'Do you speak English?'

'Of course I do,' she replies tartly. 'I need to for my job.'

'Help me get him out of here,' I say.

'Why should I?' she asks. She is certainly an operator; I'll give her that.

'Otherwise I shall have to ask you to leave the island,' I say.

'Fine,' she shrugs. 'Darling!' she says, breezing across the marble floor towards Mr Fahad. 'Let's go home. I am a little tired.'

'What?' he says, turning around.

'I am a little tired,' she repeats. 'Let's go home.'

'Good idea,' he says. 'This place is shit anyway.'

She escorts him out of the spa just as a buggy pulls up. As they flop into the back seat together, you can hear the sigh of relief echo around the Balinese pagoda. Someone turns Enya up a bit louder, another therapist changes a guest's shoes for a pair of cotton flip-flops, someone else sips on a honey-infused tisane – calm and zen have been restored.

'Hey, thanks for that,' says Geri, coming out from behind the desk. 'The last thing anyone needs now is a scene. I mean, look how busy we are.'

I follow her to the back of the reception area and look across the neatly mown grass at a few of the therapy pavilions. Diminutive huts with thatched roofs and individual therapy rooms, they are little havens of delight in these tranquil gardens. I look right out to the yoga pavilion and see a class of some eight or nine ladies, all with their feet in the air.

'Even yoga's full,' I say.

'I know,' confirms Geri. 'It was standing room only in Super Legs.'

'Really?'

'I know,' she says. 'They're that bloody bored.'

'At least Connie seems to be working out.'

'Yeah,' agrees Geri. 'Thank God for that.'

The yoga here has been a bit of a pain to get right.
Just recently we hired this sort of It girl cum yoga
teacher to work in the resort. She was certainly
attractive enough and looked the part, but she was useless. Actually, worse than that, she was very irritating.
The guests complained about her all the time.
Apparently she spent more time hitting the gong in
class than anything else. She also fancied herself as a bit
of a singer, so she spent most nights next to the piano
in the main bar, whining away like some scalded cat. It
put the punters off their drinks. Anyway, the crunch
came when she was given these weeks that she was
supposed to fill with high-profile celebrity friends and
clients on detoxing and yoga retreats. No one came. No
one signed up. No one called. No one, it appeared, gave
a shit about her and her bloody classes. She left to go
on holiday after a stressful time doing very little and the
bloke we took on as her replacement was so fantastic I
never called to ask her back. Sadly Rashi had to return
to the ashram from whence he came and now we have
Connie.

I am not entirely sure of her story, but I think it
involved a stint in PR and a dramatic career change
before she discovered her real vocation. This seems to
involve meditation at four a.m. and plenty of chanting.
No one wanted to share with her in the staff village,
which was a bit of a bore to start with, but now we

have found a place for her I have heard nothing but good. The guests respond to her enthusiasm. No one seems to mind that she will only practise on a sheepskin mat because the chi is so much better. In fact, her rota of private clients and lessons seems to increase week on week. Something little miss friend-to-the-stars never seemed to manage at all. Oh, and thankfully, Connie shows no desire to sing.

On my way out of the spa, I'm thinking about slipping off home to see Kate. It is eight p.m. and quite frankly I fancy a glass of wine and I am prepared to stare at anything on the TV, even CNN. I am waving goodbye to Geri when Mohammed comes racing through the door.

'You're a bit late, mate,' I say. 'Mr Fahad has already gone back to his villa to sleep it off.'

'No, no, sir,' he says. His face looks serious. His eyes are shining. 'It's the staff village.'

'What do you mean?'

'We have a rebellion on our hands.' The panic in his voice is real. Mohammed is not the sort of man prone to exaggeration.

'How many?'

'One hundred, one hundred and fifty. All locals.'

'Here,' I say, pointing to my buggy. 'Get in.'

On the way to the staff village Mohammed fills me in on the background to the uprising. And it doesn't sound good. We tend to have a bit of a problem with local labour, mainly because they know they have us by the balls. Legally we have to employ 50 per cent of our workforce from the local population and you can see why. There is so much money sloshing around in this place that the government wants to get their hands on some of it and distribute it within the population. So you can't blame them. But the net result is that we have a complacent workforce who know they have us over a barrel and who we find hard to sack.

Also, I have to admit there is a certain amount of underhand behaviour going on on our part. Each visa the government hands out has a job title attached to it, and they are very touchy about what are perceived as local jobs and what jobs Westerners get given. So we have managers working here on gardeners' visas, and Ingrid the PR manager is on a waiter's visa. Therefore we have to be quite careful who we piss off, and be very sensitive in our dealings.

Anyway, the story behind this rebellion sounds straightforward enough. One of the gardeners signed off to go on leave straight after coming back from his holiday. Apparently Jiwan told him he wasn't allowed to go, but he took his boat pass and signed himself out along with the rest of them. So Jiwan called him at home and asked where he was. He said that he was on leave. Jiwan replied that he had not signed the form and that if he wasn't back on the staff boat that evening he would be dismissed. The bloke never came back and ignored all other calls, only to return this evening, a week later. The rules of the staff handbook say that if you are off for more than six days in a row, you are instantly dismissed. But this bloke is refusing to go and now he has some 150 people in support of him. He is making speeches and calling for everyone to walk out. This is not the sort of news I want to hear. Especially after two days without showers and a long day of rain – and now it's dark and it's eighty twenty p.m. This could easily get out of hand.

They are all milling around the basketball hoops when I arrive. Fortunately, someone has put the emergency spotlights on, so I can see their faces. Some are looking bored, but some are looking distinctly engaged.

'Good evening, everyone!' I start out like a rock star playing Wembley. I need to get their attention quickly, establish who is boss and get them to move on. We are not allowed to get physical with the staff, so I have only got the advantage of confidence and rank. The thing to do is get the troublemakers away from the group and then talk them down in private, so they can acquiesce and save face. It is very basic psychology.

I get Mohammed to point out the slacker and I ask him to follow me into the dining room. He brings a mate along with him for moral support. Once inside, I suggest to Mohammed that he guards the door and hope that the lack of action will bore the others into dispersing. This is exactly the sort of situation I was worried about the other night. Things can turn nasty here very quickly and the managerial staff are very much outnumbered.

Then, just as I get the ringleaders through the door, it kicks off outside. I don't know who starts, but there is a massive punch-up. It is local against local. The ringleaders inside the dining room with me are shouting at me, demanding to be let out. But I am not budging. I'm guarding the door as if my life and job depend on it, which they do. If these guys get out and stir the fight up even more, then I've got no idea where it will end. I am sweating my arse off. My heart is pounding in my chest and the two blokes are shouting at me and throwing furniture around. I think it is only because I'm the manager that they don't physically threaten me.

Outside, the fight's carrying on. Through the window I can see that it is only a hardcore of about six who are actually going for it. The others have fled. Mohammed is yelling, the guards are blowing their whistles and waving their sticks. I can hear Ben shouting. He's come to join the fray.

Then suddenly, almost as quickly as it started, they stop. Mohammed's crew have got the main perpetrators by the arms. They aren't officially allowed to restrain people, but these guys are being booted off the island tonight. Their contracts were terminated as soon as they laid the first punch. So I don't care that much. The adrenalin is pumping. I need to get these six blokes and my two ringleaders out of this village and off the island before sunrise. Otherwise I might have a full rebellion on my hands. There's no telling how much resentment is stewing in those six-to-a-room dorms.

Mohammed suggests we get them on the staff ferry and kick them off the island right now, but they all refuse to go. Two of them start talking about wanting to collect their bags. One says he actually needs us to give him a bag.

Ben looks at me and shakes his head. 'We need to get these guys out of here as soon as we can,' he says.

So I opt for a bit of mollification in order to get them out of the village. Mohammed and a few of his security team will pack their bags and the rest of us will escort them to the jetty. Amazingly, they agree. I think the brighter ones realize they are running out of options and that if they are not careful I will involve the mainland police – and then there's no telling where the story would end.

So we walk through the island in the pitch black, like a reconnaissance party in some cheap war film. Ben's out front, I'm in the middle next to the prisoners, and we have guards forming a circle all the way around.

Just as we approach reception, nearing the water feature and the complimentary fruit-juice cocktails and chilled hand towels, I get a call from Mohammed. He says that it is going to take too long to get the staff ferry ready. We're stuck, he says. There is nothing else available.

I think for a second.

'Fuck it,' I say, out loud.

'I am sorry, sir?' asks Mohammed.

'Sorry,' I reply. 'Get the Azimut speedboat ready.'

'What? The one reserved for super-VIP guests?' he asks.

'That's the one.'

'Are you sure, sir?' he checks.

'I don't care if we have to hire a Learjet,' I say. 'We're getting these bastards off the island tonight!'

Thursday a.m.

I was up till two a.m. making sure the rebels were shipped off the island. They refused to leave until Mohammed arrived with all their stuff. Then one of them complained that some of their clothes were missing, that they wanted to go back to the village to collect them. I refused, of course. The last thing I needed was a bloody martyr to the underground movement returning and stirring up more trouble.

In the end we kept them in the thankfully empty reception, while I got the paperwork organized. This was a little harder than I had envisaged as none of the troublemakers' photos matched their personal files. It turned out that they had all been working under false names, with false addresses, ever since they arrived on the island. And when exactly that was, no one could be sure.

When the resort was built and the island extended some ten years ago, some of the labourers were kept on after the work was finished. So manual labourers suddenly became landscapers, gardeners, engineers and waiters at one of the top resorts in the world. And it went to some of their heads. Most of them are hard-working and conscientious, but some became ill disciplined and arrogant and difficult to manage. We came up with a personal-behaviour guide which has things like 'No chewing of betel or gum on duty', 'Don't spit anywhere in the resort', 'Don't pick your nose or ears in public areas', 'Don't shout or clap or click your fingers near guests.' For some of them the transition was too difficult. If you have spent your early adult life not sleeping in a bed, and don't know what it is like to live in a house with running water and a toilet, you can imagine how difficult it is to adjust to the demands of these extremely high-maintenance guests. Why would you care how quickly your guests' break-fast arrives, when you figure they should really be grateful for getting it at all? The culture shock has been huge.

So it was no great surprise to me to find that I have been paying staff who do not exist, handing over pay-cheques made out in totally different names. I am just delighted that I managed to get them off the island without too much bloody trouble.

* * *

Needless to say, when I got home to the villa Kate was pretending to be asleep, giving me the cold buttocks. I always get the cold buttocks when I have chosen the hotel over our relationship. I knew I was in trouble as I drove home last night. By the time I finally got to pick up my messages on my unanswered mobile, their tone was increasingly frosty. They started out quite jolly. She'd ordered room service and had opened a bottle of one of my expensive red wines. The Pud Thai was waiting and so was she. Two hours later the Pud Thai was cold and so indeed was she. Come two a.m., she was firmly on her side, facing the other way, and was not going to interact with me at all.

The alarm goes at five forty-five and she doesn't even roll over. This is bad, I think as I heave on my gym kit. I am going for my run this morning, come hell or high water.

'Morning,' I say. Nothing. 'Morning,' I try again. Still nothing. 'Look, I am sorry, there was nothing I could do.'

'Yeah, right,' she says. 'And you lost your phone.' At least she is talking, I think.

'We had a riot going on.'

'And the island's sunk,' she exhales.

'No such luck,' I say. 'But it was a nightmare. We had—'

'Save it for someone who gives a shit,' she says, rolling over and pulling the duvet up over her head.

I walk out of the door. Bollocks. I look up. It is still raining. I'm not sure that this relationship is going to last beyond the New Year.

As I drive down to the gym, the gardeners are already out in force, clearing up the debris from last night's wind and rain. Most of them bow slightly as I drive past, some touch their hearts with their left hand, others their large-brimmed straw hats. However, there are one or two who don't bother to do either. With the deportation of the Village Six, the atmosphere in the staff accommodation must be pretty bad this morning. I make a note to myself that perhaps we should get some more crab in. We buy a container of crab once every couple of weeks as a treat for the staff. It's about fifteen dollars a kilo and we ship in about sixty kilos to jolly things up a bit. But the way things are at the moment, I am not sure a whole load of shellfish is going to cut it. I might have to find some sort of excuse for a party.

Parties are a little political around here. Firstly, we can't overemphasize Christmas or any of the other Christian festivals as the locals here and on the surrounding islands are predominantly Muslim. Hence the need for a mosque and imam. But we also have Sikhs and Hindus and Jews and every other religion you can think of to consider. We have a truly world-wide community in the village and no one is favoured above anyone else. However, you would have to be Boutros Boutros-Ghali to get it right all the time. And at the moment I think I need to start a bit of a charm offensive.

I let myself into the gym and start up the running machine. Even on miserable drizzling days like today this is surely one of the most beautiful views in the world. The sun is trying its best to seep through the clouds and the pale-yellow light of dawn dances on the foam of the waves as they break over the house reef. Why anyone would ever want to work in a city, I don't know. The pollution alone is enough to make me want to get out almost as soon as I arrive. You'd be amazed how much cities actually stink. After five or six months out here, breathing in only the most clean and un-adulterated of air, it makes you gag the first time you set foot back in the Big Smoke. It also makes you feel like falling asleep. No wonder everyone is always so stressed and pissed off.

I pound away, sweating out the old sake and the tension of the past couple of days. There is a hopeful blue patch of sky on the horizon. Perhaps the weather will make a turn for the better quicker than expected.

By the time I get back to the villa for a shower and get changed into my perennial linen shirt and trousers,

Kate has already gone to work. It is quite extraordinary how little you can see of a person, even when you are living together and working on the same 150-acre island.

As I walk into the dining room at seven a.m., the place is deserted. There are a couple of cleaners putting the final polish on the grey marble floors and some waiting staff setting up the buffet breakfast. As I walk the length of the sideboard covered in plates of meat and cheese and salami, I have to say the spread is looking pretty poor. I can tell that the kitchen is on its last legs. There are no melons, no pineapples, the strawberries are looking very tired, the baby bananas are actually black and there are no tropical delights of any kind. Which looks pretty piss poor, considering we are a tropical island – the buffet should be groaning with fruit like some bacchanalian orgy. This display is distinctly four-star. Surely we can do better than this?

I give Jean-François a call. 'Jean-François,' I say, 'I'm at the buffet . . .'

'Ah, no, no, no,' he starts. 'There is nothing I can do. Chef, he wants to kill me. Me, I want to kill myself.'

'Can't we do something?'

'Not until the bloody boat arrives. I need fruit. I need the fucking pink champagne and I need it yesterday. And guess what?'

'What?'

173

'The new Russian . . .'

'Mr Georgi.'

'Yes, him. He wants a bloody sandbank tonight and I am just hoping against hope that the boat is not late, otherwise I am well and truly fucked, *en brochette*, by you, Chef and Bernard.'

'He's booked a sandbank?' I ask.

'*Oui.*'

'For how many?'

'Twenty, twenty-five, I am not sure.'

'Excellent,' I say. 'One minute . . .' That's $20–30,000 of business right there. I must make sure I send some candles, a dressing gown and a bottle of fizz around to his villa this morning and come and visit him at breakfast, or most probably at his villa. VIPs of his stature and wealth tend not to go for any of the communal meals if they can avoid them. However, just in case I tell Leila, one of our more efficient restaurant managers, to call me on my mobile if by any chance Mr Georgi and his gang should arrive. 'Right,' I say, rattling Jean-François's chain one more time. 'Meet me in the kitchen garden, right away.'

Before he has a chance to complain, I hang up. After knocking back a fortifying double espresso shot, I get back into my buggy and head off to the kitchen garden.

Maintained at the cost of some $50,000 a year, the kitchen garden is supposed to be one of those tranquil little spots where the guests can breathe in air scented by exotic herbs and taste some of the freshest produce available. It is one of those ethical green things that we advertise along with t'ai chi and yoga, which makes us appeal to the ethical green streak in every urbanite. Anyway, in the literature sitting in the villas, along with the spa guide and the room-service menu, there's a small leaflet about the garden, offering guided tours and a sunset drink in its secluded and stunning confines.

However, as I pull up by the potting shed in the drizzle, I am kind of relieved that no one has ever taken us up on this romantic offer. It looks crap. I get out of the buggy trying to remember the last time I came here – it must have been about eight months ago, when I had to approve the last $50,000 budget. Well, I think as I look around, Lord knows what they have done with the money, but they sure as hell haven't invested it here.

The tomato plants are long and rangy and devoid of fruit. The beans have no pods and the rocket looks like some three year-old's cress-growing attempts. We could hardly feed a couple of anorexics on a purge, let alone a hotel full of complacent tossers who can barely be bothered to salivate for anything less than Beluga.

The only things that are looking at all useful are the glasshouses packed with flowers, indoor plants and orchids. These are the mainstay decoration for the public areas and guest villas. We get through about 4,500 cut flowers a week, which are all imported from Malaysia. So every time the villa host decorates the couple's bed with pink frangipani flowers, forming a flower or dragon motif with folded sheets, every bud and petal has been flown in. The same goes for the orchids you see dotted around the place, in the bathrooms, on the bar. We used to rent them at four dollars a pot from this outfit in Thailand, so that as soon as the flowers dropped or the leaves went brown we just called them and they were replaced. However, during a recent cost-cutting exercise we took in an $8,000 shipment of the bastards. They all arrived without bloody pots, and are now sitting on bricks in the glasshouses while we wonder what to do with them. Somehow as I walk past the glass walls, staring in at the useless flowers perched precariously on the tables, the four-dollar-a-pot deal doesn't look so bad.

The other glasshouses are a little more successful. They are three large fifty-metre-long, three-metre-wide tunnels for nursing cuttings, which are mainly used to landscape the gardens. And bearing in mind that we change and replant between three and four hundred plants a day, the two guys who run the place are kept very busy indeed.

Jean-François speeds into the kitchen garden and leaps out of his buggy. His black leather-soled shoes look a little incongruous in the damp sand. What has he come dressed as? A food and beverage manager from the City?

'So have you found anything worth eating?' he asks.

'I am afraid not,' I say.

'Ah, *oui*.' He gives me one of those Gallic I-told-you-so shrugs. 'I don't even put this place anywhere in the equation.'

'Really?'

'I know the chef got some mint out of the garden last week and it was a cause for much celebration in the kitchen.'

'Mint? Is that it?'

'Well,' he looks around, 'you might get one bowl of rocket out of here in the next couple of weeks. Do you and Kate want it?'

'No, thanks,' I say, suddenly feeling a bit of a fool. This place is clearly the biggest joke on the island and I am the last to know. I was suffering under the illusion that my $50,000 a year was buying something more than a few cuttings and leaves, but clearly not. Someone's arse needs kicking, that's for sure.

As I walk back to my buggy, contemplating whose backside is first in line, my phone goes. It's Leila. Apparently Mr Georgi likes a buffet, he's an all-you-can-eat type of guy after all, and he and a few of his mates have just walked into the dining room. I check my watch. It's only quarter past nine. He's remarkably prompt for a billionaire.

I floor the accelerator and ten minutes later I'm shaking Mr Georgi's hand and wishing him the best morning possible. Tall, with a full head of hair and a trim figure, he is jolly and ebullient and quite unlike most of the short, porky, sour oligarchs I have to be nice to. I sit down at his table and join him for a cup of coffee, while he tucks into his eggs Benedict. This is not something I tend to do, as guests don't normally want a long chat with their breakfast. Most of them have jet lag and are barely awake, and the idea of having to make small talk is enough to make them try and avoid you altogether. But Mr Georgi is very chirpy indeed. Then again, what has he got to be miserable about? He's got some sexy girls back in one of his many villas and a cohort of goons to laugh at his jokes. Hell, even Ben might be jolly in that case.

So he tells me over and over again how much he loves the place, even though he has only just arrived. Garry seems to have charmed the underwear off him on the boat on the way over. And he is positively overexcited about the sandbank trip tonight. He's got twenty-three guests and wants to give them the time of their lives. It turns out that it is Mr Georgi's brother's birthday. Dimitri is going to be fifty and he really wants to party. Mr Georgi is keen that we get the right wine. So I offer him the chance to have a bit of a tasting on the beach this afternoon. If a bloke is going to spend at least $23,000 in one night – the full sandbank experience is $1,000 per head – then I should at least give the man the opportunity to spend a little more on some seriously good-quality wine. There's some very nice stuff that we keep back especially with this sort of big spender in mind. He seems delighted by the idea, and shakes my hand. His Breitling Bentley platinum watch flashes in one of the first rays of full sun we've seen in two days. Things are looking up.

Just as I get up to shake his hand one more time, there is a crash and an almighty groan on the other side of the dining room. Two of Georgi's goons twitch and feel for their pockets. These guys are packing pieces. But before I can work out quite how to tell them that we don't appreciate guns on the island, there's another low moan from under the far table. What the hell is going on?

I make my excuses rapidly and rush over to find Leila lying flat out on the floor, surrounded by what looks like water.

'Are you all right?' I ask. 'Did you fall over?'

'No,' she hisses through gritted teeth. 'I'm giving birth.'

I am so shocked I can't move. Leila? Having a baby? I didn't even know she was pregnant. No one did. She doesn't even look fat! Well, she *is* fat – but she's always been fat. How long has she been pregnant?

'How long have you been pregnant?' I ask, totally bewildered.

'Nine months,' she whispers, before breaking into another huge roar. She grabs hold of my hand and practically wrenches it off.

'Shit!' I say.

'Shiiiiiiiiiiiiit!' she screams.

'Are you going to give birth here?' I ask. 'By the fruit platters?'

'It sure looks that way,' she says, panting through her mouth. Her face is now bright purple.

'Will someone phone the fucking doctor!' I shout in a manner that is not entirely managerial.

'Yes sir,' agrees one of the waiters, running towards Leila's meet-and-greet lectern.

'Can you move?' I ask.

'Noooooooo!' she yells. 'It is coming right noooooooow!'

Shit. Fuck. Fuck. Shit. We didn't do this in catering college, either. I look around at the guests. Some are moving away; some are rooted to the spot, staring; and some are popping sub-standard strawberries into their mouths like they are watching a live action TV show.

'And will someone put up some sort of screen here

and give the woman some dignity?' I shout. I look back down at Leila and give her hand a squeeze. 'OK, Leila,' I say, trying to sound calm. 'I seem to remember that it is important to breathe.'

'What do you think I am doing, you bastard?' she hisses, panting in and out, beads of sweat breaking across her forehead.

'Good, good,' I say, patting the back of her hand. 'Keep it up.'

As I smile at Leila's straining face, I can't help but think that this should be the father's job. Whoever he may be. This is the first birth we've had on the island and already I am thinking about the problems we're going to have with the authorities. They don't take too kindly to men and women out of wedlock even sitting next to each other, let alone producing illegitimate children. We're going to have to come up with some sort of yarn about her husband having passed away or something along those lines. Unless the real father suddenly decides to step up to the mark.

Within ten minutes Dr Singh arrives and my hand-holding services are no longer required. He manages to persuade Leila to move, and between contractions gets her into a buggy and back to the surgery in the staff village, which is obviously an infinitely more suitable place to give birth than the middle of the main dining room.

I make a quick tour of the place to apologize for the extraordinary circumstances and say I hope that it has not put anyone off their breakfast. Most of the guests take it in their stride. Some ask who the father is and I practise the deceased-husband story on them. By the third telling, I am beginning to sound convincing. However, the one thing most of them are really interested in is the weather. When is it going to stop raining? Is this usual for the time of year? How long will it go on for? I reply to each and every one of them, 'Well . . . at least it is not going to snow.'

Leaving the dining room, I get a call from Jean-François. The *Mary Celeste* is here. The relief in his voice is audible.

'We have fruit!' he shouts down the line. 'Pineapples, mangoes, the lot!'

'That's great news,' I say. 'And pink champagne?'

There's a pause. I can hear him leafing through the invoices.

'*Non.*'

'What?'

'*Non,*' he repeats. 'We have no pink champagne.'

'Well, you're in the shit, aren't you?' I say and hang up.

I head off down to reception to meet the morning boat, which has been to the mainland to collect six guests who have flown overnight from the UK. As I walk through the lobby towards the jetty I bump into Angela, who is poured into her tight wetsuit and looks as if she is about to take one of Mr Antonov's daughters out windsurfing.

'Morning,' I say.

'Good morning,' she replies. She doesn't look like she is in a very good mood. 'Have you heard about Leila?' she asks.

'Yes, I was there,' I say.

'Who's the father?' she asks.

'I don't know.' Is she thinking what I am thinking? I wonder.

'What does the baby look like?' she asks.

'I am not sure that it has been born yet,' I say. 'She was hard at it as I left.'

'Oh,' she replies, before marching off down the jetty, dragging the little girl after her. It appears all is not well in the world of Yoshiji and Angela.

I look out to sea, my meet-and-greet face firmly in place. The guests' boat is arriving, and seeing as the weather's welcome is not particularly warm, I am hoping my jolly old smile will make up for it. But as the boat nears the jetty, I can see it is going to take more than a few cocktails and cold towels to calm this situation down. There's a tall, red-faced bloke in a short-sleeved shirt and grey slacks pacing up and down on deck, shouting at the captain, and there's a rather large woman with a tight mahogany perm wringing her hands.

'Good morning,' I say, with more than a little trepidation.

'You the manager?' The red-faced bloke turns on me from the deck.

'Um, yes,' I say.

'Well, you are totally irresponsible.'

'Right.'

'Totally and utterly irresponsible. We could have been killed.'

'Killed?'

'Look at it! Look at it!' He gestures out to sea. 'It's blowing a gale, a storm; it was too dangerous to cross by boat, the waves are too big. You should have flown us. You are totally fucking irresponsible. I want to be collected by plane when I leave. My wife here . . . my wife . . . she could have drowned. We've been flung about all over the bloody place. Haven't we? Haven't we?' He looks at the middle-aged couple disembarking, he dressed in a blue blazer and panama hat, she sporting a knee-length cotton skirt that is transparent against the light.

'It wasn't the smoothest of crossings,' the man admits, as he takes his wife's hand.

'Right,' I say. 'I am terribly sorry if you haven't had a pleasant journey. I can only apologize. This is a very

184

good boat and the captain is well used to making the trip. If it was at all dangerous then I am positive he wouldn't have set out.'

'Well, I am appalled,' continues the red-faced man. 'My wife's a wreck. Look at her!'

I must admit she looks a little peaky. 'I am very sorry, sir. Please come into reception and we'll get you something to drink. And if you feel you need to see a doctor, we do have one on the island.'

They eventually calm down enough to get off the boat and knock back their complimentary cocktail. In the meantime, I have a word with the captain. It turns out that they were hit by a couple of big waves on the way over and he had to cut the engine. I get him to take me out to sea, partly to check out how choppy the waves are and partly to get away from the guests.

As we pull out from the jetty, the rain stops. I stand at the bow of the boat, feeling the warm wind in my hair, going for the full Kate Winslet. It feels fantastic to be cutting through the water, blowing away the cobwebs, getting off the island, if only for a few minutes. There are days when it really does feel like a prison and today is one of them. I throw my head back and breathe in. My mobile rings. I am tempted not to answer it. But I do.

'Hi, it's Garry.'

'Hi there.'

'Where are you?'

'I'm on the guests' boat . . . out at sea.'

'Oh.'

'Why?'

'We're waiting for you under the pagoda on Palm Sands beach. You're meant to be officiating at a wedding.'

Thursday p.m.

Just as I am pronouncing Mr and Mrs Nogami husband and wife, the cloud clears and the sun comes out.

'Thank God for that,' I mumble, as I look towards the heavens.

'High,' agrees Mr Nogami.

'High, high,' reiterates his new wife.

I can't tell you what a difference a bit of sun makes. I look up and down Palm Sands beach and I spot the Japanese couple I married on Tuesday heading towards the sea with their snorkels. There's a lardy woman in a silver thong dragging her wooden lounger out from under the palms towards the shore. There's a couple of white Germans slathered in iridescent sunscreen walking away from us. The dank black crows have gone quiet. The sky is clearing. Things are returning to normal. I can feel the stress ebbing out of me. My shoulders are coming down from my ears. The island is becoming manageable again. Hell, I might even have time to pop into the boutique to make it up with Kate. I might suggest some dinner or something.

I shake Mr and Mrs Nogami's hands and pose for the post-vows shot under the pagoda. Mr Nogami nuzzles into my armpit, while Mrs Nogami's bridal headdress tickles my cheeks, but we all smile and pretend that we are the best of friends.

I am seeing them off on the flower-festooned buggy that will take them on a tour of the island with photo ops when my phone goes. The caller ID tells me it is the dive centre.

'Hello, it's Hans.'

'Hi, what can I do for you?'

'Please could you come to the dive centre,' he asks. His voice sounds a little hollow.

'Is it important?' I ask, as I wave off the newly-weds and check my fingernails. 'I am a little busy.'

'We have a situation,' he says.

'What sort of situation?' I sigh. There is nothing more irritating than an obtuse German.

'Someone is dead.'

Fuck. He's got my full attention now. Who? When? How? And are we liable? Actually, I am lying slightly. The liable question was the first. I leap into my buggy, and while I'm driving the full length of the island at top speed straight down to the diving bay, next door to Silver Sands, Hans fills me in on the phone. Fortunately, the dead tourist is not one of ours. The group are from a four-star resort which is about an hour away by boat, and they have requested permission to land with us so that Dr Singh can sign the death certificate.

'They were out diving,' explains Hans, 'and the bloke died underwater.'

'God . . . how gruesome,' I say.

'I think they are all still in shock,' he adds. 'From what I can tell over the radio.'

'Keep them where they are,' I say. 'I am going to contact Dr Singh and head office to see what we should do.'

It takes me a while to get through to Dr Singh. He is not answering his mobile or the surgery phone. Finally, just as I pull up at the diving bay, he picks up. For a man who spends most of his time writing sick notes for staff who have a hangover, he is having a busy day. He tells me he is in reception, waiting for a seaplane. Leila needs a C-section and he can't perform that on the island.

'It sounds serious,' I say, worried for Leila and her baby and thinking this is not the sort of day I would like to repeat in a hurry. Dr Singh tells me that it is nothing too serious. The baby is not in imminent danger of arrival. He tells me Leila is only three centimetres dilated, like I am supposed to know what that means.

'Good, good,' I find myself saying. 'That's excellent news.'

'But the baby is breech,' says Dr Singh.

'That is not such excellent news?'

'No,' he explains.

'Do you need to go with her?' I ask.

'No. I was going to go,' he says, 'but the mainland hospital is sending a doctor in the plane, and if you need me here . . .'

'We do, we do,' I say, watching the hospital seaplane circle overhead. I have never actually seen a corpse before. I could do with someone with some sort of experience, I think. I mean, what are you supposed to do? 'As soon as you can,' I add.

'Of course,' he says. 'As soon as I know Miss Leila is OK then I shall come straight over, right away.'

I sit in the buggy and look at the dive boat bobbing around off the shore. Despite the brilliant turquoise sea and the shiny white well-scrubbed decks, it looks miserable out there. Most of the passengers appear to be pacing around in panic, looking out to sea and staring back at us and the beach in frustration, while a couple are gathered around what looks like the blanket-covered body on deck. My heart goes out to them, but it is truly more than my job's worth to let them land until I have permission from head office. I put the call in.

This has to be one of the worst, if not *the* worst situation we've had on the island so far. We've had plenty of drunken falls and swimming-pool accidents. One of the worst was when a little girl nearly drowned in one of the villa pools. A villa host was walking by when the girl's elder brother ran out of the villa, calling for help. The host ran in to find her floating on top of the water. She had apparently been there for a minute or two. He performed mouth-to-mouth and she choked up half the pool. It was terrifying for all concerned. Eventually we got her to the mainland, where she spent two days in hospital followed by a further couple of days back here, as she was not allowed to fly in case her lungs were infected. We didn't charge her parents for the villa or the trips back and forth to the mainland. I don't think head office were too thrilled, but there are times where you have to put decency before profit.

We did the same thing for a bloke who slipped and broke two ribs on the dive boat. Not that we were liable or anything. But sometimes it is good PR to be nice. We comp-ed the last couple of days of his stay and gave him a back-brace to fly home in. He returned the brace along with a very nice letter, which he also sent to the big boss. We came out of the whole experience smelling of pleasant flowers, even if the hotel took a rather small hit.

Our incident rate is not as bad as the city hotels, however, because as we are an island we don't get that pissed, wired and reckless through-traffic at three a.m. We don't have much of the outside world coming in. We know who the prostitutes are, as they are registered by the guests and tend not to leave in the morning. We don't have any tramps dossing down for the night, or concierge scams where they sell on rooms, bring in drug-dealers or turn a blind eye to the wild misdemeanours of guests. In fact, we don't have a concierge at all. We have guest services, but they are there to help you spend money on this island. If we had a concierge, what on earth could he recommend? Dinner on Fantasy Island? A coffee on the mainland? A boat trip? That's hardly going to tax the golden-key motif off any well-trained professional.

Head office finally get back to me. They don't think that I should let them land. They are not our guests, they tell me, they are not our problem. The insurance company who covers the hotel doesn't want anything to do with it. They tell me that it would be a paperwork nightmare and would leave the hotel totally exposed. I try and argue that the hotel is already exposed, and if we send the dive boat on its way we are liable to have a bad PR problem as well as some sort of karmic comeback. Their snort of derision can probably be heard all across Europe. Karmic comeback? I try to explain that as an island resort we too would be at the mercy of the goodwill of others if ever we were in trouble. They ask me if I have been drinking.

I am about to go and meet Hans in the dive centre and radio over to the boat that sadly permission for them to land has not been granted, when I see Dr Singh jogging towards me. His white shirt is unbuttoned and falling out of his black trousers and his black hair is ruffled. He is dripping sweat from every pore. The bloke hasn't been this busy since he arrived on the island just under a year ago.

'Don't worry, don't worry,' I say, seeing the anxiety in his eyes. 'I've been told they're not allowed to land.'

'I am sorry?' he says, as he arrives panting and puffing, running his hands through his hair.

'I've been told they are not allowed to land.'

'With all due respect, sir . . .' He inhales. 'That's illegal.'

'It is?'

'Yes, sir. I am a doctor and I have a professional commitment to certify someone dead. If you send them off, I have not done my duty. And I can't not do my duty – that's my job.'

I have always found Dr Singh's self-important pomposity deeply irritating. The way he insists that anyone who comes to him and asks for a sick note gets one, despite the blindly obvious fact that they are shirking, drives me nuts. But today I could kiss him. I can't possibly send those poor people back out to sea, to set sail with a corpse on deck in the heat of the afternoon sun. I wouldn't be able to look myself in the eye before I go to bed tonight. That's just not the way things work out here. The sea is a dangerous place. These islands are dangerous. Some people mutter that there are still pirates who sail in these waters. All I know is that there are some islands you would never go to, some waters through which you would never sail. And if anything should ever happen to me, or any of my guests, I would hope a rival resort or a rival hotel would come to our aid. But if you are pushing paper around an air-conditioned office in Knightsbridge, I don't suppose that would make much sense.

I call head office back and explain the situation. I have to admit that I embellish it somewhat and suggest that it is actually against the law in this country to refuse another boat assistance, and they eventually tell me to go ahead, while covering my arse at every step of the way.

Hans looks relieved. He is a tanned, toned, tattooed German hippy who likes to commune with turtles and rays. He is not the sort of bloke who is going to understand risk assessment and the bottom line and I could tell he was beginning to get very twitchy indeed. After all, this is the sort of nightmare situation that he can totally relate to; he is probably even mates with the skipper of the other boat.

He radios over to share the good news. The divers' arms rise with delight and a small cheer travels across the water. The engine starts. The anchor is lifted and the boat heads towards the jetty.

My heart is beating fast. My hands are sweating. The last time I was this nervous was when I witnessed a stabbing at a hotel I worked in in Singapore. I was working late on reception and the Japanese restaurant manager rushed out and told me that one of the guests had been stabbed in the restaurant. It was some sort of professional hitman, who had luckily missed the vital organs, and apparently the guest didn't want an ambulance. Instead he'd wandered bleeding, clutching his chest, into the kitchen and asked us to find a doctor to sew him up. The ex-pastry chef was the duty manager that night. He was running around like a blue-arsed fly, unable to cope, while I had to sit there and hold the man's hand as the doctor came and stitched him up. It was very weird. The restaurant service continued all around us. They carried on cooking and slicing sushi. In the end, the only thing the man asked for was a new shirt so that he could carry on eating his dinner. We managed to find a clean shirt from housekeeping and he went back out to finish his main course and no one on any of the adjacent tables was any the wiser.

This is a little different, though just as surreal. The boat pulls in at the jetty and seven dejected souls climb off, leaving behind the captain, the dive master, a couple of local guys who look as if they can swim like dolphins, the dead man's wife/buddy/partner and, of course, the corpse. Hans springs into action and gets the other divers into our dive centre, handing out hot drinks, water and warm towels. Surly Angela's making herself useful on the boat, putting her arm around the weeping wife/buddy/partner. Her own problems are clearly paling into insignificance. She takes her off down the jetty towards the dive centre to join the others. The poor woman doesn't need to witness the jolting reality of us all trying to remove the corpse.

'Mate, mate, mate,' says the tall bronzed dive master, shaking my hand vigorously as he disembarks. 'Thanks so much for this,' he adds, pushing back his bleached-blond hair that is stiff with salt. 'My name's Shane.'

'Hello, Shane.' I nod.

'Bloody nice of you to help us out of this mess,' he continues. 'I had no idea what to do. It's my first bloody fatality in fifteen years.'

'What do you think happened?' I ask, looking over the side of the boat at the blanket-covered body.

'I'm not exactly sure,' he shrugs. 'But I think the bloke's gone and had a heart attack. I think he might have been OK if he hadn't been underwater. My theory is that he choked on his own vomit.'

'Mmm,' says Dr Singh, stroking his chin.

'D'you want to examine him here?' says Shane, pointing to the jetty. 'Or on the deck?'

'I think it might be better to examine him in situ,' says Dr Singh.

'Right you are then,' says Shane. 'Mustapha,' he shouts at one of the local guys standing guard by the corpse. 'The doctor's coming aboard.' He points at Dr Singh. 'Go ahead, mate.' He smiles. 'Be my guest.'

While Dr Singh scrambles aboard with his bag and pens and bits of paper, Shane yawns and stretches.

'Jeez,' he says to me, looking around him. 'You've got a nice place here.'

'Thanks,' I say.

'You the manager?'

'That's right.'

'Any chance of a job?' he asks. 'The place I'm working at is a right old shit hole. The food's disgusting, there's no one fun working at the place,' he adds, looking down the jetty towards the shapely Angela. Well, she does look good at a distance. 'And do you know what?' he asks, leaning in to whisper.

'What?' I ask.

'The guests are kinda boring.'

'Oh.'

'I know,' he nods, tapping the side of his nose. 'Newly-weds and nearly-deads.' He laughs. 'Or really-deads.' He nods over towards his boat. 'All they do is stare out to sea and hold hands. The dining room is like a morgue. But this place,' he sniffs, as though he is inhaling the action. 'Looks like there is plenty to entertain a simple bloke from Sydney.'

'You'd be amazed,' I say, watching Dr Singh gently lift the blanket and steel himself to take a closer look.

'I've got my Divemaster, I can teach the open-water exam, do night dives, anything you want.' Shane continues with his pitch. 'All right there, mate?' he asks Dr Singh. 'Does it look like a heart attack to you?'

'It is certainly showing all the signs,' agrees the doctor. 'D'you know if he has a history of heart problems?'

'Not according to the paperwork,' replies Shane. 'I like to keep a nice tight ship,' he says to me, by way of bolstering his job application.

'I'm sure,' I say. He grins right back, clicks his tongue and shoots me with his index finger. I can't work out if Shane really is a cock, or if he is so freaked out by what has happened he just can't stop himself from talking bullshit, because if he stopped for a second he might realize that someone has died on his boat and he is in for one hell of a ride once the corpse's insurance company get hold of him. And then let's just hope that his ship is as tight as he says it is, otherwise he is up to his neck in it.

It takes Dr Singh another ten minutes of examination before he concludes his report. Although it is obviously not his job to say how the man died, he would not be performing his duty if he didn't write down anything that might be useful to the coroner. He looks a little pale and drained as he comes off the boat; there are rivulets of sweat pouring down from his temples.

'I would say that in the end the man probably drowned,' he says, sighing loudly.

'Drowned?' asks Shane, scratching the back of his head. 'Jeez. But I thought you said it was a heart attack?'

'Most likely,' agrees the doctor.

'But you said he drowned?' Shane is suddenly looking much more concerned. Drowning clearly resonates more in his profession as a diver than a chief-executive heart attack.

'As a result of the heart attack,' clarifies the doctor.

'Oh, right,' says Shane, clearing his throat. 'Shall we get the body off the boat then?'

I hang around to commiserate with the weeping woman, who turns out to be a Belgian from Brussels who was holidaying with her husband of twenty years.

They have two children of school-leaving age who fortunately are not on holiday with them. The rest of the group all appear a little better after their water, cups of tea and fresh towels. I offer them all a late lunch in the restaurant, which everyone accepts. Even the weeping widow gets on the buggy with the rest of them, which is fortunate as it means she does not witness the fiasco that is Shane, Hans and the local dive boys trying to get the corpse off the boat without dropping it into the sea.

There is much huffing and puffing and heaving and hauling as they all take a limb apiece and try to squeeze the body down the gangplank. Unfortunately, Monsieur LeBlanc or whatever he is called seems to have been a little fond of his *moules frites* and weighs a bloody ton. They can't get him through the gap while holding on to him, as they can't get down the gangway two at a time. So they throw him over the side. On the count of three they swing the corpse together, hoping to get enough momentum to clear the sea and land him on the jetty. On another count of three they hurl him over the side. The body hits the deck with an almighty thud and Shane raises a weak cheer.

'Thank God the bloke's already dead,' he declares. 'Because that's one hell of a way to go.'

I am still fielding calls from head office about procedure and how to cover our corporate backsides when Jean-François gets through on my mobile.

'We are all set up on Golden Sands beach,' he says.

'Set up?'

'*Oui*,' he says. 'For the wine-tasting for this evening. I am expecting Mr Georgi in about five minutes.'

'I am on my way.'

I say my goodbyes and give my condolences to Shane and his crew. They shake my hand and thank me again for letting them land, telling me they didn't know what else to do. Shane pitches once again for a dive master's job, while rolling a cigarette. I tell him I'll give him a call. I have to say he does look the part, even if his attitude is deeply suspect. On my way to the buggy I give Ben a quick call, asking him to keep an eye on the rival resort's guests and make sure they get back on their boat after lunch. The last thing we need are a couple of stowaways on the island, helping themselves to a free dinner. I also check in with Dr Singh, who seems to be on top of everything. He is arranging for the body to be brought back to the surgery and taken to the mainland for a post mortem. He seems to have thought of everything.

'Oh, by the way,' he says as I am about to hang up. 'Leila has had her baby.'

'Great,' I smile.

'It's a boy,' he says. '9lb 4oz with lots of ginger hair.'

'Fantastic news!' I laugh. That's Yoshiji out of the

picture. I wonder who on earth the father could be?

I drive out of reception and up to Golden Sands. Christ, I think as I pass the spa, I could murder a drink.

About ten minutes later I arrive at the beach and I see that Jean-François has done us proud. There is a trestle table set up under the palm trees near Mr Georgi's Grand Beach Villa. The table groans with the weight of some of the world's finest wines, while the white linen cloth flaps gently in the breeze. Mr Georgi is just peeling himself off a lounger and slipping on a dressing gown as I approach.

'Good afternoon,' I declare, trying to sound breezy and relaxed.

'What lovely weather for wine,' he grins, wrapping the terry robe around his waist. 'I can't think of a better way to spend the day.'

'Neither can I,' I agree.

'Busy day?' he asks, slapping me on the back.

'Not really,' I lie. 'You?'

'So many calls, so many deals,' he says. 'These days you are just never alone.'

'I know.'

'Anyway,' he says, rubbing his hands together, looking at the array of some eight or so fine wines laid out in front of him. 'What have we here?'

'This is Jean-François, our food and beverage manager.' Jean-François nods. 'And this is Marco.' I indicate a short, handsome fellow who is prematurely jowly around the jaw. 'He is our head sommelier.' Marco smiles. He is a charming and extremely know-ledgeable man. 'Watch him,' I add, 'as he is prone to sampling too much of his stock.'

Mr Georgi laughs. He thinks I am joking. Everyone else at the table knows I am not.

'So,' he says. 'What do you suggest?'

'Well, I would suggest some red and some white for the dinner and some champagne for the boat,' starts Marco.

'Champagne.' Mr Georgi nods.

'A nice Cristal?' suggests Marco, popping a chilled bottle then and there. 'Light and fruity, perfect as the sun goes down . . . this is a 1997 . . .'

'Mmm,' says Mr Georgi, as half a flute slips down his clearly parched throat. 'Now that is very, very nice . . . How much is that?'

'The magnum is $1,800 a bottle.'

'Mmm,' he says, draining the rest of his glass. 'Now that really is very, very good. How many do you think we would need for the trip?'

'Eight, maybe seven, depending how generous you are feeling,' says Marco. 'It is only the aperitif.'

'Oh Dimitri, there you are!' exclaims Georgi. 'What took you so long?'

'I have been asleep,' says Dimitri, rubbing his creased

face and smoothing down a small strip of hair. He was clearly not first in line when it came to who got the looks in this family. 'What are you doing?'

'We're choosing wine for tonight.'

'Oh,' he says, looking puzzled. 'You're tasting wine? What for?'

'To see what is the best,' says Georgi.

'But you know how to find the best,' says Dimitri, looking from his brother back to me like we are both incredibly stupid. 'You find the fine wine section, and you cover the left-hand side with your hand – so you are not bothered with the names – and you choose the most expensive. It is very simple. Why are you wasting your time with this?'

I take a sip of my Cristal and smile. The sun is out and everything's back to normal.

Thursday Sunset

We spent the best part of the afternoon sitting in the shade of a couple of palms, sampling some of the finest wines Marco could source. And he sure as hell does have a few up his sleeve, including a Château Cheval Blanc, Premier Grand Cru 1947, which goes for just over $15,000 a bottle, and the cheeky Château Lafite Rothschild, Premier Cru 1995, for $6,500, as well as an old favourite, Petrus 1989, which is $4,500 a bottle. But Marco did actually behave himself. Apart from knocking back a whole magnum of Louis Roederer Cristal 1997 for $1,600 a bottle, we didn't really raid the cellar and drink into the hotel's profit too much. The bottle of champagne made us appear very generous. But when you know it costs us $62 a bottle before we mark it up to $1,600 we can afford to look like we are giving it away.

The food and wine mark-ups in the resort are a little steeper than you would expect in a city hotel – mainly because it is so hard to get stuff here and we are taxed through the nose by the local government. However, as the guests can't dine anywhere else and have little choice but to eat here, we have tried to play fair with the basics. So you can get a club sandwich for $25 at the beach, which, bearing in mind where you are sitting and where all the ingredients have come from, I don't think is too bad. But as soon as you enter the realm of the luxury item then you should be prepared to flex your friend like a member of the Olympic gymnastics team.

The normal food mark-up of times two and a half goes out of the window with things like caviar, for which we charge $600 a serving. Wine is usually times three or four, but as you can see with the Cristal we can name our price. If you are the sort of person who wants to quaff designer bubbles on a desert island then, quite frankly, your pockets must be quite deep in the first place. The great irony, of course, is that the biggest mark-up of all is on soft drinks and bottled water, for which we times by five. So if you're on holiday and want to save yourself a few quid, then drink the beer or save up the complimentary water you get by your bedside at night. Either that or drink from the tap. If the water is not drinkable there will be some sign somewhere telling you so. Imagine the lawyers' headache if there weren't.

I have to say, in the grand scheme of things I don't think the food prices here are too bad. If you compare them to other resorts I don't think we are at wince level yet. But we have to make money somehow. One of the usual nice little earners in the city hotel business is the banqueting room. Night after night they churn out soup, steak, vegetables, mash and ice cream for between five hundred and six hundred people. They plonk some red and white wine on the table, plus an industrial pot of coffee and a jug of milk, add some shitty petits fours and call it a banquet or an award ceremony. It's a licence to print money. Your workforce is transitory. You have no pension plans and incentive schemes to worry about. Frankly, you don't know their country of origin, let alone their name. The ballroom is one of the lifesavers in the hotel business and it is nearly always full. Here we have nothing like that. No conferences to keep us ticking over. So we bump up the price of the room, charge you six dollars for a Diet Coke and hope one day to do a little more than break even. In the meantime, thank God for Mr Georgi, his Cristal habit and his brother's birthday party.

Turns out though, come four p.m., Mr Georgi gave up listening to Marco talking about grape and body and vintage, and followed his brother's advice. He put his hand over one side of the wine list and, covering up the names, ordered the most expensive items on the page. So we could have saved ourselves a whole lot of trouble and a couple of hundred dollars into the bargain. But at least I got a few flutes to make up for my stressful day and Marco just about managed to re-tox from the night before and re-boot his system to somewhere approaching normal levels.

Come five fifteen, Mr Georgi disappears off to shower and shave before meeting his guests at the Lotus restaurant to crack open his first three bottles of Cristal. In the meantime I get on the phone to Jean-François to find out exactly how the plans for the sandbank birthday bash are shaping up.

With it costing $1,000 a head and being a great excuse to flog wines and champagnes, the sandbank dinner is obviously one of the hotel's nice little earners. It ranks up there with the catamaran dinner, which is also $2,000 a couple, and the cost doubles if you want to spend the night. So not only are you paying a couple of thousand dollars for your villa, which you aren't sleeping in, you are also dropping an extra $4k for a night under the stars. However, my favourite when it comes to guest-fleecing must be the big-game fishing, which is again a couple of thousand per couple for the day, with the added bonus for the guests that they can have Chef cook the fish they have caught that day for dinner in the evening – for an extra fifty dollars, of course. Well, Chef's a busy man and his services don't come free!

Mind you, it is not all money for old rope. These sandbank experiences are incredibly hard work to pull off well. And we do pull them off well. Extremely well. Most of the work goes into the preparation and the clear-up. The party itself is the easy bit. We sail out to what is effectively a deserted strip of sand in the middle of the ocean, in the middle of nowhere, and take it over. We bring our own generators, our own lights, we put carpets on the sand, we set up lamps with shades. There are piles of silk cushions, mattresses, bamboo arches for spotlights. There's a band, there are barbecues, there are tables and chairs and plates and crystal. It looks like the most elegant and fabulous of dinner parties. Then it is all cleared away before the next day. So if you are on a dive trip in the morning and you sail past at seven thirty, you would never know that anyone had ever been there. It is an amazing feat of organization. And when I tell you we have three sandbanks tonight, plus five private beach barbecues at the villas, which each require outside caterers, plus lights, carpets, cushions, grilled lobster, wagyu beef – the works – then you might begin to understand the sort of operation we are running here.

Not that any of the guests do. One of the biggest

complaints we get is that there are never enough villa barbecues available. Due to the number of chefs and barbecues and cushions we have, we are limited to five or six a night. So if you are staying here during high season and the hotel is full, then it can be hard to get one. During your ten-day stay, there will only be about sixty barbecues available and there are 140 villas, so some people lose out. Fortunately there are a few who are too tight to go for the private-dining option. But I am always being called up by irate guests, asking why they can't have what they want when they want it. Then again, that is an occupational hazard here.

It is also part of my job remit to visit guests during a sandbank or barbecue. It is supposed to add to the glamour of the occasion, although I am sure it just pisses them off. However, it is a job that is usually delegated to one of the senior members of staff, to check out that all is OK and that the guests are enjoying themselves. Tonight, as I am going to Mr Georgi's party, I'll be popping into the other two sandbanks while I'm out there. Thank God for the speedboat.

'So Jean-François, have you got the wine order?' I ask down the phone, while laying out alternative white linen shirts on my bed. Kate's in the shower. We are speaking, but not exactly communicating. I did give her the option of not coming tonight, but she sighed and said it would look odd if my girlfriend didn't turn up, particularly as Mr Georgi was such an important client and he was dropping so much cash. So she's pulled out some old sequinned chiffon number and is going to go through the motions for the good of the hotel.

'I think I've got them all,' he says. 'Fifteen bottles of Domaine de Chevalier 2001 at $450 a bottle?'

'Yes,' I say. My mouth begins to salivate as I think what a delicious little white Bordeaux that is.

'And another fifteen of the Château Lafite Rothschild 1995 at $1,200 a bottle. The only thing is,' he says, 'I'm here in the cellar and I am not sure we have fifteen of those, so we might have to take a few of the Mouton 1995 at $1,000 a bottle. Do you think he will mind?'

'What, we are out of Lafite '95?'

'I think so,' he says. 'Marco is also here on the case. But we haven't turned up any more. Even though there are two more on the ledger.'

'There are two missing?' I ask.

'Looks like it,' he says.

'Right,' I say. 'Let's look into that later. In the meantime, grab a few bottles of Mouton – that should be fine.'

'Oh, one more thing,' adds Jean-François.

'What's that?'

'We are on a different sandbank tonight.'

'We are?'

'Well, I went to look at the usual one this afternoon

and it seemed a little small. We've never done a dinner for this many.'

'We haven't?'

'Not in the ten years we've been open.'

'Really?'

'And I think that the usual place is too small. Once we've got the band and the tables and the serving area and the cushions out there won't be enough space.'

'OK,' I say. Shit, I think. I don't like surprises, especially when there is this much money involved and this many important people.

'But the other place is great,' he promises. 'Absolutely perfect.'

'Fine,' I say. 'See you at the Lotus in ten.'

Kate is complaining about her hair being wet as we drive to the Lotus for the champagne drinks. She keeps saying she looks shit. But I rather like the wavy unkempt look. When you are surrounded by so many overdone, enhanced ladies, with noses and tits that all point upwards, it is quite nice to have a bit of reality in the mix. But no matter how many times I tell her she looks lovely, she tells me off for being patronizing. It doesn't look like I am going to win tonight.

'And one thing,' she says as we park up the buggy. 'Don't leave me talking to the Natashas all bloody night.'

Poor Kate, she always gets left with the ladies on these trips. The sort of man who can afford to take a sandbank is not usually the sort to enjoy female company for its own sake. Women are there to be admired, to decorate, and to have sex with. But they are certainly never required to join in the conversation. I often think that one hundred years of female emancipation gets dumped at Customs here, along with the porn, the pork and the vodka.

'I promise I won't leave you,' I say.

'If I have to discuss diets and fringes for six hours, like I did last time,' she says, 'I am going to shoot myself.'

Kate and I have our happy faces firmly in place as we walk past the huge dragons and turn the corner into the bar. Just offshore, bobbing in the water, are two local fishing boats decked out with flowers and lights that are strung in ropes hanging off their masts. They look like something out of a romantic fairy tale. The weather is finally dancing to our tune and the sun is slipping down a cloudless sky, about to produce a perfectly photogenic sunset. Mr Georgi approaches in a white open-necked shirt and white trousers. He is grinning and his hand is outstretched.

'Fantastic, fantastic, fantastic,' he declares, taking a sip of Cristal. 'And this champagne is perfect.'

'I am so glad, Mr Georgi,' I say. 'Oh please, let me introduce you to my girlfriend, Kate.'

'Katya,' he says, kissing the back of her hand. 'I am delighted. Galya,' he shouts. An unfeasibly beautiful gazelle turns around. 'Come here,' he orders. She walks over, her plunge-front emerald-green jersey dress clinging to every delightful inch of her. I can feel Kate's irritation from here. 'This is Katya,' says Georgi.

'Hello,' says Galya. 'How very nice to meet you.' Her handshake appears limp; her manicure is immaculate.

'Why don't you take Katya to meet the girls? I am sure you have much to talk about.'

'Of course,' she giggles. 'Come with me.'

Kate shoots me this look of terrible loathing, before she follows Galya over to a group of stunning girls, all talking Russian and all about seven years her junior.

'I'll be over in a minute,' I say.

'Of course you will, darling,' she replies. 'If you value your life!'

I laugh loudly. Fortunately Mr Georgi is too busy watching his girlfriend's arse to hear what Kate says.

'Let me just say,' he adds, taking hold of my hand. I must stop staring at that Breitling watch. 'This has all turned out much better than I expected. I think I might have to come back and have a little party for myself here.'

'That's a great idea,' I smile. My heart races slightly. We had better not fuck up tonight.

Kate, Jean-François, a couple of key waiting staff and I help the Russians on to their Dow boat with their quails' eggs, caviar, blinis and flutes, then head off in the speedboat to the sandbank. The idea being that they leave us on the shore as they set off, only for them to find us already there when they arrive.

The sun has set by the time we get into open water and the sky is deep red. Some stars are already shining and the moon is rising. It is a balmy night, and despite the past two days of rain the air is warm but not too humid. I look across at Kate, whose hair is getting the ultimate blow-dry in the wind; she has a gentle smile on her lips. I am not sure if it is the expensive champagne that has perked her up or the fact that she can stop talking about fringes and nail varnish for half an hour at least.

We cut through the surf at full speed, taking the tops off the waves. The water turns from turquoise to a dark midnight blue and schools of fish occasionally leap out of the ocean in front of us. A couple of dolphins accompany us part of the way, but soon get bored. The boat slows down as each of us peers into the twilight to see if we can find the new island.

'It should be somewhere around here,' says Jean-François, straining ahead into the semi-darkness. 'It wasn't much further along than the usual place, which is why we found it.'

'There!' shouts Kate, pointing just to the left of Jean-François. 'Can you see the lights?'

Shimmering across the ocean we see a long rope of lights swinging in the breeze. As we approach the island, I can see they have done the most incredible job. There are large lights hanging off bamboo arches, which also have fairy lights twisted around them. There are Moroccan carpets on the beach, petrol flares shoved into the sand and cushions everywhere. The sandbank looks like some Arabic hooker's boudoir. There are three barbecues up and running, all tended by chefs in tall white hats. There are serving tables of salads, small tables of glasses, and four round tables with dining chairs and linen tablecloths right by the sea. The four-piece band is knocking out a few tunes and the white wine is in ice buckets behind the bar. However, what is truly magical about this scene is that the whole thing is surrounded on all sides by the ocean. It is extraordinary to think that none of this was here this morning and none of it will be here tomorrow.

But there is little time to dwell on how impressive the whole set-up is, as we have a couple of cases of Mouton and Lafite to unpack and dinner to organize before twenty-five Russians pitch up and demand to be entertained. Everyone is running around. Waiters are wading out to sea in their black trousers, carrying box after box on to the island, while Jean-François and I walk around the tables, making sure they've been laid properly and that things like flowers and water are in the right place.

I keep an eye on the ocean; it is calm tonight and what little wind there is is dropping. I am even a little excited. These evenings are always rather fantastic. I did one the other day for a European heir to the throne. It was a very drunken, very jolly evening that ended up with all of us popping by an enormous yacht on the way home. This is one of the largest single-mast yachts in the world and the man who owns it is a music impresario, who is obviously very rich. He invited us all aboard and with a flick of a switch he flooded the back of the boat and turned it into a swimming pool. As I was drunkenly going up the 98-foot mast in a lift, the water below was slowly changing colour due to the underwater lighting. I couldn't believe it. Everyone else tucked into the cannabis and the cocaine and looked on in awe. I remember sloping home at about four thirty a.m. and trying to look in control the next day.

I can hear the coos of delight across the water as the Russian boat arrives. They have clearly been making the best use of their $10k-worth of champagne, because they all think that it is hilarious that I have arrived before them. There is much laughing and back-slapping as they disembark on to the island. A couple of strikingly stunning girls throw themselves at the cushions like a couple of school kids. They are loving the whole thing. Mr Georgi has one of those shiny smiles brought on by sun and sea and champagne.

'Beautiful, beautiful,' he says, taking in the flares and the food and the crisp linen tablecloths. 'My brother is very happy.' One of the waiters arrives with a cold glass of Domaine de Chevalier and he claps with joy. 'And I am delighted,' he says, slapping my back a little too hard. 'I think you should come and work for me.'

'It is a team effort, Mr Georgi. It is all about pulling together at the right time,' I say.

'Yes, yes,' he says as he walks off to join his own party.

I take this as my cue to slip away. I have two other sandbanks to visit tonight, just to make sure that everyone else is having a nice time. I board the speedboat and ask the captain to open up the throttle. The idea that I might miss out on a few glasses of delicious Mouton or Lafite Rothschild is enough to make any epicurean a little twitchy. So I hold on tightly and we fly over the waves and head off to see the first couple. It is Mr and Mrs Forrest, the English couple who are renewing their vows tomorrow and for whom we are flying in twenty-seven Dolce Vita roses and the handmade ring from Singapore. Or at least I hope that is what's happening. What with matters of life and death today,

I have totally forgotten to double-check that these things are actually turning up tomorrow.

We beach the boat in the surf and I leap out, my white linen trousers rolled up around my knees.

'Good evening!' I exclaim as I march up the beach towards them. They are sitting at their small round table, surrounded by candles and flares, with two waiters dressed in black tie standing behind them.

'Who's that?' asks Mr Forrest, staring out into the darkness, concern writ large on his sunburnt face.

'The man from Del Monte,' I say. I use the same joke every time I land on a sandbank, as there is something quite ridiculous about me arriving out of the middle of nowhere to check up on their lobster.

'Oh my God, it's you!' squeals Mrs Forrest, kicking up sand with her feet. 'How funny!'

'Having a nice time?' I ask.

'Oh my God, yes,' she says. 'It is so romantic! The food is fantastic, the wine is amazing.' I clock they are having a nice little 2002 Newton Chardonnay from the Napa Valley at $220 a pop. 'And the service is amazing. I can't believe you got everything here by boat!'

'It's great,' says Mr Forrest, with the smiling confidence of a man who knows he is getting laid tonight. 'I can't fault the experience.'

'Just so long as you are happy,' I smile, shaking them both by the hand. 'Anything else I can do?'

'Nothing,' they both reply at the same time.

On the next sandbank it is a slightly different story. It is Mr and Mrs Thompson, and I could cut the atmosphere with a knife as I wade ashore. They are not entertained by the man from Del Monte and they seem positively bored by each other's company. With nothing to look at other than his wife and the dying candle on their table, you can see Mr Thompson is thinking that this is the worst $2,500 he has ever spent. I try and jolly them up a bit, ask about the sunset and the lobster, but they are both a bit monosyllabic.

'Anything I can help you with?' I ask as I turn to leave.

'When does the boat come to collect us?' asks Mrs Thompson.

'Just as soon or as late as you want.'

'Thank you,' she says.

'Have a great evening,' I reply.

'Darling, I think now would be a good time to order the boat, don't you?' she says as I get back into the speedboat. That marriage is in real crisis, I think, if they can't find any joy in this paradise.

Back on Mr Georgi's sandbank, the singing and the shouting and the band bashing out that old Russian favourite 'Kalinka' are all audible way before I can see the lights. As I draw nearer I can also hear the roars of approval every time Jean-François sets off one of his Balinese paper lanterns. They are gorgeous things that are made of tissue paper and are powered by small candles. The heat sends them flying high into the night sky and then they burn up and crash in a bundle of flame. The Russians have clearly never seen anything quite so beautiful. They are looking upwards, their mouths open in excitement, oohing and aahing like a bunch of schoolchildren. I have a feeling these one-dollar paper lights are being appreciated far more than the bottles of vintage champagne.

Mr Georgi is ecstatic when I make it ashore.

'The food, the wine, the lights!' he says, shaking his head. He is lost for words.

'I am so glad you are enjoying yourself,' I smile, looking over his shoulder at the bottles of red wine on the bar. I have missed dinner with the island tour, and could murder a glass of red wine. 'I'll see you in a minute,' I say, nodding. He is not listening to me any more. He is looking above my head. Another lantern's been launched into the sky.

The waiter gives me a very large glass of Château Lafite Rothschild and I let the delicious liquid slip down my parched throat as I watch another lantern fly up into the sky. Life doesn't really get much better than this.

'Oh *mon dieu*, there you are,' says Jean-François, tapping me on the shoulder.

'Hi,' I smile.

'We're in the shit,' he says, indicating over his shoulder towards the sea. 'The tide is coming in. The island is submerging. In about an hour we will all be under the sea.'

Friday a.m.

Last night was officially what is known as a close shave. Soon after we ran out of flying lanterns it became pretty obvious that we had to evacuate. We realized the reason why this extra-large sandbank had never been used by the resort was that it disappears at about eleven thirty p.m. The waves came lapping in thick and fast. We radioed back to the island for another boat to help us out. We had twenty-two guests rather the worse for almost $25k of booze and we also had waiters, chefs, a band, plus a whole load of carpets and cushions and crockery and glassware to shift back to the resort.

Fortunately, Mr Georgi saw the funny side of it and was laughing and toasting his way all the way back to the Lotus restaurant, which we reopened for him. His brother thought that it was the perfect end to the perfect evening, that somehow we had managed to borrow this magical island and our time was up. Sometimes I really love the Russians, they have a very strange take on most things. While any other guests might have berated us for not reading the tide book before we set up a $47,000 party, they thought it all rather marvellous.

As we set sail with the guests, the bottles of fine wine and a whole load of soft furnishings, I turned back to look at the sandbank, still covered in tables and chairs and standard lamps. There were five waiters with their trousers rolled up to their knees.

'Are we coming back for those guys?' I asked Jean-François, who was squashed up beside me in the boat.

'Who?' he quizzed.

'Those waiters.'

'Oh no,' he said. 'They are looking after the stuff. They are staying the night to make sure nothing goes missing.'

'What?' I asked. 'Who is going to rob a half-submerged sandbank at two a.m.?'

'You never know,' he shrugged. 'And anyway, we can't afford to let the stuff float away.'

'But they are up to their knees in water and it's pitch dark!'

'High tide doesn't last for long and the moon is out,' he said. 'We'll collect them at six a.m.'

So we left them there, guarding a few tables and chairs. It was going to be a long night for them.

Our night turned out to be quite long as well. The Russians went back to the Lotus and partied the night away. I woke the DJ as soon as we landed. Andy is a lovely skinny bloke from London who specializes in mixing iTunes, whatever that means. It is not exactly spinning the decks as I used to know it, but he gets old rich men to dance and all his equipment is sponsored, which is a win-win for us.

Anyway, Jean-François and I left them to it. The last thing the guests needed was the manager hanging around when they wanted to misbehave and I could kind of smell wickedness in the air as I said my good-byes. But actually in the end that turned out to be coming from Jean-François and Marco, who had some-how managed to half-inch one of Mr Georgi's magnums of Cristal and were consuming it at the bar.

'The thing to do,' said Jean-François, as he admired the yellow flute of bubbles up against the light, 'is to ask them if they want to check their empty bottles on at least three or four occasions. And then, once you have their trust, you can steal a bottle or two.'

'You are quite right,' agreed Marco, knocking back his second glass in as many minutes. 'Make them your mate and then steal. It is so much more effective.'

I have to say I stood there for all of one minute, thinking I should have made them take it back. But quite frankly it tasted delicious and if a bloke's too lazy to check his empties, then what's another bloke going to do?

However, as I walk into this morning's meeting with my mouth as dry as sand and a sharp pain behind my right eye, I think that this hangover is probably my punishment.

I sit down at the table and mumble 'Good morning' to everyone. Thankfully, Lynne, who has read my needs correctly, lumbers in soon after me with a small bottle of water and a large cup of coffee.

'So,' I say, rubbing my hands together. 'Anything terrible that I should know about?'

'Um,' says Ingrid, clearing her throat. She is looking quite fit this morning, I think. No wonder Ben has been sniffing around her all week.

'Yes?' I smile. Oh dear, I think I might still be pissed.

'Well, news of the rebellion in the staff village is all over the papers.'

'What papers?'

'The local newspapers.'

'Is that all?'

'It's the front page,' she says, showing me the lead story, with a headline which she informs me translates as HOTEL CHAOS – WORKERS REVOLT. There is even a photo of me and a huge picture of the hotel.

'Bollocks,' says Ben.

'You can say that again,' I say, staring at the newspaper. I am starting to break into a sweat. Jesus Christ, I think, taking a long glug of my water. This is all we need.

'There's a quote from the minister of tourism about workers' rights, and two of the rebels have been interviewed. They say they are going to sue for unfair dismissal,' says Ingrid. 'I have had some press inquiries already from Thailand and Singapore. What line do you want me to take?'

I have my head in my hands, and am slowly scribbling on my meeting pad. The room has gone very quiet. I look up to see they are all staring at me.

'Oh right,' I say, shifting in my seat. 'Can I have a think about that?'

'Yes,' says Ingrid, twitching with efficiency. This is the most exciting thing to happen to her since a journalist from the *Mail on Sunday* turned up to write a travel piece three months ago. 'But I have promised to get back to people before ten this morning.'

'Fine.' I nod. 'Anything else?'

Bernard clears his throat with self-importance and opens up the logbook, licking the tips of his fingers as he does so.

'Well,' he says, 'apart from a few complaints about noise coming from the Lotus restaurant, the night seems to have been without incident.'

'Great,' I say.

'One thing,' he adds.

My shoulders stiffen. 'Yes?'

'We have a French couple who want to move villa because they say it is too windy for their daughter to revise for her exams.'

'That's a first,' says Geri.

'Apparently her papers are blowing in the wind too much.'

There is always someone who wants to move villa and it is nearly always for the same reason – wind. One side of the island is much windier than the other. We are stuck in the middle of nowhere; there is nothing for miles to break the strong prevailing winds. They can blast the island for days at a time and it can be unbearable. Guests are always wanting to move out of the wind, or sometimes when it has been screamingly hot they want to move into it. Either way, they always want to move. Which of course is the prerogative of the high-maintenance guest – never to be satisfied.

'So shall we move them across?' he asks.

'Why not?' I say. 'I'm sure we have some people checking out.'

'Yeah, we do,' agrees Garry. 'Villa 131. The one next door to the German under house arrest.'

'Is he still under house arrest?' I ask.

'Oh yeah,' confirms Garry. 'Don't worry about him,' he says, with a little wave of his hand. 'He's loving it here. He's so happy, he's like a pig in shit. His villa host told me in the village last night that he's been whistling around the place. I'm sure it is a great excuse to do absolutely nothing.'

'I know what you mean,' says Ben. 'There's nothing I'd like more than to be forced to lounge around a large villa, ordering room service and occasionally lying in the sun. It sounds like heaven to me.'

'Maybe we should suggest it to all our guests?' says Bernard.

'It would certainly save us a whole load of hard work,' yawns Ben, who as far as I can ascertain has yet to pull his finger out.

'So yes,' I say, ignoring my deputy's call to slow down. 'Let's move the French next to the annexed Germans . . .'

'And occupy the Sudetenland,' laughs Bernard.

'What?' asks Geri.

'Oh nothing,' he sighs, looking down at his logbook.

'Anything else?' I ask, trying to get the meeting back on track.

'Um, yes,' adds Bernard. 'What are we going to do

with Mr Antonov's boat? It has been sitting in the harbour for three days and he has not been on it, asked for it, or even suggested that he might be interested. In the meantime we are feeding his crew and trying to entertain them in the village, which is frankly not our job.'

'I agree,' says Garry. 'They are hanging around cluttering up the place.'

'Why don't we dismiss them?' says Ben. 'It's costing the bloke $10,000 a day for them to sit there scratching their arses.'

Everyone's looking at me again. I'm feeling dreadful. I can barely choose between the coffee and water sitting in front of me, let alone decide whether to dismiss Mr Antonov's boat.

'Um, I think we should get rid of it,' I say. 'We can always get them to come back if he shows any interest, can't we? There's hardly going to be a run on luxury yachts, now, is there?'

I am just about to pack up the meeting and hopefully disappear to shovel a couple of croissants down my throat when Bernard reminds us about the Forrests' wedding this evening. He checks with Jean-François that the catering has been taken care of and that Marco knows about the wine.

'And the ring and the flowers are on their way?' he asks me.

'Oh right,' I say, flicking through my papers, pretending to be checking. 'Has anyone spoken to Kate? She should know what is happening.'

They all look at me as if I am mad. I sleep with Kate, I should know what is happening.

'We try not to talk shop at home,' I laugh.

'Right,' nods Geri.

In fact, truth be known, we are not talking at all. She is still fuming at being forced to talk about hair and handbags all night to a group of women who, although much younger than her, appear to have greater access to cash. Needless to say, I got the cold buttocks again last night and the forked tongue this morning.

'It is not good for my self-esteem,' she claimed, striding around the room in her underwear. 'It makes me doubt my career path. I could have done so many other things with my life and because of you I am managing a shop in the middle of nowhere, selling kaftans to hookers and banker wives when I could have been doing something else. You should remember that when you sit me next to a gangster's moll dressed head to foot in Dolce and Gabbana.'

Amazingly, the normally supercilious Bernard senses my embarrassment and offers to take over negotiations with my girlfriend. However, Garry then drops the bombshell that he has had inquiries from our Japanese travel agent as to whether we could cope with a further twenty-five weddings in February.

'Twenty-five?' Bernard turns up his nose. 'In what is effectively four weeks? That's almost one a day for the whole month – I don't think we can absorb that many.'

I hate to say it, but I think Bernard is right. 'Absorb' really is the word. The words of dive master Shane are ringing in my ears about his resort being dead as a dodo, full of nothing but stiff mutterings and soppy hand-holders staring out to sea. It is extremely important to get the balance of guests right in a place like this. Otherwise you're stuffed. The sheen goes off the place. You lose your world standing and the great and the good and the super rich jet off somewhere else. Just as you don't want screaming kids dive-bombing the blue-rinsers in the pool, you don't want too many of the evening-slacks brigade asking for dinner jazz and Baileys on ice. Equally, we can only take a certain amount of high-spending Russians and their flamboyant girlfriends before the place begins to resemble a knocking shop. And the Arabs always try and take over when they arrive.

All it takes is for seven Japanese newly-wed couples to all decide to take their complimentary candlelit dinner for two at the same time for the atmosphere in the dining room to be killed stone dead. I've seen it happen. I have seen table after table of silent lovers all savouring their prawn starters only for other people, groups of mates, to walk into the dining room, turn and take one look at each other and walk straight out again.

I also have to say they are not exactly the most lucrative of guests. Gone are the days when the yen was riding high and the Japs were loaded, snapping up Impressionists for their offices. Now they are like the rest of us and their one-dollar tips in the spa are the least of their tight-fistedness. Time and again, these newly-weds leave the hotel with as little as twenty dollars in extras on the bill. We used to think that they must have been living on fresh air or something, until we worked out that they were bringing suitcases of Pot Noodles into the hotel, which explained why they always asked for a kettle. We found their plastic wrappers on the beach, which is kind of revolting. We try and keep the place as pristine as possible, so the last thing we need is cheap rubbish on our shores. And another thing, which I also find slightly irritating, is that we have to cater specifically for their tastes. More than any other nationality that we have on the island, when the Japanese travel they expect their country to travel with them. Perhaps their cultural identity is just that bit stronger than ours, but they expect everything to be translated for them. They want their bento boxes and beer for breakfast, but they also want other things like paper covers on their loos and new toothbrushes every day.

233

Other nationalities have their quirks. The Brits are rude as well as tight and they can spread dissent in a hotel very quickly. Like the freebie cancer at the manager's drinks, they can sit and moan to each other all day and convince themselves en masse that the hotel is shit and the service is terrible. The French are arrogant, the Germans are a little bizarre and the Americans have lots of money and very little opinion. They can usually be persuaded to try things out. If you take them by the hand and direct them to spend $4,000 on a sandbank experience, or $200 each on an early-morning reef outing, then they invariably go for it. New Yorkers, on the other hand, are a different breed. They are high-maintenance, aggressive, opinionated and never satisfied. Rather relaxingly, the Russians just want to have fun. I think they've suffered under the yoke of Communism for so long that if they have two dollars to rub together they will spend them both, as who knows what will happen tomorrow? And the Arabs – well, they just turn up here, go to their room and expect everything to arrive – immediately.

'So are we saying no to this many weddings?' asks Garry, looking up from his agenda.

'I think we are,' I say. 'I think the most we can really cope with is three or four a week. We don't want to create another alternative community.'

'Talking of which, have you seen what's been

happening at Mr McCann's villas?' asks Geri. 'Rumour has it it is like one big orgy. Those innocent villa hosts' eyes are on stalks. They'll be selling tickets soon.'

'I tell you,' says Ben, puffing out his cheeks, 'if you hang around the pool you get to see some of the most amazing erotic dancing I have seen outside of Spearmint Rhino.'

'Really?' asks Hori. 'I think I'd better check up on the pool's filter system.'

'It usually kicks off at about four,' says Ben, tapping the side of his nose. 'After a nice liquid lunch.'

'OK, I think that's it,' I say, tapping my hands together. 'At least the weather is a whole lot better today.'

'True,' says Bernard.

'Um, if you could think about our response to the rebellion before ten,' says Ingrid, clipping her files together, 'it would be very helpful.' She looks at me and gives me a tight little smile. Suddenly she doesn't look so attractive.

Walking towards the staff canteen, I am contemplating a second breakfast of sorts and wondering if I might try and slip back to the villa for the briefest of lie-downs. I know I've got to make a tour of the dining room to check on the guests, I have got to sort out what I am going to say to the local newspapers and I have stacks of paperwork to catch up on, plus a few personnel meetings to get through. Also I should really have a word with Ben about how he is settling in and perhaps invite him round for lunch on Sunday. That would be friendly. But I am feeling woozy and tired and in need of a kip. My phone goes. It looks like it's Garry. What the hell can he want? I have just had a meeting with the bloke. What's he got to get off his well-worked-out and waxed chest now?

'Sheikh attack!'

'What? When?'

'Now!'

'Fuck!'

'I know,' says Garry. 'ETA this afternoon.'

Now I'm awake. I call Bernard.

'Sheikh attack!'

'When?'

'This afternoon. What have we got free?'

'How many?'

'Shit, I don't know. Call Garry. But I presume at least three.'

'We've got one Grand Villa with a pool near the Samurai, on Palm Sands beach. Villa 225.'

'Cool, see you there.'

I hang up and call housekeeping.

'Sheikh attack!'

'Where?'

'Villa 225.'

'When?'

'This afternoon.'

They hang up and I go on to call Hori, Youssif the chief villa host, Jean-François, Ingrid, Ben; even Geri gets a tip-off just in case. In fact within about ten minutes of the initial call from Garry, the whole island knows we have a sheikh, plus entourage, on their way. And most of them turn up to villa 225.

Walking along Palm Sands towards the Grand Beach I can't believe how many people are crawling all over the place. It is like a crime scene. The chief gardener is there replanting the garden with fresh shrubs, Bernard is running all over the place issuing orders. Garry's shouting at everyone, telling them he needs four more villas. Housekeeping have decided to give the Grand a deep clean, which means they are steaming the curtains and doing a full maintenance check, including things like whether the lights in the cupboards come on when you open the door. Hori is hovering about arguing with his men about how to clean the pool and make sure there are no leaks. Christ, I think as I stand and take in the mayhem, you'd have thought that there was no one else in the whole hotel.

Ben saunters over, looking a little bemused.

'Who is this bastard and why are we making so much fuss?' he asks, squinting through his shades.

'He is one of the twenty-five richest men in the world. He flies in on his Boeing 747 jet for a long week-end every so often for some R&R with his mates. And last time he was here he gave me a $3,000 tip.'

'So he is worth being nice to?'

'Definitely,' I say. 'I'd bend over backwards to accommodate him in every way.'

'Let's hope it doesn't come to that,' says Ben, tapping me on the back. 'Anything I can do?'

'Yes. Make sure that all the buggies are washed and scrubbed and lined up outside reception when he arrives.'

'What time would that be?'

'Around three p.m., or so I've been told.'

'What happens to the other guests in the meantime?'

'Oh,' I say, turning around to look at Ben, 'tell them it's better if they walk.'

As I make my way towards the villa, the shouting and the ringing of mobile phones becomes unbearable, especially for a man in my fragile state. Everyone is shouting at someone and trying to call someone else, but everyone's phone is either ringing or engaged, so no one is really achieving anything at all. This happens every time we have a sheikh attack. It is like releasing a fox in a pen of chickens and watching them run around flapping in every direction. I have this theory that there are always so many executives and their followers running around issuing orders that none of them can do anything unless their number two is there.

As I walk through the villa, there are so many people being terribly busy I almost don't know where to start. Jean-François grabs hold of me beside the bath. What the food and beverages manager is doing here I don't know. Perhaps he is seeing to the minibar.

'Ah ha,' he says, his long dark hair flopping forward. 'So I have booked out tables for sixteen at the Lotus and the Samurai and the main dining room, just in case.'

'OK.'

'And I have asked the head chef in each to cook up a special menu.'

'Right.'

'Last time he came the Samurai was full and it was terrible, don't you remember? So we have a special menu in place in all the restaurants.'

'Well done,' I say, patting him on his back.

'Thank you,' he says, exhaling into my face. 'Oh, by the way,' he adds. 'We only lost one lampshade last night. We collected the waiters at six thirty and everything was fine.'

'OK, guys, OK!' shouts Garry at the top of his voice, clapping his hands over his head. 'No need to panic. He's not arriving until four. We've got plenty of time.'

In the sitting room the stench of bleach is

overpowering. The air-con is doing battle with the curtain steamer and is definitely losing. There are three cleaners polishing the mirrors. A villa host is checking the TV for sound and vision. There are guys in the pool outside. There's someone spraying for mosquitoes. The beds are being remade. More pillows are arriving, fresh flowers, fruit. The minibar is being stacked with champagne. There's a complimentary bottle of VSO brandy sitting on the table. Everyone is bumping into everyone else, thinking their job is the most important.

I can't bear it any more and escape to the shoreline. I'm the boss, so everyone thinks that I am off to do something very important, not that I am getting the hell out of here. I walk along the beach, looking out to sea. I am hoping the air might improve my hangover. But it's warm and humid and nowhere near bracing enough. It's just like standing in the steam room with the door half open. However, looking out to sea I suddenly notice something. There's a whole load of rubbish floating in the water. It's not the usual packet of beef Super Noodles sailing by – there's loads of it. Plastic bags, packaging, rotten fruit, all sorts of stuff, and it looks rank.

'Jiwan! Hori!' I shout back at the villa. Amazingly they both hear me. 'Get your arses down here!'

Within ten minutes I've got seven guys up to their waists in the sea, fishing shit out of the water. No one can believe it. Look at all this stuff. It is like some industrial rubbish bag has burst and is threatening to land its contents on Palm Sands beach, just as the sheikh arrives.

'It is all about having an eye for detail,' I find myself opining to Ben. 'You know, looking at things from a different perspective.'

Just as I am in danger of boring even myself, there is a positively girlish scream from the villa.

'Fucking hell!!!!' It's Garry. 'The sheikh's already landed at the airport! He's on his way. He'll be here in less than an hour.'

Friday p.m.

Ben, Bernard and I are standing in a row like the three stooges, waiting for the sheikh to arrive. Our man on the mainland radioed over about forty-five minutes ago to say he had boarded the Sunseeker yacht we'd sent and was on his way. Its top speed is thirty-six knots, so unless the captain is taking the scenic route we should expect him here any minute. We are trying to look relaxed and failing miserably. Bernard's phone keeps going off, Ben won't stop scratching and complaining there are mosquitoes in the staff village, and I am sweating so much old alcohol in the boiling-hot afternoon sun I can smell it on my skin.

'*Merde*, there he is,' mutters Bernard, pointing at the horizon. 'Let me just make sure everything is ready.'

'What happens now?' asks Ben, turning to me and frowning over the top of his *Miami Vice* shades.

'We meet and greet and give them drinks and towels and then take the sheikh and his entourage to the row of buggies outside,' I explain.

'Are there enough?' asks Ben. 'I've got ten outside.'

'They all washed?'

'And scrubbed and hand-dried,' he adds.

'Ten should be enough,' I say. 'They're sixteen, so some will have to go in together, but that's fine. I'll travel with the sheikh up front, in case he has any questions, and you can go with his number two.'

'Who's that?'

'It will be obvious.'

'Fine.' He nods. 'Jesus Christ! Look at that!'

Ben stares out to sea, his mouth slightly ajar. Standing on the top deck of the boat are the sheikh and a gaggle of about ten of his men, all dressed head to foot in their white flowing robes. There are acres of white cotton flapping in the sunshine. It is quite an amazing sight. A couple of the guys at the front are holding firmly on to their headdresses, while the sheikh, sporting a golden dishdash, seems to be loving being blasted by the wind; he gives us a cheery wave from the boat. All three of us wave back.

'He seems jolly,' says Ben.

'He likes a party,' says Bernard.

'Really?' asks Ben.

'Oh yes,' replies Bernard, talking out of the side of

his mouth, staring straight ahead. 'He is one of those sheikhs who ask you to fill the fridge with alcohol, not take it out. I wouldn't be surprised if there are some ladies coming over later.'

'Travelling at a discreet distance,' I smile.

'*Ah oui, très, très discrète,*' agrees Bernard.

'Good afternoon, sir!' I shout across at the yacht as it slows towards the jetty. 'How lovely to have you back here with us again.'

'It is great to be back,' says the sheikh with a broad grin. 'I have brought some friends.' He gestures to the group behind him.

'You are all very welcome,' I say, putting my hand on my heart and bowing. '*Salaam alaikum.*'

'*Alaikum salaam,*' they all reply, bowing slightly and putting their hands on their hearts.

They disembark in a flurry of cloth and luggage; half the buggy boys on the island are ready and waiting to carry their bags. The sheikh leads the way, heading off up the jetty and into reception. He ignores the trays of complimentary drinks, plucks a chilled hand towel and heads straight out to the buggies, which are all buffed and polished and lined up like they're in a car showroom. The first buggy driver leaps out of his seat like someone has shoved a cattle prod up his backside and grins with attentiveness. His arm is out, indicating where the sheikh should sit. But instead of going to his seat as planned, the sheikh veers off to the right, towards the grass roundabout and the view to the sea.

'Come,' he says, turning to me, beckoning me towards him. 'Let us walk.'

'Walk the whole island?' I query, looking somewhat longingly at the rows of shiny buggies.

'Yes,' he says. 'I would like to see the resort, look at what you have done to the place, and you can answer my questions.'

So we set off in the searing heat of the afternoon. I'm almost at half jog as I try and keep up with the sheikh. He bobs along, muttering and mumbling quick-fire questions at me, while I fall over myself, stooping forward trying to catch his every word. Meanwhile, his entourage of sixteen male friends follow on behind him, and in the wake of their robes follow Ben, Bernard and a long line of buggy boys and helpers, carrying their luggage. If the sheikh is walking, then so is everyone else.

The sheikh doesn't appear to notice the stares of Mr McCann's bikini-clad babes or indeed the slack jaws of the Thompson children. He is intent on firing off as many questions as he can, and I am just trying to keep up with him.

It takes us forty-five minutes of power-walking to reach the villa. By the time we turn the corner and head up the path, my shirt has stuck to my back with sweat and I have skinny rivulets of the stuff snaking down the side of my face. I keep mopping my forehead with my handkerchief but nothing seems to stem the flow. All that happens is that I look increasingly knackered and out of control. The sheikh, on the other hand, is cool as a cucumber and doesn't have a bead of the stuff anywhere. One thing's sure – at least the island yomp has bought us some more time, which we clearly needed. For as the sheikh walks in through the front of the villa, I spot three cleaners and a gardener disappearing out the back.

'This is perfect,' says the sheikh, looking around. 'It is the same place as I had last time I was here.'

'Of course, sir. We want you to feel quite at home.' I smile and nod. Thank Christ for that, I think.

'Home is the place I am flying away from!' he laughs. Sixteen other men join in.

'Of course,' I smile, adding my laugh to theirs. 'Anything you need, please call me,' I say, handing over my card. The sheikh looks the other way as someone else picks up the card. A man of his importance doesn't do paper.

'Thank you,' he smiles.

This is obviously my cue to leave. I glance over at Ben and Bernard and then across at the door. They get my drift and we all back out of there. This man is keen to get his party started.

We all blink in the hot sun.

'*Mon dieu*,' says Bernard, mopping his neck with a handkerchief. 'I didn't need the walk.'

'I know,' huffs Ben. 'Who'd have thought that a guy like that would want to walk to his villa? Especially after I'd gone to all that effort to clean up those buggies.'

'I know.' I shake my head. 'I am bloody exhausted.'

'What a fucker,' says Ben.

'That's sheikh fucker to you,' I say, wagging my finger.

'I hope there are no more surprises,' says Bernard. 'I hate surprises.'

'Oh shit,' says Ben as we head off down the path.

'What?' I say.

'All the buggies are in reception – we've got to walk all the way back again.'

'Think yourself lucky,' I say. 'At least you don't have a hangover from hell.'

'Are you kidding? I was knocking back the beers in the staff bar until they kicked me out. I feel like a small dog has shat in my mouth.'

'Oh God,' says Bernard, shaking his head. 'You English are all the same.'

We head off down the path and out on to the open road. Hot and sweaty and exhausted, we must look like three blokes in search of an oasis. Who would have thought that a forty-five-minute walk could have wiped us out so completely?

Just as I am about to really lose my dignity along with my cool, a laundry buggy comes by. It is piled high with dirty sheets and damp towels from the five or six villas the bloke's just cleaned. Bernard flags it down. Ben hurls himself straight into the sheets and Bernard perches pertly on the back. I debate for a second if I should join them before remembering my position. I ask the driver to move over and join him in the cabin in the front. The sun disappears behind a cloud and I exhale. Things are looking up – all I need now is a litre of water and a change of shirt.

Showered and refreshed, I return to the staff dining room for a late lunch. The atmosphere is buzzing. It is amazing what a sniff of sheikh and all the tips that entails does for morale. The Russians are all well and good and I have a feeling that Mr Georgi will certainly be generous when he leaves, but sheikh money is oil money and that tends to flow so much more easily. I wouldn't be surprised if in the next couple of days almost everyone in the hotel will find the need to go and make themselves useful in and around the Palm Sands Grand Beach Villa.

I am just about to sit down with Mohammed, my head of security, to chat about things and check that all is OK post the staff village uprising. A local himself who has worked his way up through the ranks, he has his ear to the ground more than anyone else and always knows what is happening. We are sitting down with our red trays of salad from the bar when my phone goes. I pick it up straight away, just in case it is the sheikh.

'Hello? Hello?' comes this shouty voice. My first thought is that it is the bloody nanny again, asking for another bloody buggy.

'*Hola?*' I say.

'*Ciao, ciao,*' she says. 'This is Countess Donatella di Cassucci.'

'Good afternoon,' I say. 'How can I help you?' I'm trying to remember which villa she is in. A Beach? A Water? I'm not sure. All I can recall is that she's only been here a couple of days.

'The sun has gone in,' she declares.

'Has it?' My heart sinks. Here we go.

'Yes, it has,' she says. 'And I am on my holidays and I want sun.'

'I'm sure it will come back out again, madam. It always does. We're an island and the weather changes . . .'

'I know that!' She is sounding increasingly irate. 'But I have been here for three days and every day it rains and rains and now it is cloudy.'

'I am terribly sorry, madam,' I say. 'But at least it is not snowing.'

'I don't come here for snow. If I want snow, I go to the Alps. I want sun. I have come for sun and there is no sun.'

'I am sure it will be sunny later,' I say.

'Later is no good. I want sun now. I want to fly to Mauritius. There is always sun there.'

'You want a flight because it is not sunny?'

'And it's too windy here. So much wind . . . and no sun. I want a flight this afternoon.'

'OK.'

'And I want to fly to Mauritius.'

'OK. The only problem is that I'm not sure if I can get you out of here today.'

'What? Why not?'

'Because there might not be any flights.'

'Oh.'

'I could always get you a private jet.'

'Yes, good idea.'

'But what happens if the sun comes out in the meantime?'

'It will still be windy. Call me back when you have done it,' she says and then hangs up.

Mohammed looks at me. 'Someone not enjoying themselves?'

'Apparently not,' I say, shovelling in a forkful of

salad. 'I'm afraid I am going to have to go to the office.'

I spend the next hour and a half calling up various private-jet companies, trying to organize transport for the countess. It is not so much the flight to Mauritius that is the problem, but trying to find a jet that is able to get here today. Or at least some time this evening. In my experience, if someone has made up their mind that they want to leave, it is usually a good idea to try and get rid of them as quickly as possible, otherwise they just end up kicking off about everything. Finally I pull a favour with an old mate of mine who has a couple of jets on the tarmac at Mombasa airport. He says it would take him a couple of hours to get here and we could definitely get her out today. So I call her to give her the good news.

'What type of plane is it?' she asks, neither delighted nor gracious about my efforts.

'A Learjet 25,' I say. 'Nippy and neat. It will get you there in no time.'

'Is it small?'

'Um, yes,' I say. 'Well, it is for you and your daughter, I presume, so it is the perfect size for two.'

'I don't want it,' she says. 'I don't like the sound of it.'

'But they can get here tonight and have you in Mauritius before midnight.'

'I don't like it,' she says. 'I don't want to be a cork in the ocean. I want a big plane.'

'But there are only two of you.'

'I want a big plane. I don't feel safe in a small can in the sky, bobbing around in the wind. Find me something else.' She hangs up.

I am tempted to call her back and tell her exactly where to stuff her jet and her stroppy old attitude. But she has a little star next to her name on the guest list, which means she knows the owner or at least a member of his immediate family, so it's my head rather than the jet that is popping up her backside. I rope Lynne in on the mission and together the two of us manage to track down a Falcon 900 that is sitting in Dubai. The company says that for $98,000 they can pick up the countess and her daughter and get them to Mauritius by tomorrow morning. I call her back, but she doesn't sound that impressed. I give her the blurb about it being one of the most technologically advanced large business jets available. That it has the latest innovations in aerodynamics and flight systems and a cruise speed of over 550 mph. And finally she accepts my kind offer. I tell her the jet will be ready at around ten o'clock tonight and that she should be at the airport a few minutes before. She doesn't thank me and doesn't even ask me how much. But then again, if you're the sort of person who drops nearly $100,000 on a flight just because the place where you are staying is a little bit windy, then perhaps manners are not high on your agenda.

Lynne and I are celebrating our marvellousness with a cup of tea and some chocolate-chip cookies that she ordered in from the kitchen when Kate calls. She tells me that the wedding ring has arrived off the midday flight from Singapore, as have the Dolce Vita roses.

'And I have to say,' she adds, 'the roses are amazing. I have never seen anything like them before. The stems are as long as your arm.'

'You're sounding very well,' I say.

'I've had a good day,' she says. 'Mrs Antonov was in this morning and spent $3,000 on bikinis and some beaded Matthew Williamson tops. She is a nice woman.'

'So they are not all just interested in haircuts and nails?'

'Well, this one isn't. But then again, she was married to him before he owned all the aluminium in Siberia. I think she is looking forward to going on the boat later on this afternoon.'

'Yeah,' I say, dunking my biscuit into my tea. 'Sorry? What did you say?'

'She's going on the boat this afternoon?'

'Shit!' I drop my biscuit into my tea. It splashes up all over my shirt. 'Shit, shit, shit.' I stand up, trying to brush the tea off. I look down – there's a great big milky stain across my left pec. Not another bloody shirt.

'What's the matter?' Kate sounds sweetly concerned for a girlfriend with the hump. It is amazing what a little business can do for a girl's mood.

'Can I call you back?'

'Sure.'

'Lynne!' I shout.

'What's the matter, sir?' she asks, popping her head around the office door.

While Lynne takes my buggy back to the villa to get me my third shirt of the day, I scrabble around at my desk trying to turn Mr Antonov's yacht around. I manage to get the charter company to radio the skipper and find out where the hell he is. Fortunately for me, he is taking the scenic route home and can be back at the resort in about an hour to an hour and a half. Which is not too long to keep a well-connected Siberian oligarch waiting. As it happens he has yet to request his yacht, so I'm sure I can think of some technical hitch that needs sorting, ready for a lovely sunset cruise with lashings of complimentary champagne.

I'm on my way to have a word with Hans about the yacht plan when I bump into Geri outside the spa.

'Thank Christ you're here,' she says, stubbing out a cigarette in the sand. I have told her off about this before, but somehow it always slips her mind.

'Why, what's happened?'

'I don't know what to do,' she says, shaking her dyed blonde hair and crossing her arms underneath her ample bosom. 'We've got a couple having sex in the spa.'

'Really?'

'Yeah,' she sniffs. 'It's like some live porn show. The therapist ran screaming from the pavilion about two minutes ago, and I came out for a fag to decide what to do.'

'Show me,' I say.

Geri and I walk through the spa lobby. Enya's still on a loop and a couple of Japanese newly-weds are exchanging their sandals for towelling flip-flops. We walk out into the garden. The sun is peeking between the clouds and there are a few birds singing above the bubbling of one of the many water features. Geri beckons me towards the couples' suite cabana. It is made of wood with a thatched roof and opens on one side, facing the sea.

'There,' she whispers, pointing though the leaves of a palm.

I step forward to see a middle-aged couple going for it hammer and bloody tongs. She is sitting on the treatment table, legs akimbo, while he shags her while admiring the lovely sea view over her right shoulder. Also admiring the view is the whole of Connie's yoga class. Connie appears to be trying to divert them with a quick downward dog, but none of them are having any of it. They are mostly standing with their hands on their hips and their eyes on stalks, drinking it in.

'How long have they been at it?' I ask.

'I don't know,' mumbles Geri. 'Five minutes.'

'Well, um . . .'

We both turn back to take another look. The man has now buried his head between the woman's breasts and is banging away at full speed. His pink buttocks are rippling and wobbling like tripe in a plastic bag.

'It shouldn't be long now,' I say.

'D'you think?'

'Well . . .' I nod towards the bloke. 'A man of his age can't keep that sort of thing going for long.'

'Tell me about it,' sighs Geri.

At which point the woman starts to moan '*Yah! Yah! Yah! Yah!*' with increasing volume, while ruffling the man's hair.

'German,' I whisper helpfully.

'I thought as much.'

The pounding increases, as do the yells of delight, and Connie gives up on her class. The whole of the yoga class are staring now, as are about three other guests in the spa who have come out of their treatment pagodas to see what all the noise is about.

'*YAAAH!*' the man shouts suddenly, accompanied by

a totally unnecessary caveman roar. He collapses forward on to the woman's shoulder while she sits there, staring straight ahead, looking a little disappointed.

'Honestly,' sniffs Geri, pulling her tight dress down, 'you would have thought they hadn't had a shag in years.'

'Maybe he hasn't and he just took the opportunity while he had the chance.'

'What shall we do now?' she asks.

'Let's see what happens.'

The woman gets down off the table and throws back her hair. She bends down.

'Oh Jesus Christ, no!' winces Geri. 'She's going for a blow job . . . how disgusting is that? . . . Oh no . . . No . . . OK, that's OK. She's putting on her paper pants.'

'So's he!'

'Weird.'

'They don't strike me as a terribly normal couple. You know, what with the live sex show.'

'That's true,' agrees Geri. 'It is usually the honeymooners who get carried away.'

'What?'

'Not like that,' she says. 'But you know, they get all hand-holdy after a treatment and you know things're going to happen as soon as they get back to the villa. Oh look,' she adds. 'Here they come.'

The racy Germans appear out of their cabana dressed

in his-and-her dressing gowns and they walk, bold as brass, through reception and ask for someone to call them a buggy. They look neither embarrassed nor mortified. In fact, it is almost as if someone else has just been having wild penetrative sex in full view of half the spa. Geri and I exchange looks. The longer I am in this business the more I realize just how extraordinary human beings are. What is it about hotels and resorts that makes guests leave behind the normal rules of behaviour at the jetty or on the other side of the revolving door?

The Germans take their buggy back to their villa, looking like butter wouldn't melt in their mouths. Just as I'm about to leave, a diminutive Shirley Temple type comes kicking and screaming into the spa, rapidly followed by one of our villa hosts, who is trying to corral her out of the place.

'Oh bugger,' says Geri, her shoulders slumping. 'The kid's back. She's been in here every bloody day this week, causing chaos.'

The girl looks like an angel. She has blonde curls and blue eyes, but she kicks and screams like a vixen.

'I don't know what to do,' says Geri, shaking her head. 'Hassan has tried everything. Every day the minx runs out of the kids' club, calling everyone everything under the sun, and runs in here demanding to see her mother. Who bizarrely has booked in for more treatments than the Bride of Wildenstein, simply to get away from the brat.'

Spoilt children are one of the worst aspects of this job. What you really want to do is give them a clip around the ear and tell them where to get off, but instead you have to bite your tongue and get them another six-dollar scoop of Valrhona ice cream. They are usually banned from the spa, but somehow we always seem to have a couple of irritating ten-year-olds demanding massages. They are normally Russian and they are usually poisonous. They are rude and their parents don't seem to care. We had some teenagers running amok only the other day. They were running in and out of the cabanas, shouting and screaming. You don't really want to be paying $280 for a massage with that sort of noise going on. Eventually we had to call security to get them removed. I complained to their parents, but as per usual they didn't do anything.

We do see some of the oddest parenting skills here. I suppose it is because they are used to having fleets of nannies, but I can't help thinking that the super rich have forgotten how to enjoy, relate or even talk to their children. All they do is dump them on us. At Christmas and New Year, one of our major worries is how we are going to entertain the children. We put on barbecues, we have fishing competitions, and we have pirates' battles between the boats out at sea, where everyone dresses up and we have a party afterwards. But the problem is that half these children don't know how to play. Last year we gave up trying so hard and bought a whole load of Game Boys, which seem to keep them all happy.

It makes you wonder why some of these people have children in the first place. A couple of weeks ago, when I was doing one of my evening tours of the restaurants, I saw this couple having dinner with their son in the Samurai. He must have been about seven or eight years old. They were sitting at a round table eating supper and the little boy was sitting there watching a DVD at the table, with a pair of earphones on. No one was talking. Not even the parents. I found the whole thing kind of depressing.

Geri goes over to the blonde minx and tries to reason with her. There's more shouting and screaming. I can see Geri wants to send her to her room without any supper, but in the end the little girl gets her own way and is escorted off to her mother's treatment room. She is terribly pleased with herself as she walks away.

I leave the spa and have just hung up on Hans when my phone goes again.

'Hi, it's me.'

'Hi Ben. What's the matter?'

'The sheikh has just called through to villa dining and asked for a beach barbecue.'

'What? Fuck! No!' My heart is racing. 'Are there any available?'

'I'm not sure.'

'Oh shiiiit.' I sink into the driving seat.

'What?'

'We've only gone and block-booked both the restaurants. Chef is going to kill me.

Friday Sunset

Oh dear. I thought I'd thought of everything. The villa had been cleaned, the sand raked and the sea cleansed. I'd block-booked both the restaurants just in case, but somehow I had overlooked the idea of a bloody party. The head chef, Antonio, is so furious he has hung up on me. He's hung up on Jean-François. And he's called Ben every name under the sun, including ones I never knew existed. The thing is that the chefs at the Lotus and the Samurai have been working on specials all afternoon. They have been coming up with little *amuse-bouche* dishes to tickle our sheikh's jaded palate, for which they were obviously going to charge him through the nose. And now they are fucked. We don't have any beach-barbecue slots available and no one's even given lobsters and wagyu beef a single thought.

So now we have to spirit a soirée for seventeen out of

thin air. There is so much shouting and ringing of telephones that it makes this morning's efforts look like a throat-clearing warm-up. Chefs are taken off restaurant duty and assigned to the barbecue. Carpets and cushions are stolen from empty villas and lifted from less important barbecues. Fortunately, thanks to yesterday's big resupply from the *Mary Celeste*, we have enough beef and lobster to feed an army of sheikhs and their friends. But there are still salads to make and marinades to prepare, not to mention dips and bits and starters. We need cooking stations, dessert stations and a salad bar. We need to set up the bar, dress the beach and fix the lighting. Fortunately, the sheikh doesn't want an early kick-off. He's happy to eat at around nine p.m., as I have been informed he is expecting some other guests.

Antonio calls me again. He is still spitting his dummy, moaning on about his food budget and how I have buggered up his accounts. He is supposed to balance his books like every other department on the island. He has $20 million a year to spend on food and he has to make it pay. He's complaining that he is going to have to absorb the cost of my mistake. That the restaurants are now down on the night because guests have been turned away, and he has made all this extra food. When I point out that he is sounding hysterical and that everyone knows he can sell the sheikh's delicacies on as specials, he tells me to get my big nose out of his business. I never understand what it is with chefs – why are they always prone to such histrionics? Their life never seems so bad to me. They get backhanded by suppliers, they get a percentage of the cash flow of the restaurant, and these days plenty of the big stellar names don't even get their hands dirty.

Anyway, I can't hang around and listen to his Sicilian ranting any more. I have another wedding to get to. Mr and Mrs Forrest are renewing their vows in the pagoda at Palm Sands at six p.m. and quite a few members of staff have been invited. While it is of course terribly nice and kind and sweet of them to invite us to witness – or in my case perform – the ceremony, most of the key staff need this like a hole in the head. We've got a beach barbecue to organize and a sheikh to entertain and the clock is ticking relentlessly.

Bernard is already suited and loafered by the time I arrive at the beach. The pagoda has been decked out with pink frangipani and there's a short row of white chairs in the sand.

'How quickly can we get through this?' asks Bernard, shoving a Dolce Vita rose in my buttonhole.

'I'm not sure,' I say.

'Thing is, you're going to have to go through the

whole thing properly, as they are English. No skipping to the end like with the Japanese.'

'I know,' I nod. 'Who else is coming?'

'Ben, Jean-François, Garry, Geri, Kate's the bridesmaid . . .'

The sun is settling behind a cloud and the wind picks up slightly as Mrs Forrest arrives. Kate is standing behind her in the same dress that she wore last night for Mr Georgi's party, but she still looks remarkably fresh. The bride, on the other hand, looks a little uncomfortable. Instead of the usual floaty silk number we tend to get in the tropics, she has plumped for the sort of meringue with corset that is favoured for an English country church wedding and she appears to be regretting it. She is breaking into a sweat and looks short of breath. Her satin heels sink into the sand. The rest of my gang don't look that much better. They appear hassled and itchy and twitchy. Not even the $600 worth of roses they're sporting makes them look any more celebratory.

DJ Andy starts the music and Mrs Forrest walks across the sand to the tune of 'Angels' by Robbie Williams. Mr Forrest smiles broadly as she approaches the pagoda. She arrives before the end of the first chorus and we stand and stare at the sea, waiting for the song to finish. I whip through the ceremony at a politely decent speed and hand over the handcrafted

$1,500 ring that we had made and flown here, at $1,000 extra cost to the client. But it does look fabulous and it fits perfectly. I say the magic words 'You may kiss the bride' just as the sun hits the horizon, which is going to look great in the all-important wedding shots.

Then before you can say Congratulations and I'll see you at the bar, the crowd has dispersed to various corners of the beach to listen to their messages on their mobile phones. I am still talking to the bride and groom, who seem delighted by the way things have turned out – the ring and the roses were more than they had hoped for – when Geri comes and taps me on the shoulder.

'I am terribly sorry to bother you,' she says, a tight pink-lipsticked smile on her face. 'Can I borrow you for a second?'

'Of course,' I say. 'Forgive me.' I nod my excuses to the couple.

'I'm sorry,' she says. 'But something's happened at the spa. D'you mind coming down?'

'No, sure,' I say. 'Let's go.'

On the way, Geri fills me in on what's been going on. Turns out that one of the masseuses, Melinda, has been doing a bit of extracurricular on the side.

'She is queen of the happy finish,' says Geri. 'And it has taken us this long to realize why she is so goddamn popular with the Arabs and the Russian men.'

Friday Sunset

* * *

The girls get propositioned for sex in the spa all the time. At least once a day someone oversteps the mark, but the girls have been trained to deal with this. If some bloke starts getting fresh or suddenly whips off his paper pants, or, as is more usual, refuses to put them on, then the girls are instructed to leave the room and ask the client to calm down, otherwise they will not resume the massage and will report the matter. The frisky bloke is then marked down as a man who enjoys a happy finish and is forever after given a male therapist. This usually takes the wind out of their sails and the lead out of their pencil, and they cancel all their massage appointments.

However, there are some girls for whom a quick hand-shandy is not a problem and obviously a sure-fire way to get repeat clients, endless popularity and plenty of tips. Some of them dole out happy finishes if they are required, whereas some girls actively seek them. Massaging is quite a hard way to earn a living. It is very physical and if you are performing six or seven a day, like most of the girls in the spa, it can be exhausting. So a quick way to cut your workload to a minimum is to get a bloke all excited, massaging him in all the right areas, the ones you are told professionally to avoid, and then jerk him off. The session is over in about twenty minutes and the girl gets an hour off to have a cup of tea, put her feet up and read *Hello!* magazine.

Geri knows this goes on – it is just very hard to know who is doing what and to whom in those cabanas. Unless they go al fresco like the Germans earlier today, it is hard to catch them at it. However, according to Geri, it seems that Melinda has taken the happy finish to a whole new level.

'She's slept with half the staff, you know that?' says Geri.

'No?'

'Oh yeah, everyone's had Melinda. Anyway, apparently she's been going over to stay with one of the guests in Dubai.'

'Really?'

'Yeah, he's been employing her as personal masseuse with the optional extra, as it were, and he's back here this week with his pregnant wife.'

'That's nice.'

'And now the shit has hit the fan because he has just refused to pay Melinda and she has kicked him out of the treatment room.'

There's a lot of very unrelaxing shouting going on when we arrive, which is not at all conducive to a well-run spa. The Saudi businessman is marching up and down the lobby in his white fluffy dressing gown, pointing his finger and shaking his head. Meanwhile, Melinda is standing firm in her white therapist's uniform. She looks like some diminutive dominatrix and it is not hard to see why half the resort's had a go on her. The poor receptionist is bright red and sweating. She is stuck in the middle of a fight and she doesn't know what to do. She is trying to get the businessman to pay up for the massage on principle and he is having none of it.

'You don't own me!' hisses Melinda from across the lobby, her pretty Thai face contorting.

'I have given you enough money,' says the businessman. 'I have paid you already this week.'

'I don't think this is a buy-one-get-one-free scenario,' says Geri, wading in where I would certainly fear to tread.

'What?' he says, turning around to glare at her.

'I think perhaps you should pay for the massage, with no tip perhaps, and then we can call an end to this,' suggests Geri in a very calm and measured voice.

'Why should I?' he asks. 'She didn't finish the job.'

'I think we both know that is not quite the case, sir,' she replies. 'She finished one job, just not the one she was officially booked to do.'

'Well, she is not a very good masseuse,' he says.

'That didn't seem to bother you when you booked her ten times during your last stay, and you booked in another seven at least this time around.'

'She has lost her touch,' he sniffs.

'I will call your wife,' announces Melinda from the other side of the lobby, placing her hands defiantly on her slim hips.

I have never seen a man pay up more quickly in my life. He walks straight over to the receptionist, scribbles his name on the chit and marches out of the building.

'You,' says Geri, turning an accusatory finger at Melinda, 'are terminated.'

Melinda smiles, flicks her long black hair and flounces off towards the staff lockers.

'Fraternizing with guests is a sackable offence,' Geri calls after her. 'Going to stay with them and bringing the relationship back into the spa means I want you off the island tonight.'

'Actually, it'll have to be tomorrow now,' I mutter.

'Oh?' says Geri.

'Paperwork,' I shrug. 'And the staff ferry leaves in less than an hour.'

'I want you off in the morning,' says Geri to Melinda's back and a closing door.

I leave Geri to her staff problems and head off to the bar to have a glass of champagne with the renewed and reconnected Mr and Mrs Forrest. On my way I get a call from Hans to say that Mr and Mrs Antonov made their sunset cruise without a hitch and they are busily quaffing back the complimentary champagne.

Friday Sunset

As I walk into the bar, the place appears to be rocking. DJ Andy's sunset collection seems to be doing the trick, and there are people dancing around the bar stools and plenty of guests knocking back the cocktails.

I always find it fascinating that resort guests fit firmly into two types: those who see their holiday as a time to get sloshed, let their hair down and have a good time, and those who want to sleep, sip mineral water and lose a few pounds. The whole dynamic of the hotel changes depending on which group is dominant at any one time. Sometimes the personal-fitness coach is booked up all week, the Super Legs classes are oversubscribed and the dietician can't get half an hour to herself for love or money. At other times we get complaints that the place is too boring after dark. We do try and put on something every night, even if it is just an outdoor movie and cigar smoking in the Lotus. Half the time there is no one about after ten p.m. and the other half the time we've got extra security on to stop plastered guests drink-driving buggies and having orgies in the swimming pool.

Talking of which, I remember we had to get rid of a whole load of the spa staff due to their penchant for topless bathing. They were Brazilians, of course. It's always the South American girls who like to get their kit off. But these girls who were here to do mani- and pedicures were also quite keen on a party. They were found once too often in the pool with only their pants on at three in the morning, wrapped around guests or one or more of the gym guys. They were fired, along with a girl in watersports who was found taking a guest out on a jet ski at two a.m.

Tonight there's one of those heady atmospheres at the bar, which I know is going to end with someone having to call Dr Singh. Just so long as it is in the realm of knee scrapes and nothing more tricky than that, we should be OK.

Kate is at the bar and is on good form. She is two glasses of champagne in and has that glassy-eyed twinkle of someone who is on a bit of a mission to enjoy themselves. It has been a long week and she needs to decompress. She coils herself around me at the bar and suggests that we might go home and crack open one of our many bottles of wine. It does sound tempting. There's nothing I'd like more than to collapse on my sofa and watch some TV, while drinking one of the many wines I bought at knock-down prices. When I first arrived here as manager eighteen months ago, I had an extensive wine collection that I had acquired over the years from working at various establishments all over the world, and as part of my contract here I negotiated the wines' safe arrival. However, they also suggested that I might want to buy some of the stock we have here. But looking down the list, it was clear that someone didn't know what they were doing. Apparently ten years ago when the sommelier was first buying stock for the place, they bought some cases of very expensive wine that was not invoiced for correctly, and as a result some of the wine in the cellar was unaccounted for. Over the years various managers and sommeliers have purchased some very expensive wines at knock-down prices, myself included. So when Kate suggests we stay in and crack open a bottle of something lovely, it usually is something very lovely indeed.

We are just discussing which cheeky little bottle we might open when my phone goes. It is Youssif, my chief villa host.

'Excuse me, sir,' he says. 'But we have a bit of a problem at the Grand Beach Villa at Silver Sands.'

'Mr McCann's villa?'

'That is correct, sir.'

'What sort of problem?'

'Well, sir, it is a little sensitive.'

Less than five minutes later I am walking towards Mr McCann's villa, being serenaded by the loud thumping sound of disco music. In amongst the shadows I can just pick out Youssif and Mr McCann – Mr McCann appears to have another villa host by the scruff of the neck.

'Honestly, sir, it won't happen again,' says Youssif.

He is hopping from one foot to the other in his desperation.

'Is there anything I can help with?' I ask, approaching through the darkness.

'Ah, there you are,' says Mr McCann. 'Look what I have found here.'

He waves the villa host in front of me, who has a pair of slippers on his hands.

'This guy here has been sneaking around the place like some sort of special agent,' says Mr McCann, his golden neck chain shining in the light coming from the villa. 'Look at his hands, for chrissakes. I don't know what the hell he expected to see. Some sort of live sex show . . . although come to think of it . . .' He starts to laugh. 'Hey, Yulia?'

'Hello honey,' comes a heavily accented voice from the villa.

'This guy here was hoping to see you and me at it!'

'Oh really!' she laughs. 'Oh very funny, no?'

'It just cracks me up,' says Mr McCann. 'I mean, just how bored is he?'

If you only knew, I think. 'I am terribly sorry, sir,' I say. 'I shall have him removed immediately.'

'Immediately,' adds Youssif for good measure.

'You sad old bastard,' says Mr McCann to the villa host, taking in the slippers one more time. 'I found him over there, near the open-air shower. I sneaked up on him, which was kind of weird. He wasn't very awake for a peeping Tom.'

'What have you got to say for yourself?' I ask him.

His head is hanging in shame. 'I am very sorry, sir,' he says. I can see him thinking, trying to come up with some sort of excuse. But being caught with a pair of hotel slippers on your hands to dull the sound of your crawling approach is something of a give-away.

'And so you should be,' I say. 'Mr McCann, I can't tell you how sorry I am. We take the privacy of our guests very seriously indeed.'

'Sure you do.'

'We really do. We've only once had anyone snapped by the paparazzi here, and that was an heir to the throne and his girlfriend. We try to keep things as discreet and private as possible.'

'Yeah, right.' He nods and then grins. 'Next time I'll have his balls.' He makes a scissors gesture towards the villa host's trousers. 'Snip, snip, snip.'

I have to say, for such an important man who is so very obviously letting his hair down in a very public way, he is taking his invasion of privacy in very good humour. Maybe he kind of admires the bloke's initiative. Or perhaps the idea that on an island with so many movers and shakers and multi-millionaires, his is the villa the staff are interested in tickles him.

But Mr McCann's moment in the mirror is going to

be short-lived. Having left instructions that the junior
villa host should receive a written warning, I am on my
way back to my villa when I get a call from Bernard,
saying that the sheikh has ordered in some company
and they are on their way over from Singapore. He is
sending a boat to collect them off the evening flight.
They should be on the island as of about ten o'clock
tonight. We did kind of expect this, and it is always nice
in this business to have one's suspicions confirmed.

But then again, it is always nice to be surprised. Kate
and I are sitting in our his-and-hers hammocks, staring
out to sea, when Ben calls me. He tells me that there has
been a terrible accident near the boutique and the
restaurant and he would appreciate my help. I leap up
and head for my buggy, leaving Kate sighing and
staring at the stars, about to crack open another bottle
of champagne.

When I arrive at the scene it is quite difficult to work
out what is going on. Mr and Mrs Thompson are red-
faced and furious, and their Spanish nanny and two
children are crying.

Ben comes rushing up towards me. 'Shit, man, shit,'
he says, shaking his head. 'I don't know what
happened. One minute I was talking to Mr and Mrs
Thompson, explaining that we were going to pick up
another couple before heading out to reception and

getting the boat, so they could catch their plane, and the next thing I knew the buggy was in the sea.'

'What?' I say, peering over the edge of the jetty, looking down at the swell and the surf and the pile of suitcases. 'With all their luggage?'

'With all their luggage,' repeats Ben.

'And the buggy driver?'

'Over there, a little shaken. He jumped as the thing went over,' explains Ben.

'So . . . ?'

'He hit the accelerator instead of the brake,' says Ben.

'Oh, right.'

'We need our bags to get on the plane,' demands Mrs Thompson.

'Right now,' reiterates Mr Thompson.

Just as they are stamping and complaining and shouting and making demands, a couple of the buggy boys climb up with their suitcases. They are full of water and sand.

'Listen,' I say, 'I've got an idea. I'll get the dry-cleaning crew up and active in the laundry and we'll dry-clean all your stuff for you and send it back.' They look dubious. Like I am going to run off with their stuff. But it is only when I reach the laundry that I realize why. The buggy boys and I open each of their suitcases to find they are stuffed to the brim with little bits and pieces that they've half-inched from the hotel. It is a bloody treasure trove. There are dressing gowns and slippers, towels, hangers, soap dishes, candles – they have shoplifted the whole villa.

We always expect a little bit of stealing. The robes are usually the first things to go, followed by the hangers and slippers. But weirdly, people here take the incense burners, which are made of solid brass and are really rather heavy. We have put a price list in the room, which is supposed to deter all thieving. Sometimes I think people steal stuff in the expectation that it will appear on the final bill. However, when your room rates are as high as ours, we have factored a few soap dishes and hangers into the $2,000-a-night bill. It costs us as little as ten dollars a night to turn the rooms around, because labour is so cheap out here. And it does seem a little churlish to add a $300 dressing gown on to a $40,000 hotel bill.

But this does seem to be taking the piss somewhat. They've got everything that hasn't been nailed down. I go through it with the guys in the laundry – there's piles of the stuff and altogether it comes to about $3,000 worth. We stare at it all and then one of the guys asks me what to do.

'Clean and wrap it all in tissue paper,' I say. 'Just to make them realize that we know, and now they know that we know. That way we won't be getting any complaints about losing their stuff in the sea.'

I leave them to it and call Ben on my way home, just to make sure he's coping with the problem of trying to get $24,000 of buggy out of the sea without damaging it any more. He tells me he's called in a crane and that he and six blokes are working on getting it on the beach before high tide. I wish him luck and head home. I could really murder a drink.

Kate's nowhere to be seen when I get back to the villa. I half expect her to be asleep. But the bed is empty. Finally I discover her out the back with a bottle of wine, two glasses and a pair of binoculars firmly trained on the villa across the bay.

'Oh my God!' she hisses. 'You've got to come and look at this!'

'At what?'

'This!' she says, handing me the binoculars. 'Straight ahead.'

I squint through the lenses and focus them. There on the beach are the sheikh and his mates, having a party. The sheikh is sitting down on one of the carpets, looking straight out to sea. Next to him is his number two. They are both talking away and smoking a hookah pipe.

'They're smoking,' I say, handing back the binoculars.

'Look again.'

Beach Babylon

I take another look, and as I stare more closely I realize that each of the men is not only smoking a hookah, but also being blown by a hooker at the same time. They are lying on the carpet, looking out to sea, chatting away normally, while the heads of two prostitutes bounce up and down on their cocks.

Saturday a.m.

God, I slept badly last night. By the time I did finally get my head down, I was just falling into a deep, delicious sleep, fantasizing about a double-hooker experience, when the phone went. It was Geri and the conversation went something like this.

'Hi, it's Geri. Sorry to bother you.'

'What? I rolled over to look at the clock. 'It is two in the morning.'

'I know. But the thing is, the sheikh has called me up and wants a massage.'

'At this time of night?'

'I know.'

'Hasn't he got a whole load of girls to do that for him?'

'You would have thought.'

'Well, what do you want me to do about it?'

'Tell me what to do.' She sounded all worried and perplexed.

'Wake up one of the girls. The sheikh wants a massage, he gets a massage.'

'How about the happy finish?'

'Make sure that the villa host is near by, so if the girl needs some help all she need do is scream.'

'Right,' she said.

'Oh,' I said, just before I hung up, 'and for God's sake don't send Melinda.'

Of course, the girl we did send is now claiming to be traumatized. She's been in my office for an hour, telling me just how sensitive a soul she is and how the sheikh gave her quite a turn. I am nodding away, sympathizing with her, telling her that she will get an enormous tip just as soon as the sheikh dips into his pockets, and all the time I am thinking what a lucky bastard the man is.

So last night, after his double-hooker experience, he and his mates fancy a few nips of cognac so he orders up Hennessy Ellipse at $1,220 a shot – which take it from me, as a man who knows and likes his cognacs, is worth every penny. He downs three or four shots of the stuff and then clearly feels he needs a little more relaxing, so calls up for a massage. He gets Maria, who is one of the best deep-tissue girls we have. And he also has one of his Natashas working his other end. So whatever Maria does to his shoulders, a topless

Natasha imitates on his lower back. They cover him in oil and work his muscles in unison. Eventually the Natasha mounts him and is on all fours, topless, on the massage table working in the oil, while Maria carries on tweaking his pressure points around the back of his neck. It is only when the Natasha crawls up the bed and eventually edges Maria to one side that she is allowed to leave.

'Oh dear,' I say, shaking my head at Maria. 'That sounds absolutely, totally and utterly terrible.'

'It was,' she says, nodding away in her white therapist's dress. 'I wish never to have to do night massages again.'

'You won't, love, you won't,' says Geri, putting her plump arm around Maria's slim shoulders. 'You don't have to do anything you don't want to do.'

'Well . . .' I say. Geri shoots me a look. 'Absolutely. Whatever. You go and have a nice cup of peppermint tea. Put your feet up and calm down.'

'You will tell me how much is the tip?' asks Maria as she heads for the door.

'Of course.' I nod.

'And I won't share it with any of the other girls in the spa?'

'No, of course not,' says Geri. 'It's all yours.'

Maria leaves a little more pleased than when she arrived.

'D'you know?' puffs Geri, plonking herself down on the sofa in my office and picking up one of the many glossy magazines that we feature in. 'When I was running the spa at this resort in the Maldives, we used to have the masseuses on sheikh standby all the time.'

'Really?'

'Yeah, they used to sleep next to their uniforms just in case they were needed in the middle of the night. It was a great way to earn extra cash, they loved it.' She stands up and drops the magazine back down on the table. 'Why are therapists so goddamn sensitive?'

'God knows,' I say. 'Sounds like a top night in to me.'

'Yeah,' smiles Geri, raising her overly plucked eyebrows. 'You blokes are all the same.'

Geri leaves and I sit at my desk, trying to eradicate the image of the relaxing sheikh from my mind. Leafing through some departure-and-arrival info should do the trick.

Saturday is a busy day for arrivals and departures, especially from Europe. During low season our weekend intake is a little less marked, what with weekenders from Singapore and our steady stream of Japanese weddings to keep us ticking over. But right now it is prime season for Euro trash and they don't come more trashy and flashy than Formula One racing drivers. We love a racing driver. They have plenty of cash and know how to spend it. Unlike other sportsmen we have had here, like

284

Roger Federer, who just drank fruit juices and knocked up every day with our tennis coach, the Formula One guys really do party. Last month we had one F1 driver who shelled out over $30k on wine for one dinner. He ordered fifteen bottles of $2,260 Richebourg 1990, which made for one hell of an evening.

Anyway, today we've got a few other guests coming on the same flight as the F1 driver, so I think I might send Ben to meet and greet, and then I shall pop myself at the jetty and give them the big-manager handshake when they arrive. I have too many things to organize this morning to spend the best part of the day on the Sunseeker yacht. Although looking at the sun and the crystal-smooth sea outside my office window, there is nothing I'd like better. What a shame the Countess Donatella di Cassucci left last night, she might have enjoyed the gentle on-shore breeze today.

I dispatch Ben to the mainland and go to see a man about some crows. We have a bird problem here and I have invited some guys on to the island this morning to try and deal with it. They are a group of six hunters from the mainland, and I have to say they look a little intimidating in their rough clothes and reflector shades, with their shotguns slung over their shoulders. None of them speaks much English, so I talk to them through their boss, who is a tall red-faced forty-something Australian bloke called Mike.

'G'day, mate,' he says, shaking my hand. His grip is firm and rough – it is like being exfoliated by sandpaper. 'So how many of the little blighters d'you think you've got here?' he asks, pushing back his leather hat and looking up into the canopy, chewing tobacco.

'A couple of hundred?' I suggest.

In fact, I have no idea at all. Just enough of the bastards for them to be constantly hovering around, screeching their heads off, lowering the tone of the place. Enough of them to really piss me off.

'I'd say you've probably got a few more than that.' He inhales through the back of his teeth, like a cowboy builder about to hoick the price up.

'Jiwan here, the head gardener, will have more of an idea,' I suggest.

'Three hundred and twenty-seven, more or less, sir,' he says, with alarming precision.

'There you go,' I say.

'A shit load,' nods Mike.

'You could say that,' I reply.

'So do you want us to shoot the lot of them?' he asks.

I look at Jiwan. He looks at the sand. For a Muslim, Jiwan seems to have gone all Buddhist on me and is waiting for me to give the orders.

'OK,' I say. 'I'd like you to kill as many as you can.'

'Ten bucks a bird?' he asks.

'That was the deal.'

'Great,' he sniffs. 'Let's get on with it.'

Mike and his team of sharpshooters are not our usual form of pest control. We actually have a reassuringly expensive outfit that comes over three times a year from Bangkok. For $37,000 plus air fares a year they come and clear the island of anything unpleasant. When the resort was first built, they had a deal with the builders that they got a dollar a rat. They caught the rats alive, then at the end of the day they were supposedly shipped off and released on another island. However, it was the same rats that kept returning. The builders were simply storing them in containers overnight, only to reclaim them and be paid again the next day.

But the guys from Bangkok are very professional. They go over the island with a fine comb. They check the rooms and the surrounding grounds for anything that should not be living there. And in the meantime, if we find anything unsavoury between visits then we photograph it and email it to them and they tell us how to get rid of it. It is, I have to admit, an ongoing battle. Every time anything comes on to the island it brings something with it. We are always weeding beetles and spiders out of the food supplies. But it is the building materials that are more problematic. Bamboo arrives on the island untreated. It is full of small animals and weevils and creatures. The worst is the thatch. It comes off the boat in rolls and is full of rats and all sorts of shit. We flog it and spray it and smoke it and still a whole load of wildlife comes ashore. The island was bat-free until we purchased some 20,000 trees. Now the place is teeming with them. Come dusk they are flapping around from palm to palm. Fortunately, most of the guests are so unobservant they don't notice.

People don't come here to commune with nature. They come here to relax, recharge and hopefully spend an obscene amount of money on very decent wine. This is not the sort of place to come to if you want to get back to basics. There is nothing basic about our $2,000-a-night villas with hot and cold running villa hosts, a plasma and surround sound. However, if nature does try and bite back we never hear the end of it. The other day I got a call from this woman complaining she had a fly in her villa. We get calls about mosquitoes and bugs, asking us to get rid of them. Some people actually complain on their guests' questionnaires that they saw something fly past.

We do spray the shit out of the place. We say it's all organic but I have no idea if that is true or not – I suspect not. The last thing any self-respecting millionaire wants is for a couple of flies to ruin his open-air lunch. The same goes for mosquitoes and your early-evening cocktail. But some guests can be very unforgiving. They live in an air-conditioned, controlled environment 98 per cent of the time and they don't see why being on an island in the middle of the ocean should be any different.

Mike and I are standing on Palm Sands beach, listening to the shots rain in the vegetation behind us. I have chosen a major change-over day in the hope that not that many guests will be disturbed. It is also eleven a.m., so most of them will be having a late breakfast or be in the spa, at the pool or in the gym, i.e., nowhere near this beach.

'So how long do you think you'll be here?' I ask Mike, watching another black flapping bastard fall out of the sky. That's the sixth or seventh so far. These guys are good shots.

'The whole day,' he says. 'We might have to come back later. The evening is a little better as they are coming home to roost then and the words sitting duck spring to mind.' He spits his chewing tobacco into the sand and rubs it in with his boot.

'That's a difficult time,' I say. 'You know, with guys having showers and that sort of thing.'

Another shot rings out. It echoes around the island. We both look through the trees, waiting for the thud of bird on sand. Nothing.

Then through the undergrowth I see a woman running towards me. She is middle-aged and wearing a

289

bikini. It is not the prettiest sight I have ever seen. She appears to be crying.

'Stop! Stop! Stop! How could you?' She is shouting and waving her arms. Oh fuck, I think. This is all I need – a bloody animal-rights activist. 'Stop! Stop! Stop!' She is bright pink with emotion, touched up with sunburn. 'What are you doing?'

'Our annual cull, madam,' I say, trying to sound as dispassionate as possible.

'But you can't! These animals have as much right to live here as you or me,' she says.

'The thing is, they shouldn't be living here,' I try and explain. 'They were brought on to the island by mistake. They are not natives.'

'But they are now and you can't kill them,' she says, wringing her hands, tears rolling down her cheeks.

Another shot echoes through the trees and a half-dead bird comes flapping towards us. A second shot is fired and it falls to the beach like a stone. The woman screams and covers her ears. She stamps her feet in the sand like a small child.

'Oi! Stop that!' shouts a roly-poly bloke, dressed only in a small yellow pair of Speedo pants, from the edge of his pool. 'It's a bloody disgrace! Stop it right away.'

'Mike,' I say.

'Gotcha,' he replies, moving towards the undergrowth.

'Another time, eh?' he suggests. 'When there are fewer sensitive souls around.'

'I think it would make life easier,' I say.

Mike marches up the beach and lets out an extremely loud whistle and the shooting immediately stops.

'Thank you!' sighs the woman, shaking her head. 'I just couldn't bear it.'

'It is just one of those things that has to be done, madam,' I explain.

'Yes, but not when I am here,' she replies. 'It's like a nightmare.'

'I am sorry. We don't mean to ruin your holiday,' I say.

'Well you have,' she says, her shoulders shaking. 'You very nearly have.'

'Let me send you and your husband a bottle of wine to compensate,' I suggest, nodding towards the jelly belly in the yellow pants.

'Wine?' she says, her face creasing again.

'Champagne?'

'That would be lovely.' She smiles and practically skips back up the beach to her husband. Amazing how a bit of liquid compensation can make you forget your troubles.

Mike and I, plus his six sharpshooters, are walking down to the jetty and trying to work our way around the crow problem. He asks me if there is a period when the hotel is empty and the answer is no. This is one of the problems with this place – it is impossible to do any maintenance or essential repairs without putting out guests who are paying through the nose for some very expensive R&R. And they don't expect to hear sand machines pumping all day long, or see pin barges tugging piles of rocks through the sea, or indeed dead crows falling out of the sky. They want a good view, good weather, good wine and a good seeing-to by their wife and/or anyone else.

Mike and I are negotiating a call-back in April, when the guests are mainly Japanese and less likely to complain, when my phone goes. It is Ben.

'Hi,' I say. 'Can I call you back in a minute?'

'Um, just a quick one,' he says. 'Have you heard from Mr Van de Berg?'

'Who's Mr Van de Berg?'

'One of our guests. We are waiting for him at the airport.'

'And?'

'And we've lost him.'

'Lost him? Lost him? How can you lose a guest? Are you sure he arrived?'

'Oh yeah,' says Ben. 'I have checked the passenger list and his luggage is going around and around on the carousel.'

'Have another look. He can't have gone far. The airport's bloody tiny.'

'OK,' he says. 'Oh, by the way, our F1 driver is here.'

'Excellent. Speak to you in a minute.'

I am seeing Mike off to his seaplane when Ben calls again.

'Christ!' he huffs down the receiver with exhaustion. 'You won't believe what has happened.'

'What?'

'The guy was only so drunk that he set up shop next to all the confiscated alcohol and was ordering drinks like he was at a bar.'

It transpires that our new Dutch guest had drunk so many vodka and tonics on the plane that by the time he landed on the mainland he could barely see straight and could certainly not walk straight. And although the airport is tiny – barely larger than a couple of rooms cobbled together – he somehow managed to miss the left turn to immigration and so was waylaid by the tables of contraband booze that had been confiscated off unsuspecting tourists. He then sat down next to the tables, presuming them to be a bar covered with drinks. The poor old pisshead had helped himself to half a bottle of vodka and was just starting on some Jack Daniel's when they found him.

It took all Ben's powers of persuasion for him to get Mr Van de Berg through Customs and out of the

airport. But seeing as he was so plastered and a little
difficult, airport security insisted on escorting him right
to the reception of the hotel. This put Ben in a bit of a
quandary. Should he put the plastered Dutchman on
the yacht with our VIP F1 racer and the other guests?
Or should he and his poorly humoured police escort
find another means of transport? Eventually, after some
to-ing and fro-ing with the airport staff, he has put the
drunk and the cops on a speedboat, and the VIP and
the others are sailing glamorously over on the yacht.

'I hope I did the right thing,' he says above the noise
of the speedboat. 'So can I rely on you to meet the
yacht?'

'Of course, mate,' I say. 'Sorry you've had such a
nightmare.'

'Yeah well,' he says. 'Surely the best person to deal
with a drunk is a fellow pisshead. I tempted him up the
gangplank using a bottle of tequila.'

So I get my arse down to the jetty to meet the
Formula One driver and his girlfriend, plus a couple of
Brits who won a week here after entering a competition
in the *Sunday Times*. I can see the boat coming over the
horizon as the reception staff ready themselves with
drinks and smiles and chilled towels. Then just as we
get into position, the speedboat with the pissed
Dutchman nips in from nowhere. I am not sure if we
were all so transfixed by the prospect of a Formula One

celebrity that we missed the speedboat coming in across the wake, or whether the thing is so small and quick that we failed to spot it. Either way, we are now faced with meeting and greeting the two parties that we were trying to separate at exactly the same time.

'Ben!' I shout over the top of the engine noise. 'Let's get Mr Van de Berg ashore first.'

'Roger that!' he shouts back.

I watch him take Mr Van de Berg's shoulders and start trying to walk him in the direction of the gangplank. The man seems to have gone beyond the stage of the escapist drunk which he was earlier, and has now become a plain old drunk drunk, which means his head is hound-dog, his limbs are loose and he is very suggestible, if a little unstable. I can hear Ben shouting instructions. Mr Van de Berg puts one step very carefully in front of the other as he edges his way off the boat. A wave crashes against the jetty. The boat rises and falls in the swell.

'Whoa!' shouts Ben, as the Dutchman swings back and forth on his feet. 'Keep going, keep going.'

The man edges his way closer and closer to shore, shuffling like some old bloke in a pair of slippers. Meanwhile, the Sunseeker yacht moors up next to the speedboat. I am torn. Do I see off the drunk and get him through reception as soon as I can? Or do I gladhand the F1 star? In the end I go for the star. I am all smiles and waves and exuberance, in the hope that my enthusiasm will disguise the car crash that is going on behind me.

'Hello! I hope you had a wonderful trip. The boat was OK? Isn't the weather perfect?' It is stream-of-consciousness verbiage, but anything to stop them from looking over my shoulder.

'Great trip,' he says, shaking my hand so firmly I think he is going to crack the bones. 'What a nice place you have here.'

'Well, we've had quite a few of you guys,' I say.

'I know,' he nods. 'Schumacher, Hakkinen, Barrichello, Alonso, even Eddie Jordan, they've all been here.'

'We're quite the F1 hangout.'

'Jesus Christ!' exclaims the driver, pointing over my shoulder. 'Look out!'

I turn around to see Mr Van de Berg swaying like a pendulum on the jetty. His feet are right on the edge and he is about to fall over backwards into the sea. The F1 driver and I stand and stare, rooted to the spot, while Ben sprints down the gangplank and catches him in his arms like some swooning nineteenth-century heroine. Ben pushes the bloke perpendicular and he walks on as if nothing happened. F1 and I watch him zigzag his way to reception, relieving the waiting girls of two drinks as he goes.

'What's wrong with him?' asks F1.

'Seasick,' I say.

'Poor bloke,' nods F1.

'I know,' I agree, ushering the buggy boys towards the waiting Louis Vuitton luggage. 'It can really affect some people.'

We check the F1 driver in without any other incident. He seems delighted with his Water Villa and loves the pool. His girlfriend is stunning and clearly quite expensive to run, because the first thing she asks about is the spa, and then where she might have a glass of champagne.

I am walking back along the wooden walkway that leads to the F1 villa when my phone goes. It is Ben.

'Hi, it's me again. I have got to Mr Van de Berg's villa.'

'Excellent,' I say, looking up at the cloudless sky. 'Well done.'

'The only thing is that some fucker has gone and stolen the bed.'

Saturday p.m.

How can anyone steal a bed? Why would anyone *want* to steal a bed? Granted our beds are nice, they are a nice bit of Italian designer living. But all your average guests do is ask where we got them and who made them. Is it really necessary to steal them? And how can anyone get a bed off the bloody island? But more importantly, what the hell am I going to do with an extremely drunk Dutchman with nowhere to sleep off his booze and a wife turning up in six hours on the flight from Singapore.

I ring up the guys in housekeeping to try and find out what is going on. They sound decidedly shifty. Hassan tells me some very long-winded story about how a guest fell in love with the bed and how they asked and asked for it and how eventually housekeeping sold it them. And I'm afraid I don't believe a word of it. He has no explanation for how the guest took it off the island, who the guest was, or indeed how much the bed was sold for or where the money is. Basically a couple of bastards who work here have taken a boat, loaded it up with a bloody bed and half-inched it off the island. I can't believe it. What would any of the locals want with $900 worth of bed?

This is the first bed that has actually been pinched. But I know there are plenty of nights when the dive boats are filled up with goodies from the hotel and sailed off the island. But it is usually DVD players, plasmas, stock for the minibar. There is also a huge amount of shrinkage and seepage from the stockrooms to the staff villas. Knives, forks, salt and pepper cellars are always going walkabout, as are teaspoons. We are always having to reorder teaspoons. Don't tell me they have all been lost in the sand. Like the pink linen napkins earlier in the week? Theft is an occupational hazard within this business and I do think that it is kind of up to the hotel to make things as hard to steal as possible. Everything here has to be signed in and out, so at least there is some sort of paper trail. Even if it does go cold rather quickly. It is partly a game of cat and mouse. They see how far they can push and I try and outdo them. We have regular raids on the villas in the village and spot checks of the lockers. In the end, I have to justify my numbers to the boardroom and I am damned if a couple of light-fingered bastards are going to make me look bad. But not even I thought it was worth nailing down the beds. Silly, silly me.

Now I have got a villa I can't rent and it's going to cost me $2,000 a night. Not cost me, exactly. But I can't make any bloody money on it and I am very pissed off, to say the least. Fortunately we are currently running at 97 per cent capacity so we do have a few villas spare. However, as a result of his having no bed, I'm going to have to upgrade the bastard by way of apologizing. Not that he is going to remember ever having been here, if he carries on putting back the shots the way he is at the moment.

It's happened before. I had a Britpop rock group who lost a whole week when they came and stayed at the Four Seasons in Bali. They were with some London hip crowd and they all dropped acid tabs on the second day of their stay and only really woke up again when they paid the bill. They were all seriously sunburnt because they'd passed out on the beach, and they'd ended up spending about £5k each on meals and beverages that none of them could remember ordering or even eating and drinking. We could have shoved anything under their noses and they would not have known the difference. Personally, I can think of better ways to drop £5k.

I get Garry on the phone and ask him to sort out Mr

Saturday p.m.

Van de Berg's accommodation. I advise against a Water Villa, as we could do without waking up to a floater in the next couple of days. Other than that, he and Ben can get on with it, while I try and sort out the elusive bed problem.

I go down to the staff village and have a word with the guys in carpentry. They are rushed off their feet at the moment; they've got twenty sunbeds to repair before the Christmas rush. Half of them have rotten or broken slats, which are not conducive to an executive backside, particularly when it is plonked down from a great height. They don't seem at all surprised or perturbed when I tell them they have to make a bed for villa 126. I could almost swear they were expecting it. But then I am feeling a little paranoid. What does it say about Mohammed and our security, if thieves can walk off with an emperor-size bed in the middle of the night?

The carpentry boys tell me they can make something quite similar within a week. I say three days, which means it might happen in a week, and I head off to my afternoon meeting.

We wouldn't normally have a meeting on a Saturday afternoon, or indeed any afternoon, as Saturday is just another working day on the island, except perhaps a little busier. But we need to discuss the plans for Christmas and New Year, finalize a few things and make sure we all know what we are doing and that we have all the correct things on order. Because if we screw up and don't have the right amount of drink, food, presents, decorations and wrapping paper, there's no popping down the corner shop to pick up a few items that have been missed off the list. I tried to explain this to a Russian guest we had staying last year. He wanted a sound system and speakers – a bit of a disco outside his villa for him and a few of his mates. He couldn't understand when I told him that it was going to cost him a small fortune to get it all flown over from Dubai. He kept on asking why we couldn't pop out and pick it up somewhere. Eventually he gave us the keys to his private plane and we sent a couple of the guys to go and source it all in Dubai. Well, his plane was sitting on the tarmac doing nothing at the airport and the man said he wanted a party. Sadly for us, we don't have fleets of Lears at our disposal, so preparation is very much our friend.

Garry, Bernard, Hori, Jean-François, Antonio and Marco are all in my office, eating biscuits and tucking in to cups of coffee by the time I arrive.

'Sorry I'm a bit late,' I say. 'But some bastard stole a bed and Ben's trying to sort out an alcoholic with a room.'

'An alcoholic?' Marco perks up. 'A rich alcoholic?'

'He doesn't appear to be,' says Garry. 'I Googled him and came back with nothing. Anyway, you've got a

Formula One driver to worry about – the civilians are not going to shell out anywhere near as much as him.'

'We need some more Russians to really shift the wine,' sulks Marco.

'We've got plenty of those,' I say.

'Sadly we're losing Mr Antonov today,' says Garry. 'But thankfully his bill looks like it's coming in at around the $130,000 mark.'

'I thought it would be more,' shrugs Jean-François, already starting to doodle on his pad. 'With the boat on standby.'

'I don't call that very bad going for a family holiday,' I say.

'Well, Mr Georgi's bill is looking more like $400,000,' says Garry with a little smile that wrinkles his nose. 'That's more like it, *n'est-ce pas?*'

'How much longer is he here for?' asks Marco, clearly looking to shift some old stock and make space for his Christmas stash.

'A few more days. I think he's leaving on Tuesday,' says Garry.

'But that's less than a week?' queries Jean-François.

'That's a private jet for you, isn't it?' says Garry. 'Gadget rich, time poor. He's probably got some chickens to look at in Siberia or something very pressing.'

'Siberian chickens,' says Bernard with a Gallic shudder. 'Do you think they have three legs?'

'You'll be finding out soon if we don't get on,' I say.
'I've got an oligarch to see off the island and—'

'And six hundred lifejackets to take delivery of,' adds
Bernard.

'Six hundred lifejackets?'

'In case of another tsunami.'

'Oh Christ,' I say, putting my head in my hands.
'When did they arrive?'

'More important than that,' says Bernard, 'where the
hell are we going to store them?'

'Actually,' chips in Garry, 'even more important than
that, there are eight hundred staff, 140 rooms and only
six hundred lifejackets. Aren't we a little short?'

Garry's right, of course. We are more than a little
short; we are totally and utterly unprepared. It is not
that no one takes a tsunami seriously – we were hit by
the last one and although we didn't lose anyone, it did
enough damage for head office to take it seriously.
We've had endless calls back and forth from the big
cheese in the plush penthouse in Piccadilly, saying that
we need to have things organized and an evacuation
plan. But it is just a question of finding time for it all.
I've got a whole load of walkie-talkies that we are
supposed to have practised how to use in an emergency,
but if I am honest they have been here for three months
and we have yet to charge them up. I am inclined to
think that if our mobiles aren't working then we're all

dead anyway. Quite how me being able to shout at Hori is going to help matters when we're halfway to Antarctica on a killer wave, I don't understand. Just as there is not much point in handing out lifejackets. The safest thing to do in a tsunami is to run like fuck to higher ground. The highest point on this island are the optics behind the bar. Which means that in the event of a sudden tsunami this evening it is highly likely that the only survivor would be Mr Van de Berg, who I am sure would be found safely clinging to a bottle of gin. The rest of us can only pray.

Health and safety on this island are not that brilliant. In fact they are shit. All the fire extinguishers are rusty and corroded, and in the event of a fire they would prove to be utterly useless. The fire hydrants are no better. Dotted around the island, they are painted red and look very impressive, like something out of an American movie. The only problem is that when they were building this place, someone forgot to connect them to the water supply. We only discovered this last month when we were doing a random inspection. Fortunately, as the Countess Donatella di Cassucci will attest, it can be rather wet here and the undergrowth has never become tinderbox dry. Or at least that has been the case so far.

'So where shall we put them all, then?' asks Bernard, looking up from his notepad.

'How about the store cupboard near villas 210–220 on Golden Sands beach?' I suggest.

'Oh, we've looked in there,' sighs Bernard, 'and it seems to be full of pink linen napkins.'

'What pink linen napkins?' asks Jean-François.

'I don't know,' he shrugs. 'Just some napkins.'

'I have been looking for those for over a week!'

'You have?'

'Yes!'

'He has,' I add. 'I was about to write them off as stolen.'

'Stolen?' says Bernard. 'Why would anyone want to steal a load of linen napkins?'

'They've been stealing sheets,' says Garry.

'They have?' I ask, my heart sinking.

'Yeah,' he says. 'It's been really fucking up my turn-around. That's why the German couple were so pissed off when their room wasn't ready. That was down to the sheets.'

The laundry here is a nightmare. Tucked away in a corner of the staff village, it works 24/7 and it never seems to crack the backlog. The sheer amount of stuff it has to launder makes it impossible ever to get on top of. Each and every one of the villas has clean sheets and towels every day. So that's towels from the beach, towels from the spa, six big towels from the bedroom plus five bath mats, two hand towels, two face towels, one under sheet, one top sheet, a duvet cover, six pillowcases and four bathrobes from each villa, which all have to be loaded on to a tricycle to be taken to the pantry, where they are all transferred to a buggy, like the one Ben, Jean-François and I hailed down, and driven to the laundry. There it is all washed, ironed and aired and put on another bed within six hours. The same happens in 140 villas all over the island. The people who work there do twelve-hour shifts from six a.m. to six p.m. or six p.m. to six a.m., with one day off a week. It is cheaper for us to pay them three hours' overtime every day than employ extra staff, as we don't have room in the village to accommodate and feed any more. So you can imagine how finely run the place is. Lose a whole load of sheets and the system is brought to its knees very quickly.

'Will you ask housekeeping to keep an eye on that for me if you see them before Monday's meeting,' I say, 'because that could get quite serious.'

'Will do,' says Garry, making a note in his book.

'Now, Christmas,' I say, rubbing my hands together, trying to muster some enthusiasm. 'Any ideas?'

'Umm,' says Garry.

'Umm,' agrees Bernard.

'Well . . .' says Hori.

'OK,' I say. 'I'll ask a question. How is Santa going

to get here this year? He can't come down a chimney, so . . . ?'

Last year we had half a dozen Santorinas in tiny little red skirts with sacks on their backs water-ski behind a red speedboat and land on the beach. It worked a treat, but I have a feeling the dads were more excited about it than the children. Which is good. But not really the point.

'We could have Santa parascend in?' suggests Hori. 'Get one of the watersports guys to dress up and come in with a big sack.'

'But you always dress up,' I say.

'I'm not doing that, mate,' he says.

'I didn't have you down as a scaredy cat,' smiles Garry.

'I'm not.'

'Well then.' Garry purses his lips. It's enough to send Hori over the edge.

'I'll do it. If those bastards down in watersports can do it it can't be that difficult.'

'OK,' I nod. 'But we'll need a trial run. The last thing we need is to have to fish Santa out of the sea. It's enough to put everyone off their turkey.'

And we do have turkey. We do the whole goddamn thing. We have a dinner on Christmas Eve for the French and the Germans, who like their foie gras and champagne the night before. We have turkey in the middle of the following day for the Brits, who can't do without their stuffing and sausages. We also have carol singers. There are twenty-two members of staff who have been practising for the past couple of weeks to get the words right. We have also managed to find two guys who can play guitar to keep them in tune, and someone is hard at work making them all uniforms. They are going to sing when Santa arrives and during the manager's drinks.

'Which reminds me,' says Jean-François. 'We definitely won't be able to get the pink Dom Pérignon this year for manager's drinks.'

'What is it with the pink Dom?' I say. 'They seem intent on fucking things up for us. We haven't had any here for a week.'

'We've had no pink bubbles at all,' moans Marco. 'It is fucking my bottom line. Everyone knows you pay through the bollocks for pink.'

'I know,' I agree.

'I don't know what is happening,' shrugs Jean-François. 'We could always have a pink Cristal?'

'Not at $3,900 a bottle we won't,' I insist.

'But we get it for $1,000.'

'That is still way too much,' I say. 'We don't want to go over the top.'

There's a fine line here between going overboard and trying to keep the guests happy. Some of them have come to the other side of the world for a reason – to get away from the festive period altogether. So we have to be quite careful not to be too Santa-ed out in case they get pissed off. We are always having this debate about where to put the Christmas trees that we have flown in from Singapore. We've got three of them at a price of $3,850 each so we want to make them sing for their supper. Everyone says that we should put one of them by reception. There's the perfect place by the pagoda as you look across the island towards the sea. But I think the last thing you need to see as soon as you arrive in a place like this is a bloody Christmas tree. You've done the office party, you've said goodbye to your staff, you fly fifteen hours and you arrive to a thirty-foot spruce. It's enough to make you get straight back on the boat.

But then equally we have families who have flown here *because* it is Christmas, and all their children need presents. We go shopping for them in Singapore, fly the whole lot out, wrap them and mark them up with their names on. There are no guns, no water pistols, no drums, no noisy gifts of any kind. Just nice stuffed toys and dolls. We have thought of everything. As you can see, we really do earn that Christmas supplement.

But New Year is the big one, as I remind the meeting. This year we have got a huge party planned around the pool, with a thousand candles, a red carpet to the event and hundreds of purple and white satin cushions all over the beach. When you come out of the buggy at the top of the red roped-off areas, there will be a photo moment for you and your family, which of course we will send framed to your room the following day. They are all wisely taking notes, as I tick things off. Then there is the drink. It'll have to be normal Moët at the rate we're going, but I am hoping that Jean-François can order some Dom. Then we'll have some canapés, caviar, oysters, foie gras, followed by a small buffet with lobsters, the usual sort of stuff. Come ten p.m. boats full of fireworks will set off into the bay. At around eleven fifteen we'll hand out the hats and the bangers, just so no one sets them off too early, and at midnight we'll have an eight-minute firework display. Well, at least that's what I'm hoping to do. I am not flying it all out again like I did last year. I am hoping that right now it's all on a container on a slow boat from Thailand. After the fireworks, DJ Andy has promised a music-and-laser show over the horizon pool. He keeps saying he'll work it out and I keep asking him to give it a trial run through one night. But somehow he hasn't managed to find the time so far.

'So you and DJ Andy really need a run-through,' I suggest.

'That's fine,' says Hori, jotting down notes.

'You need to make sure all the Dom is turning up,' I say to Jean-François. 'And that we have enough foie gras and caviar for the season, because we won't be the only people using it on the night. Guests will be ordering it left, right and centre during the festive period.'

'Sure,' says Jean-François.

'And we are full?' I ask Garry.

'To the freaking rafters,' he says. 'I am waiting to be bribed!'

'So do we all know what we are doing?'

'Um, I'm not that busy,' admits Bernard. The whole room looks at him like he is insane.

'You can help organize the singing,' I suggest.

'You'll be good at that,' winks Marco. 'I've heard you late at night in the bar.'

With Christmas and New Year nearly on track, I rush out of the meeting to see Mr Antonov and his family off to their private jet. We are standing in reception and I am shaking his hand. He is being very effusive about his stay. He tells me how much he enjoyed himself, how much his wife and his children loved the food and the watersports. The sunset cruise last night on his $40,000 yacht was just perfect. Then he gets out his briefcase and lays it on the table in reception. He rummages around in it for a minute before taking out a wad of envelopes. He asks for the names of the people who have been looking after him and hands over $500 for Bernard and $200 for each of the waiters; he gives his villa host $2,000 and then he gives me an envelope containing $4,000. I know how much we all have because he has written the amounts on the front. I am very effusive and tell him it is not necessary to be so generous, but he doesn't seem to hear. He then reaches back into his briefcase and gives me a small box. I have to say that I am beginning to feel a little embarrassed at this point. I have hardly bent over backwards to accommodate the man. The most difficult thing he asked for was a yacht and even then I nearly buggered that up.

'Honestly, Mr Antonov, I really don't think this is necessary.'

'Please,' he says with a dismissive wave of his hand. 'If we only ever did things that were necessary, life would be very, very boring.'

'Well, thank you,' I say.

'Thank you,' he nods. 'We have had a wonderful time.'

'I am so glad,' I say. I open the box. Holy shit! It is a Patek Philippe watch worth about $10,000. I know this because one of the many codes you learn in this job is how to read watches. Breitlings are two a penny, unless they are like the one Mr Georgi is wearing, then they are a pretty penny. An IWC means the bloke has a bit of class. A Rolex means he doesn't. I have been given plenty of Sector watches at about $800 a pop – I have a box of about fifteen gift watches that I've received in the last year. But never have I been given anything quite this fabulous.

'Do you like it?' he asks.

'Like it?' I ask. My eyes are round with joy, my mouth slightly parched with lust. 'It's truly beautiful.'

'I am pleased you are pleased,' he says, nodding away. 'Oh, there is one little thing that I wanted to ask you.'

'Oh yes?' I say, looking down at the watch.

'My wife, my children and I, we want to come back.'

'Great,' I smile.

'At Christmas,' he says.

'Christmas?' My voice goes up at least an octave.

'This Christmas.'

'Oh,' I smile back breezily, 'I am sure we can squeeze you in.'

Saturday Sunset

I stand on the jetty waving off Mr Antonov and his family with a wide, stiff smile. I'm an arse and a twat and a sucker for an expensive watch, and now I have got the resort and myself into a bit of a pickle, to say the least. Quite what I thought I was doing telling the bloke we could accommodate him in six weeks' time I have no idea. I was momentarily blinded by a beautifully crafted precision timepiece and I don't know what came over me. Plus the man is clearly a crafty devil. He wouldn't own most of the aluminium in Siberia if he didn't know how to make people do things they don't want to do.

So on the way back to the office, I give Garry a call and tell him to get his arse over as soon as he can.

'You've done *what*?' he says as soon as he walks

through the door. Somehow the tan and the teeth aren't so bright and shiny now.

'I am sorry.' I shrug. 'It was hard to say no.'

'Well, try a bit harder next time,' he says, flapping out the expansive Christmas bookings sheet. 'It's a small word,' he adds. 'And sometimes quite effective.'

'I am very sorry,' I say, getting up from behind my desk to look over his shoulder. 'Do we have any room at all?'

'If we had room, I wouldn't be doing my job, now would I?' he says sarcastically. 'This is the busiest time of year. If I can't fill this place over Christmas I may as well shove a couple of cocktail sticks up my nose and be done with it.'

'Right,' I say, looking down at the mass of blue, green, purple, red and yellow stripes. 'What does all this mean?'

'Dark green means direct, firm without deposit; purple is paid by agents; yellow is luxury tour agencies; dark blue is direct, firm and fully paid; and pink is agency, no deposit.'

'What is the turquoise?'

'Press.'

'Great, let's ditch the press.'

'If you look at the chart, you have villa numbers down the left and dates across the top. The turquoise is not booked in for Christmas.'

'Oh.'

'Yes – oh . . .' Garry runs his finger up and down the chart, mumbling to himself. 'We don't want to fuck around with any rack guests,' he says.

He is quite right about that. We love rack guests. They are guests who are paying the full rate nicely through the nose. The full $2,000 a night, or the full $6,500. They have booked through one of our agents and have money, will tip and will probably take in a sandbank, a barbecue or something charmingly profligate like that. They'll be keen on nice wine and their children will happily sup on the six-dollar-a-scoop Valrhona chocolate ice cream.

It is the guests who book through travel agents that we are less keen on. We charge them rack minus 5 per cent, although their travel agent will notch it up, thereby ensuring that they make some sort of profit on the exchange. The idea being that the travel agent fills the place up and we give them a deal on the rooms. However, sometimes it can be cheaper for the guest to book directly with us. There are plenty of last-minute deals to be had, or offers to be made. If you come straight to us, you'll be offered rack minus 10 per cent; sometimes we go up to minus 25 if we have plenty of villas standing empty. Obviously we would prefer to have guests than empty beaches and no one to drink our champagne.

But bargains are, of course, dependent on the season.

'How about this guy?' I ask.

'No,' says Garry. 'He is one of the hundred riches men in the world.'

'How many villas has he actually got?'

'Twelve,' he says. 'Some are for bodyguards. One for his doctor. Then there are his nannies.'

'Can we put the bodyguards on Fantasy Island?'

'How are they going to protect him from there?'

'No one is going to do anything here,' I say. 'We're in the middle of bloody nowhere.'

'I know that, you know that, but maybe he can't sleep without them. Like Wayne Rooney and hi hairdryer. Maybe he needs the white noise of their snoring to send him off. What do I know? There!' he says suddenly, pointing to a pink stripe. 'If we move him once during the stay we can do it.'

'Can't we move someone else?'

'I'm sure we can,' he says, squinting at the chart 'Look – we have an agency, no deposit. Right there! can't believe it.'

'Which agency?'

'I don't know. Elegant Travel, Sunfinders, who cares If we haven't got the cash yet then I am bumping them Happy bloody Christmas!'

'You are a fucking star!' I say, slapping Garry very firmly on his back.

'I know,' he says, wagging a finger at me. 'And don't you ever do that again.'

'Consider myself suitably admonished.'

'Mr Antonov,' says Garry, writing over the pink stripe. 'So what did he give you?'

'Give me?'

'Yeah,' says Garry.

'How do you mean?'

'Watch? Money? Villa in the south of France?'

'Don't be stupid,' I say, walking out of the office. 'He just asked nicely.'

'Yeah, right,' he sniffs. 'And Posh's tits are real.'

'You can believe what you want.'

'Oh, by the way,' he says. 'Haven't we got a few of the guys doing the FLAG programme tonight?'

'Shit, have we?' I ask, stopping and turning around.

'At least that's what my booking sheet says.'

The Feel Like A Guest or FLAG programme is something we devised for the staff as a bit of a treat. It is supposed to help them realize what it feels like to be a guest in the resort and show them what things look like from the guests' perspective. It is also a nice thing for them to look forward to in a place where, let's face it, there are not that many perks once you've smoked the pot and had a squeeze of Melinda. It is no wonder that we had the smack problem, the rebellion the other day, and the staff keep being terminated for fighting.

Anyway, the FLAG idea is a perk that we wave to keep everyone a little more focused. Although that's not to say it has been without incident. A few villa hosts were given a FLAG night a few weeks ago and abused the hell out of the place. They were checked in like proper guests at reception and then driven to a villa, where they proceeded to drink the minibar dry and have a party. But instead of letting their hair down subtly, they invited all their mates over and took the piss.

We did talk about cancelling the programme altogether. But then a couple of the middle-management guys complained. They pointed out that it wasn't fair for them to be punished for someone else's misdemeanour and that they wanted to be given the chance. It is not as if they never get a sniff at the glamour of the resort. Executives and assistant department heads – and that includes people like Connie, the yoga teacher – get to dine out once or twice a week, depending on how senior they are. They can choose between any of the three restaurants and have a soft drink or a glass of wine included in the meal. Anything after that they get at half price. So they do get some small perks. However, the FLAG night is clearly a big one and something to look forward to.

'Who's having a FLAG night tonight then?' I ask.

'I am not sure exactly,' says Garry. 'But I know Keith is going.'

'Keith?'

'Yeah, he's packed his weights and has been making extra biltong for the occasion.'

'Note to self,' I say. 'No need to pop by.'

'Yeah,' agrees Garry.

'Will I be seeing you later?' I ask.

'How could I resist?' he says. 'It is the highlight of the week.'

Saturday night is disco night on the island and it is sadly the highlight of most of our weeks. Every week Kate and I say that we won't go and nearly every week we end up there, throwing some shapes on the sand with all the drunk and disorderly guests in the resort. It is mainly because Saturday night is a big entertaining night for me. There is always some millionaire, billionaire, magnate or celebrity who needs entertaining and tonight is no exception. It was a toss between Mr Georgi and the sheikh as to who should have a beach barbecue, and seeing as the sheikh had one last night and is here for a few more days, it is Mr Georgi who is having the pleasure of the company of Kate and me, in our lovely home.

I swing by the boutique to pick Kate up. We have about half an hour before Mr Georgi, his girlfriend, his brother and his brother's partner arrive, and we need to shower and down at least two glasses of Dom to get into the mood.

Kate is just packing up as I walk in.

'Christ,' she says. 'I've just had the Chief Desperates in. They've been twittering around the place for the past half-hour, trying on various bits and pieces.'

'Who was it?'

'Monica and Alison,' she sighs. 'Do you know, they actually arranged to meet each other here? They told me they'd called each other and had suggested they went on a shopping trip.'

'But there is only one shop!'

'I know. But they've both had their hair and nails done at the spa this afternoon.'

'Really? I thought we were full up at the moment,' I say. 'I must talk to Geri about this.'

'Apparently Monica insisted and Geri found them both a treatment room.'

'She'll be pissed off.'

'Furious,' says Kate, stapling the last of her receipts together.

'God, it is cold in here,' I say, shivering. 'How low do you have the air-con?'

'As low as I can,' she says. 'It is the only way to keep awake.'

'So what else did the Desperates have to say for themselves?' I ask, opening the heavy glass door for her. We are both blasted with hot air from outside.

'God, it's hot,' she says. 'Sometimes I spend so long

in that fridge I forget I am on a tropical island selling bikinis for a living. I could be in some shitty precinct in Melbourne.'

'What did the Desperates say?' I ask again, putting my arm around her slim shoulders, trying to cheer her up a little. Kate is always a bit depressed at the end of the week. Selling Liz Hurley flip-flops was not exactly her dream when she spent three years studying the hospitality industry in Sydney.

'Oh,' she sighs. 'They've had a coffee in the bar and lunch at Alison's house, where room service took over an hour to come, as per usual. Anyway, they are very excited about disco night tonight.'

'They are?'

'Oh yeah,' she smiles. 'It is the highlight of their week.'

'Really?'

'Yup. They've bought new outfits and everything.'

'Good,' I say, turning the buggy around.

'Oh, remind me tomorrow – we've had a run on kaftans, we need to order some more for the shop.'

Twenty minutes later, Kate is in a much jollier mood. She is showered and champagned and sitting in a hammock watching the last rays of the sun disappear behind Fantasy Island. The barbecue team have trans- formed the house. There are flares in the sand, carpets on the beach, salad and dessert stands all ready and waiting, and a table laid for six sitting near the shore. We have linen tablecloths, polished glasses and a candelabra. There's wagyu beefsteak and lobster waiting to be thrown on to the hot coals, there's wine and champagne chilling on ice, and both of us have remembered there are worse ways to earn a living.

The lights on Fantasy Island are twinkling away across the sea and the moon is on its way up when Mr Georgi, his wife Yulia, his brother Dimitri and his wife/partner/special friend, usefully called Natasha, all arrive. The women look like they are dressed for a black-tie dinner in tight dresses, heels and real diamonds, while the men are very much dressed for a barbecue on the beach. I suppose if your job and your livelihood was dependent on looking good and keeping your man interested, you might have a blow-dry and slip into something distinctly less comfortable of an evening.

We exchange pleasantries and news of our day. Turns out that Mr Georgi has been diving and appears to have personally rented over half our boats to accompany him on his jolly day trip. While he runs through the flotilla of boats that followed him and the exciting fish, turtles and rays that he saw, I mentally tot up that the man has blown about $19,000 in an afternoon.

'That must have been fantastic,' enthuses Kate.

'Well,' he shrugs, 'I have seen better fish in the Maldives.'

'Oh,' she smiles. 'We try our best here.'

'Yes,' he agrees. 'Maybe it is global warming. But somehow you just don't have quite the variety.'

'Perhaps. But at least you had a lovely day out, and that is what is important,' I say. 'Shall we have some dinner?'

Dinner is five courses long, with a change of wine and/or champagne with each course. There are starters and salads and pudding and cheese, as well as all the usual surf and turf. By the end, Dimitri is knocking back the VSO cognac and burping loudly, the ladies are looking a little more louche and a little more un-comfortable in their tight dresses, and Kate and I are plastered. Drinking a large amount of alcohol after a heavy week at the coalface of hospitality is enough to make anyone think that a boogie at DJ Andy's beach disco is a truly excellent idea.

'Dance? Dance? Dance? Dance?' Kate questions each of our guests in turn.

'Fantastic,' agrees Mr Georgi, who I suspect might be quite a mover. The women are just as keen. Only Dimitri needs peeling off his high-backed chair and leading up the beach. In the end it is the lure of tequila cocktails that seems to do the trick. The wine and the cognac are not sitting well in his stomach, he says. He

needs something a little stronger to settle things down
nicely.

I drink-drive the buggy to the Lotus restaurant with
one of the richest men in frozen chickens – and indeed
Russia – clinging on to the back. He and his wife are
laughing and shouting, pretending to fall out of the
back of the thing, while Dimitri and Natasha are
squashed in with Kate and me in the front. This is
totally illegal, but seeing as I am the boss and the leader
of the legal system on the island, I don't care.

We park up outside the restaurant and fall out of the
buggy. We weave our way between the other buggies
towards the giant dragons, tea lights and the Chinese
lanterns. The music is loud and funky and there seems
to be a bit of a crowd, which is much more happening
than usual. Most Saturday nights it takes a combination of Kate and me hitting the floor along with a
couple of classic toe-tappers like 'YMCA' or 'It's
Raining Men' before anyone so much as shuffles out on
to the sand. But tonight there are enough plastered
guests throwing themselves around for DJ Andy to play
a few of his more eclectic tracks. And boy does he look
pleased; I can see his skinny-arsed smile from here. He
is even allowing himself a couple of waves above his
head to get the crowd going.

I look around the beach restaurant area and smile.
This is when the design of this place really works. It is

a perfect night, there is hardly a breath of wind and there are plenty of rich people flopped out on cushions, drinking cocktails, smoking cigarettes, chomping on cigars and enjoying themselves. At this time of year, Saturday nights are a laugh. Come April, when it is Kate, me and three Japanese newly-weds dancing to 'Say You, Say Me', that's when I want to throw myself off a very tall building. If only there was one.

Mr McCann and his bevy of beauties turn up soon after us and scatter themselves like elegant cushions around the disco. He orders four magnums of Cristal and invites everyone to join him. Not to be outdone, Mr Georgi does the same, except this time he orders six and suddenly many more managers appear to crawl out of the woodwork. Ben turns up a little worse for a night in the staff bar. His face is all sweaty and pink and soggy. His eyes are covered in a film of alcohol.

'Wotcha,' he says, clicking his tongue and going for a subtle wink. His whole face complies. 'So this is Saturday. The big night. The one.'

'That's right,' I say, standing at the bar, watching one of Mr McCann's girls effectively lap dance another.

'This it?' he asks.

'What do you mean?'

'Does nothing else happen?' He is slurring his words quite badly now.

'What else do you want to happen?'

'I dunno,' he burps. 'But this feels like a school disco.'

'I don't remember those two being in my year.' I nod over to the two girls who are now wrapped around each other and seem to be on the point of kissing.

'No!' says Ben, taking in the floorshow, his mouth slowly falling open. 'They're fit.'

'And expensive.'

'And worth every penny.'

Ben and I are now actually staring. It is pathetic really. Two grown men gawping at a couple of pretty girls who are showing off. Or bored. Or just trying to get the attention of the man who is paying for them to be here. It must be quite galling to be that beautiful and that finely put together and for no man to be paying you any attention. It is no wonder that they are resorting to getting off with each other.

'Put your tongues away,' says Kate, approaching us at the bar. She snaps my jaw shut with her hand. 'You look like a couple of schoolboys.'

'That's funny,' says Ben. 'Because that's just what we were feeling like.'

'Yeah, well,' replies Kate, thrusting her empty flute towards a passing magnum of Cristal. 'I can hardly blame you. They are gorgeous. I mean, I'm half tempted myself.'

'Oh don't,' I say. 'That image is just way too much.'

'So's that,' says Ben, pointing to the other side of the dance floor. 'Am I seeing double or is this really happening?'

'Oh, that's really happening,' smiles Kate. 'I sold them both stunning ensembles just this afternoon.'

Across the dance floor, through the writhing bodies and lesbian floorshow, are Alison and Monica, both dressed in exactly the same clothes. This of course wouldn't matter if they were sporting white T-shirts, but they are both wearing bright-pink-and-yellow-striped Juicy Couture tube dresses. Alison, being the taller and more bohemian of the two, is pulling it off. Just. Monica, who is short, wide and past her prime, looks like a little mobile marquee. Weirdly, neither of the women looks embarrassed. It is almost like they are affirming the fact that they are in some sort of club that sets them apart from the rest of the gang.

'New dress?' I say, going over to Alison.

'Yes.' She smiles, running her hands covetously over her stomach. 'What do you think?'

'It's great,' I nod. 'So is yours.' I smile at Monica.

'I know,' she says. 'Do you like our little joke?'

'Hilarious!'

'Isn't it?' says Monica. 'We've been planning it all day.'

'Busy?'

'Oh,' she says, shaking her head. 'D'you know, I just

329

don't get a moment to myself these days. And poor Alison can never find the time to paint.'

'Terrible,' I say. 'Have a nice evening.'

I circulate and drink. Circulate and drink. I dance to Boney M and all the Russians go crazy to 'Kalinka'. It is one of those merry tunes that seems to bring out the inner Cossack in everyone. I look around and everyone seems to be enjoying themselves. I think I can actually make a move and call it a night. I walk over and whisper into Kate's ear and we sneak off, leaving Mr Georgi wrapped around his wife on the dance floor and his brother passed out on a nearby carpet.

The stars are shining, the moon is high in the sky and it is a romantic, stunning evening. As I weave the buggy gently home, Kate rests her head on my shoulder. At times like this, I do feel king of this extraordinary millionaires' theme park.

The villa is dark as we gingerly pick our way towards the front door. I look at my new watch and see by the light of the moon that it is two thirty a.m. We are standing outside the villa, fumbling around for the key. I manage to get the door open, but before we can go inside Kate grabs hold of my hand.

'Let's do it on the beach,' she says. There's a wicked glint in her eye. The champagne has clearly gone to her head.

'Well, I'm not . . .' I hesitate.

'Come on,' she says. 'Who is going to see us?'

'Well, I'm . . .'

'Oh come on,' she insists, pulling me towards the beach. 'You're the boss. No one can tell you off.'

She runs towards the shore, peeling off her white dress, and wades into the sea in her underwear. The light of the moon catches her back and dances on her shoulder blades. I follow her towards the surf, taking my linen shirt off and hopping out of my trousers. I am down to my Calvin's, paddling towards her. She has lost her pants somewhere in the surf and she immediately pulls at mine to remove them. I can feel her cold wet breasts against my chest and her hard flat stomach against mine. She kisses my lips and I can taste salt water and champagne. I have my hands over her naked buttocks as she throws my underwear away in the water. I am kissing her lips and running my hands all over her naked flesh when I hear the distant ringing of a phone.

'That's the villa phone,' I say into her parted lips.

'Ignore it,' she mumbles.

'But what if it is important?' I ask, pulling away, holding tightly on to her shoulders. I am so torn between shagging her brains out in the surf and worrying about what the call might be about, I can hardly breathe.

'Don't go,' she says, leaning in for another kiss.

'Oh fuck it,' I say, pushing her away in the surf. I run stark bollock naked with a rock-on up the beach to the villa. I swiftly pull aside the sliding doors and hurl myself on to the bed.

'Yes?' I blast down the phone.

'Is that the manager?'

'Yes!'

'I am the sheikh's assistant . . .'

'Yes?' I am just beginning to get my breath back. My heart is thumping in my chest. My erection is subsiding. 'How can I help?'

'Um . . . this is a little delicate . . .'

'Right . . . OK . . .'

'The sheikh has run out of condoms.'

'What?'

'The sheikh needs some condoms.'

'But it is two thirty in the morning!'

'Precisely.'

'I'll call you back,' I say, hanging up. The bastard, I think as I dial up the duty manager's number. I gave you my card in case you wanted anything important. I didn't expect a bloody call just to inform me that he was getting his end away.

By the time I have spoken to the duty manager and told him to open up the boutique and where the condoms are, and which size to get – Super Trojan, of course – Kate is out of the sea, wrapped in a towel and as cold as the iced water she is drinking. Sometimes I have to wonder if this job is really worth it.

Sunday a.m.

Normally I love Sundays. I get a lie-in, a shag and breakfast on the beach with my girlfriend. I get to lounge around in my dressing gown and my pants for most of the morning. I might take in some news on the TV, read the headlines, and I might even try and chat to a few of my old mates on Skype. However, today is not going to plan.

I have already missed out on the lie-in because I got a call at six a.m. to come and sort out some sort of incident in the staff village. Thereby ensuring the shag went out the window at the same time. So you can understand that I am pretty pissed off by the time I turn up at the village and find that Marco has driven a buggy into the sea.

Apparently last night's disco and sniff of a couple of free flutes of Cristal set him off on a drinking binge of gargantuan proportions. He roped in Hans and Yoshiji and together they troughed a fair way through Marco's secret stash of fine wines, which he's been squirrelling away for a while in his villa.

Anyway, clearly bored of each other's company, they decided to steal Antonio's buggy and drive it at full pelt around the staff village. They would have got away with it if Hori had not been up with a team of engineers mending a broken water pipe. So they come crashing through the water, all legs and screams and cheers and splashes, which of course really pisses the team off. Hori stops the buggy and orders them all to bed. Hans and Yoshiji rather weirdly go off to bed together and Marco appears to comply, only to escape from his room five minutes later and try and drive off in the buggy. Hori then decides to disable the buggy and calls security to babysit Marco outside his villa. They leave after ten minutes, presuming him to be asleep. However, Marco reappears, steals Hori's buggy and drives it straight through the burst water pipe, down the beach and straight into the sea.

Which is when I got called, and precisely when my Sunday morning got buggered.

I spend over an hour talking to Marco, Hans and Yoshiji. Marco and Hans both blame Yoshiji for the idea of stealing the buggy and drink-driving it like a bunch of nutters around the island. It is his last night here as he and Angela are leaving this evening to go and start a new life together in Japan. Although quite what he was doing spending his last night in the arms of Hans is anyone's guess. Marco does take the blame for driving the buggy into the sea, which is big of him, and receives another written warning. He now has two. One more and he is off the island, which would be sad as I like the bloke. He is also very good at his job. It is usual for a sommelier to have a fondness for his own stock, but Marco appears to be developing quite a penchant. The rate of alcoholism is rather high in this business. Most of us are functioning alcoholics, in that we rarely have a day when we don't drink a little too much and we almost never have a day when we don't drink at all. But it is when you cease to function, you can't take the hangovers and you start driving $24,000 buggies into the sea that things go a little pear-shaped.

Standing in my office, his hair all washed and combed straight from the shower, Marco is the image of contrition. He tells me it was his way of giving Yoshiji some sort of send-off and that he is upset the man is leaving. Although I have to say I wasn't aware the two of them had even had a conversation. He does the whole innocent-schoolboy thing about how he is so sorry, he doesn't know what came over him and it won't happen again. In the end I am almost totally taken in. Until the point when I go over to shake his hand and he stinks of old sweaty booze. I have got my eye firmly on him now – one more fuck-up and he'll be on the boat before he's had time to pack his bags and indeed steal half the cellar.

Back in the villa, Kate is giving me the silent treatment. By way of protest she hasn't waited for me to get back from the office before ordering our usual Sunday breakfast. She has long since eaten her fresh-fruit salad and *pain au chocolat* and she's left my two fried eggs to sit in the sun and go dry and crisp. My butter has melted, my coffee is cold and my toast is a springy mattress. It is clearly time to apologize.

'I'm sorry,' I say.

'It is your day off,' she replies. 'Can't we get some time to ourselves?'

'I know, but there is nothing I can do.'

'Yes, there is,' she says, looking up from her month-old *Hello!* magazine. 'Tell them you're off duty and that it is not your responsibility.'

'But it *is* my responsibility. I'm the manager. I run the place. It is all my responsibility.'

'You're not that fucking indispensable,' she says, getting out of her seat and walking over to her hammock. 'They could get rid of you just like that.' She clicks her fingers.

'Maybe that's what I am worried about,' I say, sitting

down to my congealed breakfast. I slice one of the eggs in half. The yolk oozes across the plate. Sod it, I think, it's flown all the way from Germany – I may as well eat it. I grab a piece of cold toast and mop the egg up, shoving it into my dry mouth. My mobile rings on my bed.

'That'll be another arse that wants kissing,' shouts Kate.

'I am not going to answer it,' I shout back. 'I'm eating my breakfast.'

'Are you sure?' she asks. 'It could be the sheikh wanting another condom.'

'The shop's open,' I say.

The phone keeps ringing. On and on. I can feel my heart beat faster. I look across at the bed where it is lying. It is taking all my will power not to run over and answer it. Eventually it stops.

Kate starts to clap slowly from the hammock. 'Bravo!' she says. 'Some guest can take their where's-my-breakfast crisis elsewhere.'

'Absolutely,' I say with an exaggerated yawn as I get out of my chair. 'I'm just going for a shower.'

'OK,' she says, sounding quite chirpy. 'Don't be too long.'

I go inside and slip my mobile into my pocket on the way to the shower. I check the screen to see whose call I've missed. Ben. Thank God for that, I think. He's left a message.

'Hi there, mate,' he says. 'Ben here. Christ, I've got a hangover. Whoever said good champagne doesn't hurt your head was talking bullshit. I only had about a bottle of the rapper's favourite tipple and I feel shit. Anyway,' he yawns, 'what does one do around here for fun? What happens on this piss-poor island on a freaking Sunday? I'm bored. Call me.'

'Kate,' I say, walking back out on to the terrace.

'Mmm?'

'I think we should invite Ben over today.'

'I wondered how long you'd resist checking your message,' she says. 'Well done – that was less than forty-five seconds.'

'You've made your point,' I sigh. 'I am sorry. What more can I say? I find Sundays hard. I hate being out of the loop. I hate not knowing what is going on. I think it is going to go to shit while I'm away. I worry. I am worried. I am always worried. I can't help it. There. So now you know.'

Kate gets out of the hammock and comes towards me. She kisses me on the forehead.

'I have always known,' she smiles. 'Now take your shower. Invite your mate over and get a move on. We've got to have our walk before lunch.'

Every Sunday morning Kate and I walk around the whole island. It takes about an hour and it is the only time that I get to see the place from the point of view of the guests. I take a bit of paper and a pen and make notes on what I see, then bring them in to the Monday-morning meeting. Bizarrely, Kate doesn't seem to mind this part of my obsessive-compulsive behaviour. Possibly because she switches off and just enjoys the walk. But I think mainly she likes it because it is the only real time during the week that we get to talk and hang out together, without any interruptions. We often chew over the gossip of the week and try and work out where we might be headed.

As we set off down towards Palm Sands, she appears to be in a much better mood.

'Can you believe that Yoshiji and Angela are actually leaving today and are going off to live in Japan?' she says. 'I mean, has she ever been to Japan? It is such a weird place. I wonder if she'll cope. I bet you she'll be back here before you know it. You know, there was a rumour that Leila's baby was his.'

'I know,' I nod. 'But it is not.'

'How do you know?'

'Dr Singh told me it was a red-head.'

'Are there any red-heads on the island?'

'Not that I can think of.'

'Hans is a bit red.'

'He's blond.'

'That's a bit red,' she says. 'Oh look! A baby shark!'

We walk along Palm Sands beach following two baby

340

sharks as they swim in and out of the shallows. The sun is beating down; the cool seawater is rippling up the beach. Kate is transfixed; she paddles on after them, while I make a quick note that the sand is all hard underneath the palms around villa 150 and that it needs to be broken up properly and then raked.

We carry on past Mr and Mrs Forrest's villa. The curtains are drawn and the blinds are still down – no doubt they are enjoying the fruits of their renewed vows. Next door to them is the German industrialist who is still under house arrest, not that he appears to mind. He is the colour of mahogany and is laid out on a lounger, slathered in oil. He gives me a little cheery wave as we walk past and raises what appears to be a cocktail. He is certainly enjoying his holiday. On past the recently vacated villa 162, where the Thompsons and their extremely demanding nanny were staying. I notice that the garden needs sorting. The hedge needs putting back between the two villas. I had quite forgotten that we'd pulled it out, and now of course if a guest in either villa wants to take a naked wash in the outdoor shower, they can be seen quite clearly from the path.

We round the bay and approach the boutique and restaurant area, where I just want a quick glance at the horizon lap-pool. Hopefully we'll be getting those very expensive rocks in place next week and I want to have a quick look to see if there is any more damage to the pool after the bad weather earlier this week. Kate says she doesn't mind me having a look around and takes herself off for a cup of coffee at the bar, while I poke my nose around the pool.

Mr McCann is lying on a lounger, passed out in the sun. He has taken over the couple's sunbed and is flanked by the girls who put on the lesbian dance display last night. They are curled up next to him like a couple of cats. I can't help feeling a small pang of jealousy as I walk past. For a short, fat, ugly bloke, he is certainly having a lovely time.

At the lap-pool there are a couple of banker wives doing lengths, trying not to get their heads wet. Their chins are trained towards the sky and they've got bull dog clips in their hair. They are definitely having a constitutional.

Connie walks past in her white yoga turban, carrying her sheepskin mat under her arm.

'Morning,' she says.

'Are you having a nice relaxing day?' I ask.

'Two classes and five a.m. meditation,' she declares.

She's raking it in, I think as I smile and head down the beach.

Looking up at the side of the pool from the shore, it is obvious we need to put the expensive rocks in place sooner rather than later. There are small leaks and

cracks all down the side wall that faces the sea. All it's
going to take are a few huge waves to hit the side and
the whole thing will come crashing down. That has got
to be the number-one priority this week, and I don't
care how many VIPs I piss off in the process.

Coming back up the beach towards the bar, I see
Kate's been cornered by the Desperates. Sunday is a
good day for them as they are now on a par with the
majority of management. Everyone's bored and happy
to chat. Even Kate is talking away.

'So did you stay late?' I hear her asking Monica.

'Not very,' says Monica, pushing her large golden-
framed sunglasses to the top of her head. 'It all got a
bit, you know, frisky after you left.'

'Really?'

'Those ladies that are with the TV man started doing
all sorts of dancing.'

'Really?'

'Oh yes,' adds Alison. 'And quite a lot of it was very
pornographic.'

'Well, at least they were enjoying themselves,' I say.

'That's true,' says Kate.

'I know, but really,' says Monica, turning up her nose
slightly. 'There I was thinking that we're a five-star –
sorry, six-star – resort.'

'All the more reason for people to be having a good
time,' I say. 'They've all worked hard to get here.'

'Some of them more than others,' says Monica.

'Oh, I don't know,' I say. 'Some of those girls look like they've worked extremely hard to me.'

'Yes, well,' sniffs Alison. 'I've got Sunday lunch to organize.'

'Oh, what are you ordering?' asks Kate.

'I won't know until Alan gets back from the gym,' says Alison.

'I didn't know Alan is working out,' I say.

'We both are,' she announces. 'We've been to see the dietician. Can't you tell?'

'Yes, of course,' both Kate and I reply at the same time.

'I knew there was something,' Kate adds.

'Amazing,' I smile. 'Come on, darling.' I take Kate's hand and lead her off down the beach.

We walk past the spa and the gym, both of which are relatively empty, but then that is to be expected, seeing as it is early and such a lovely day. There will be a few more takers in the spa this afternoon and this evening, but the gym will only have the likes of Alan in there spending time away from his wife. Kate and I are just about to turn right to Silver Sands when we see a buggy careering towards us at full speed.

'If that is a member of staff I am going to fucking kill them,' I say, eyeballing the driver, who appears not to notice me as he is talking on a mobile phone.

'Jeez, that was fast,' says Kate as the buggy and bloke shoot past. 'Who the hell was that?'

'It's that sodding Formula One driver,' I say. 'Who let him get his hands on a buggy?'

Kate starts to laugh. 'Do you think he's hot-wired it or something? I have never seen one of them go that fast.'

'I drive mine that fast,' I say.

'Of course you do, darling.'

We walk the length of Silver Sands, paddling in the shallows. The sun's high in the sky now and I am beginning to sweat. I am half tempted to hurl myself into the sea with all my clothes on. But it is sadly not becoming of a man in my position. Even when I am off duty I can't completely let my hair down. My phone goes in my pocket; Kate is far enough up the beach not to notice, so I answer.

'Hi, it's Jean-François.'

'Hello.'

'Sorry to bother you on your day off, but we've run out of presents.'

'What do you mean?'

'I am in the storeroom now and I can't find any presents for the departing guests.'

Every guest leaves here with a little something – candles, incense sticks, even kaftans. We put them on their beds the night before they go as a goodbye gift. It costs the hotel almost nothing and makes us look delightfully generous. It depends on what rate you have paid, how many times you have been here before and how long you have stayed as to what you find on your bed.

'I can't see anything in here,' he says, his voice echoing slightly as he looks around the warehouse.

'What do you expect me to do about it?' I ask.

'Um . . .'

'Come down and help you look?'

'Well, I was just . . .'

'It is my bloody day off. I only have one a week. Improvise!'

I hang up and turn my phone off. He is a grown-up – he can work it out for himself.

'Darling!' I look up. Kate is waving at me from the end of the bay. 'Come here! Hurry up. There is something you should see.'

I run up the beach towards her. 'This way,' she says, climbing over the dunes. I follow her along the beach a short way before she stops and points. 'Take a look at this.'

As I walk away from the shore towards the villa, I am first hit by the smell. It is hot and sweet and high. The stench of some fifty beer cans sweating in the hot midday sun. Secondly there's the mess. Bottles and cans all over the place. There's a table in the sand that is covered in empties. There are cans of Coke and Sprite and tonics in the sand too. There are Haribo wrappers and tubes of Pringles floating in the pool. And then there are bodies asleep everywhere. The TV has been taken out of the villa and now faces the beach. A fishing net has been strung up over the pool. Suspended in the net are two blokes, fast asleep on a pile of cushions. The mattress has been pulled off the bed in the villa and dragged on to the beach, and so have half the chairs and pillows. Basically, it is as if an American thrash-metal band has held an after-show party in the place. All it needs are a few motorbikes in the pool or a corpse in the bedroom and the look would be complete.

'What the hell happened here?' asks Kate, whispering behind her hand as she tiptoes towards the debris.

'It was supposed to be some of the middle-management guys having a FLAG night.'

'No!' she says, her eyes round with shock. 'These guys are middle management?' She looks a little closer. 'Is that Keith?' She turns her head around so she can take in the upside-down face. 'It *is* Keith,' she whispers. 'And he looks pretty shit. What have they been doing?'

'Well, it looks like they took the TV outside so they could watch the football or some films, and kind of let their hair down.'

'You can say that again.'

'I'm calling Bernard,' I say. 'He was the one who

persuaded me to give them a chance. He can come and clear up this shit.'

Poor Bernard is about to sit down to his lunch with Monica when I call. He tries to slip off the hook, but I'm afraid I am not having it.

'Get your fat French arse down here right away,' I say. 'Before I really blow my top.'

'Of course, of course,' he says down the phone. 'I'll be there as soon as I can.'

'He's on his way,' I say to Kate.

'Thank God for that.'

Keith starts to stir. He yawns and stretches. He farts and then opens his eyes. He sits up and runs his hands through his stringy long hair, as he takes in the inordinate mess.

'Shit,' he mumbles.

'You can say that again!' I say.

He turns, looks at me and leaps right out of his skin.

Sunday p.m.

Keith and his gang of merry fools spend most of the afternoon clearing up after themselves. It is a sad and sorry thing to watch. For not only have they incurred my wrath, but also that of everyone else on the island – as henceforth all FLAG nights have been cancelled. The decision was swift, easy and final. I am not being taken for a twat and indeed a ride for a third time. Which is a shame, really, as the idea was only beneficial to staff. But if they are too stupid to see that, then they are too stupid to be trusted with an expensive villa, executive plunge pool and surround-sound system. And if they are really too stupid to clear up after themselves and are caught by the manager then they can have nothing to look forward to except their weekly trip to the mainland and their annual holiday home.

As Kate and I walk back to the villa, after busting their arses, their balls and all other aspects of their family jewellery, I am seething, to say the least.

'They are a bunch of fucking arseholes,' I say, kicking the sand as I walk. 'I mean, one of the major perks of this business is living like a king, when you are paid like a pauper. It's about having the lifestyle without the responsibility that goes with it. But it is also about doing it cleverly and subtly and without pissing off the management. And I'm the management and I am extremely pissed off. Also, what's worse is that they've made me look like a fool.'

'I know,' agrees Kate, nodding as she walks along next to me. 'We used to have great beach parties in Bali and half-inch all the alcohol from the hotel's storerooms all the time and no one ever knew.'

'That's the point,' I say. 'Once you start taking the piss then it is game over. How they thought they were ever going to get away with leaving that villa looking like a fucking cesspit dump, I don't know. I am furious. I thought they were cleverer than that. Arseholes.'

'They are worse than arseholes,' says Kate. 'They are lazy arseholes.'

'Well, they can sweat off their hangovers cleaning the place up and no one is going to help them, because everyone is pissed off. And I mean bloody everyone.'

Sunday p.m.

'That's true.'

'It's lucky for them that half the staff are on the mainland today, otherwise there'd be no end of grief waiting for them.'

For those who have the day off, Sunday is mainland day. Although I have to say I've never really understood the appeal of going to the mainland on your day off. The staff ferry leaves at around nine thirty on Sunday morning and comes back again in the evening, bringing those on day-release back to the island. Each member of staff is given a pass, and they are counted out and counted back in again to make sure that everyone returns and we have no escapees or smugglers onboard either. But quite what they do between the hours of nine thirty and sunset I have no idea. There's bugger all happening there. There are a few cafés, where I know some of the Filipino and Thai girls meet up with other Filipino and Thai girls who are also on day-release from the neighbouring resorts. But apart from that, who knows? There's not even a cinema in town. I imagine there is a lot of walking around, sitting about and chatting. Not the most exciting way to spend your day off, I grant you. No wonder then that most of the Westerners who work in the resort spend their day off lounging around, drinking beer in the staff village. Occasionally someone summons the energy to rustle up a barbecue, but most of the time they sit inside,

351

drinking beer and watching DVDs. You would have thought that with some of the universally acknowledged 'most beautiful beaches in the world' on your doorstep, most people would spend their day off swimming, snorkelling and catching fish. But there is something about spending all week working in paradise that means come your day off you're utterly sick of the place. Also, anything that requires effort is obviously totally exhausting.

'Shall we take a boat out this afternoon?' suggests Kate, as we turn the corner on the beach towards our villa.

'Or we could just hang out,' I reply.

'But we did that last week, and the weekend before,' she says. 'Let's take a boat to another resort. Have dinner, or a late lunch. We could take Ben.'

Kate and I have done this a few times. We get the boat boys to take us out on the catamaran we use on the sunset cruises, and sail over to another five-star resort for the day. It can be a right laugh. The other manager or deputy comes out to meet and greet us and we have some sort of fabulously boozy lunch at the expense of the other place, of course. They are sort of obliged to comp us, out of good manners, and then we sail back, dozing on the deck. We had such a laugh at the Four Seasons a few weeks ago that the manager offered to put us up for the night. He was a delightful chap, he cracked open some very nice wines for our delight and delectation. Kate and I only wished we'd thought about it in advance. We could've packed ourselves a little bag and told the boat to leave and come and collect us early in the morning. It would almost have been like a holiday. Although strictly speaking I'm not allowed to slip off and spend the night on another island, when I'm in charge of this place. My cage may well be golden, but I am still bound to spend every bloody night here in case of fire, tsunami or another pissed guest falling into the pool. Still, at least I get the use of an $800-an-hour boat for the whole day for nix. I can also disappear off for a day's diving with the dive master and take any number of the speedboats waterskiing, have a spin on a jet ski or order myself up yet another lobster-barbecue lunch.

I suppose as fringe benefits go, my manager's perks are pretty luxurious. As well as access to yachts, speedboats and free diving, I also get my aforementioned Club Class flights home to London every year, plus as much wine and champagne as I want to drink at any meal in the resort, whether I'm entertaining or not. I tend not to push my luck too much when putting my fine-dining expenses through, though. I tend to slurp inexpensive bubbles like Moët or Veuve or a cheeky red, something that is about $160–$180 a bottle. Unlike last night's FLAG boys, I know how to push things without taking the piss. Sometimes Kate and I will box a little clever and we'll have Jean-François and Marco over, with Garry maybe, and possibly Bernard, and we'll crack open some fairly expensive bottles in the region of $600–$1500, which we will write off as a stock tasting, a staff-relations dinner or a guest complaint. Due to the terrible way the wine travels here – freezing itself sour in the hold of an aeroplane, only to boil its balls off on the quay for three days waiting to be shipped to the island – we do get a fair amount of corkage, which we occasionally use to our advantage. But that said, I still have to justify myself to the board of directors every year, and if my spreadsheets are skew it is my arse that gets it.

As well as food, wine and free boating, I get any massage, manicure or pedicure that I want, plus free use of the gym, steam room and sauna, all of which makes for a more pleasant way of life than travelling to and from work like a veal calf with your nose in someone else's armpit on the Tube.

'So what do you think?' asks Kate.

'I think it sounds like a great idea.'

'Shall I call them up?'

'Great,' I say. 'I fancy getting away from it all today.'

'We've had quite a tough week.'

'You can say that again.'

'And I think that it might be a good idea to show Ben

that we know how to have a good time. This being his first week. All he's had are problems and nightmares.'

'Good idea,' I say.

Kate is busy organizing a boat and a late picnic lunch with champagne and a bit of Lebanese food from the main restaurant, while I lie back and enjoy the sun for the first time in a week. It's weird, I almost never sunbathe. The sun is usually a hindrance to what I am trying to do. I am either too hot, or boiling bloody hot, or it is pissing with rain and then I have a crisis on my hands. Either way, it is rare that I am enjoying the sun in my swimming trunks just like every other punter on the beach. In fact, it is so rare that when I go home to see my mum in north London I have to make a special effort to get a bit of tan beforehand, just to prove that I do actually work abroad.

It is bliss lying here, soaking up the rays, flat out on my sunbed, warming my bone marrow. You can see why exhausted businessmen and overtired billionaires shell out a fortune to pass out on these white sands. Sometimes it is good to remember what being on a desert island is all about. I am yawning and stretching and contemplating a short snooze when my mobile goes.

'Hello?'

'Hi, it's me,' come Bernard's implacable Gallic tones.

'What is the problem?' I ask, rolling over and looking at my watch. It is twenty to one.

'We've got a super yacht wanting to anchor.'

'Oh God, really?'

'Eh, *oui*.'

'How super?'

'I am not sure.'

'Who's requested it?'

'Some Russian,' he says.

'Have you got the boat's name?'

'*Sea Breeze*.'

'Isn't that the name of a cocktail?'

'And a super yacht,' he sighs.

'Have you run it through yachtmati.com yet?'

'No.'

'Do that and then get back to me,' I say. 'If it is under seventy metres, they can fuck off.'

I have a bit of a love-hate relationship with super yachts. They can look fabulous moored off the resort, their expensive hulls glistening in the sunshine, their glamorous crews dressed head to foot in white and their helicopters flying back and forth, choppering in the owner and all his fabulous guests. But quite a lot of the time they are a nightmare.

Firstly, they are so bloody huge that they often have a tender and then a tender off the tender in order for any of the passengers to get anywhere near shore. We had Abramovich's super yacht *Pelorus* here last year. His other rather large baby *Le Grand Bleu* has also anchored here, but since he very generously gave it to his mate Eugene Shvidler it has yet to return. But quite frankly, one at a time is enough. Not only is *Pelorus* 115 metres or 377 feet long, but it also has a 65-foot Sunseeker on the back, plus another yacht and a crane to lift them into the water. It also has two helicopter pads, one for personal use and one for guests, and there was such a song and dance about the thing that it almost made me wish it was not there.

Ambramovich himself was rather nice; he didn't speak much English and was flanked most of the time by bodyguards, who were never more than a few feet away from him. And his fifty-six full-time staff on the boat were perfectly pleasant. The boat is incredible. The deck is made with such beautiful wood that as you arrive on board the staff give you a pair of shoes to slip into. There are swimming pools, jacuzzis and all the usual luxury suspects. The boat even splits open when you dock with the tender, like something out of a James Bond film. They also have this fantastic piece of design, so that one half of the boat is for the guests and the other half is for the staff – unlike, say, on the *Titanic*, where the hoi polloi were on the lower decks – so the staff are never more than a thirty-second dash from the guests. The service is therefore quicker and slicker and altogether more efficient.

But there are plenty of downsides to the super-yacht experience. They cause such a buzz here that the atmosphere of the place totally changes. The staff get into a tizz. The other guests either get curious or pissed off. There is nothing discreet or low-key about a bloody great yacht moored off the beach, so everyone in the resort knows who is here, where they are and what they are doing, no matter how much you try to play these things down. Plus there's the inconvenience of looking after so many more guests than the resort was designed for. And when *Pelorus* was here, there were something like 140 airlifts off the boat, with guests arriving, leaving and faffing around. Every time one of the choppers took off we would get a flood of complaints to the switchboard.

Also, we tried to put on a bit of a show for them. We gave them a delicious spread in the restaurant, a barbecue on the beach, that sort of thing – which of course doesn't go down well with your average paying guest, who has been waiting for a beach barbecue for a couple of days. All billionaires are equal in the resort, but some are more equal than others.

Although having poked around *Pelorus* and all the other enormous boats that have tipped up here in the last year and a half, I don't know why some of them ever bother to come ashore. They are so goddamn swish inside that anything we can offer here is pure Mickey Mouse. If I were them I'd never bother to leave the elegant and very expensive confines of their own launch. Anywhere else has got to be a bit of a disappointment.

Bernard calls back.

'So,' he says. 'The man is in the top one hundred on the Forbes list, his name his Ivanov, he made his money in steel and his boat is eighty-five metres.'

'Right,' I sigh. 'I suppose we'd better say yes.'

'Looks like it,' he says. 'These things rent for $455,000 a week, so let's hope he has a few dollars to spare.'

'Wad is not going to be a problem.'

'So I'll radio over and OK?'

'Absolutely.'

I peel myself off the sunbed and walk into the house. I open my wardrobe and work out what dull piece-of-linen shit I can put on to meet and greet this flash Harry in his big boat humorously named after a vodka drink.

'What's going on?' asks Kate, who is sitting on the bed, still organizing our day out.

'Some tosser has just arrived in a big boat and I'm going to have to meet him as he lands,' I say.

'Can't Bernard do it?'

'Not really,' I sigh. 'When you're on the Forbes list and you have big toys you kind of expect the manager.'

'Really?' she says, putting down the receiver.

'I'm afraid so.'

She knows I am right. In fact, she knows I am right to the point where she doesn't even bother to argue.

'Bang goes our Sunday,' she says.

'We'll only have to do drinks, or a handshake and a bit of chat.'

'Don't lie. If the bloke has gone to the trouble of making all that money and spending it so wisely on a big boat, don't tell me we are not going to be forced to look around every sodding inch of the place.'

Kate is right, of course, and an hour later we find ourselves sitting in the back of the most stunning Italian motor launch, which has been sent to collect us and bring us over to look around *Sea Breeze*.

Mr Ivanov meets us on deck in a jaunty pair of white yachting shorts, with his gut hanging out. He is your classic short, stout, fat-necked Russian who made his money creaming his country of its natural resources while Yeltsin was having a vodka and the rest of the world wasn't looking. He is polite enough, and has the requisite entourage of heavies to suggest that there are powerful people in the world who want him dead. He also has a collection of what Kate would refer to as 'skirts' – i.e. pretty girls with pretty legs, pretty tits and pretty little else. He appears to have a significant skirt, who is perfection in a bikini. She wafts around the top deck and makes me a drink and Kate feel inadequate.

'So,' says Mr Ivanov. 'Would you like to take a look around?'

'Really?' says Kate, feigning surprise.

'If you would like to,' he suggests.

'That would be very kind,' I say, sipping a delicious glass of champagne.

So Mr Ivanov and the significant skirt take us on the tour. The yacht is designed to carry up to thirty-six passengers with thirty-four crew. With a range of over seven thousand nautical miles, it is capable of crossing the Atlantic, navigating the Panama Canal and reaching the west coast of the United States and Mexico. On the top deck there's a bar, a barbecue and an eight-person jacuzzi. In the saloon there's another bar, two seating areas, both with forty-two-inch plasma televisions, DVD and CD players, plus a library/cinema with a hundred-inch screen, overhead projection and surround sound, as well as a dining room with yet another bar, a Yamaha grand piano, a fifty-one-inch Sony Wega plasma television, surround sound, DVD and CD players. Below decks there's a health centre with the main indoor jacuzzi, separate male and female studios with sauna, steam room, showers and changing rooms, a post-treatment relaxation area with hair/nail salon, massage room, treatment room and two fully qualified beauty therapists. And a children's play area/crèche, plus gym with treadmill, multigym, bicycles, step and free weights. And that's even before Kate and I are taken down another deck to the various bedrooms and bathrooms and suites and relaxing areas. It takes me three glasses of champagne to get around the vessel.

Mr Ivanov is pleasantly effusive while he gives us the grand tour and thanks me at least twice for allowing him to weigh anchor here.

'You see, some resorts can be a little unfriendly,' he says.

'Really?' I say. 'I can't think why.'

'I can,' says the skirt. 'I had a friend who was on a super yacht in the Seychelles. They turned up to a place, took over fifteen villas and the presidential suite, and they brought in so many prostitutes and so much cocaine that the manager just stood on the beach tearing his hair out. They stayed for a week. I think half the hotel checked out.'

'Who was that?' asks Kate.

'Just some oligarch,' shrugs the skirt.

'Well, you won't get that sort of behaviour from us,' smiles Mr Ivanov. 'I am far too old for drugs.'

'You are not old,' smiles the skirt, wrapping one of her unfeasibly long legs around her rather short partner.

'Ha, ha, ha,' chuckles Mr Ivanov, giving her backside a quick squeeze.

'Well, I shall leave you to it,' I say. 'Do come and go as you please. We can arrange a barbecue, dinner, drinks, whatever you want.'

'Actually we have arranged a small drinks party on the beach with your assistant,' says Mr Ivanov.

'Oh good,' I say. 'I am glad Bernard has been useful.'

'Very,' nods Mr Ivanov.

Kate and I get back to shore to be met by Bernard and a host of helpers organizing drinks on the main beach in front of the bar and restaurant. There is already a bit of an audience gathering to watch the tables and rugs and flares being set up for the Russians in some style.

'You didn't tell me about this,' I say to Bernard, who is overseeing the proceedings.

'They organized it while you were sailing over in the million-dollar tender,' he says.

'That tender is worth a million?' I ask, watching the boat disappear off towards the mother ship. 'Who told you that?'

'One of the guys here,' he replies.

'Christ,' I say.

'It doesn't mean the man has taste.' He shrugs. 'Look at the shit his people have brought over for his guests to eat.'

I look down at the tables and chairs and plates of canapés, expecting to see foie gras, caviar, smoked salmon at the very least. Instead there are bowls of crisps, sausage rolls, sesame prawn toasts and some carrot sticks.

'It is like a fucking children's party,' says Bernard, walking off, his aquiline nose firmly in the air.

Sunday Sunset

ate and I finally get back to our villa with a little time
relax before Ben and Jean-François come over for
nner. With the afternoon sailing trip totally buggered,
m even more determined to have a pleasant evening.
ate sets to work trying to organize for our Lebanese
cnic to mutate into a dinner and making sure that we
ve enough wine to make our soirée go with a swing.

In the meantime, I pour myself a nice fat glass of
mé de Pouilly 2004, which sells here for $200 a
ttle. It is delicious and fruity and just what the doctor
dered after the three glasses of Krug I quaffed on the
at. I settle down at my computer to see if I can con-
ntrate for a second on booking my own holiday. Kate
d I have a week off at the beginning of December,
hich is the lull just before the Christmas storm, and
e are not sure where to go.

At the moment Australia is on the cards. Kate wan
to see a few of her relatives and I just want to be in
city. I want cars, I want noise, I want people and caf
and things to look at. Obviously the last place we wa
to be is in another bloody hotel, but sometimes it
unavoidable. In the summer we usually do a grand to
of Europe, taking in as many friends with as ma
villas as possible, so we can avoid hotel hell. B
Australia is so huge and Kate's relatives are only
Melbourne and on the east coast, so we might have
book into a few places. We do get a discount within t
chain, or we get put up in places for free. I also have
large network of buddies who can shove us in
presidential suite for a couple of nights while we cat
up, drinking brandies late into the night. Last time Ka
and I visited Tokyo we had a ball, going from one fiv
star establishment with views to die for to anoth
without ever having to open our wallets. But it does
exactly make for a private holiday. Most of the tir
both of us are perched at the bar singing for our supp
talking about old times, or quickly going around t
hotel pretending to be on some sort of fact-findi
mission in order to justify our swanky suites.

However, at the moment I think our relationsh
might need a bit of work and I am not sure a we
ligging our way around Oz is quite going to cut it wi
Kate. And anyway, I am not sure my liver will be at

cope with the inevitable boozathon that accompanies
ll that freeloading. Which brings me to the problem of
where to book. When you are used to charging people
2,000 a night and checking out guests whose weekly
ills regularly top a quarter of a million dollars, you
end to lose all sense of proportion. Last Sunday I
ound myself booking us into some Sydney hotel where
he rooms were $1,250 a night. It seemed a perfectly
easonable idea to me. After all, it was a lovely hotel,
ith views of the Harbour Bridge. And if you live in
ne of the top resorts in the world, you've got to go
omewhere quite nice for your holidays. It was Kate
who pointed out that I wasn't an oligarch, the $10,000
was about to drop for my four days in Sydney was a
month's wages, and who the hell did I think I was?

And that was before she'd seen what car I'd hired. I
now it's lame, but I am a bloke and I only get to drive
nce or twice a year. Can you imagine what it is like to
pend your days driving a bloody golf buggy? All day,
very day, up and down one bloody island on the same
itty little paths? Giving way to guests? Slowing down
or their children on bicycles? Never to hear the purr of
n engine? Never to get that feeling of thrust? Never to
el the wind in your hair or the thrill of the open road?
orever condemned to do nought to twenty in two
inutes? It's enough to make anyone feel like a eunuch.

But imagine feeling like a eunuch, and at the same

time having to smile and applaud all these big boys who
arrive with their expensive toys, with helicopters and
speedboats and million-dollar tenders. Don't tell me
that as soon as you were given the chance, you too
wouldn't rent a Porsche 911 Carrera S convertible? It
was only $850 a day. I thought it was a bargain! I've
got some air miles, I could have whacked the Hertz bill
through on my credit card and it wouldn't have hurt
too much.

Anyway, my lack of proportion and the apparent
ideas I have above my station made Kate cry with
laughter. She called me all sorts of names that included
the words 'sad' and 'pathetic', she asked me if I was
having some sort of penis crisis and went on to assure
me that I didn't have anything to worry about. I tell
you, if I wasn't feeling sexually inadequate at the beginning of the night I was at the end. Not only do I hardly
ever get to sit behind a wheel, when I do I now have to
choose something sensible and within my budget.
Christ, where's the romance in that? It's enough to drive
a man to drink.

I help myself to another slurp of Fumé de Pouilly
2004 and take a half-hearted look at modestly priced cars
and sensible hotel rooms. I am half tempted to raid my
tips box and blow the whole eighteen or so grand I've got
sitting in there. That would give us a week to remember.
But it's nothing compared to being able to blow $98,000

on a private jet somewhere, just because the place you are staying is a little bit windy. Or even shelling out $55,000 on a jolly night out for your brother. I sigh. Sometimes it is hard not being able to afford to keep yourself in the manner to which you are very much accustomed.

My phone goes. I immediately move to answer it, thinking that Kate and I have long since given up on keeping this Sunday 'special'.

'Hello?' I think I must sound a little depressed, because the caller asks me twice for my name. 'No, no, it is me. Yes. I am the manager.' After a bit more to-ing and fro-ing I realize that it is someone calling on behalf of the Crown Prince of Saudi Arabia. Turns out he wants some rooms.

'He wants two Grands, one Beach, one Water and twelve villas for the entourage for four days. What do you think?' says the assistant down the phone.

'Right,' I say. 'When for?'

'Next weekend.'

'Coming when?'

'This Thursday.'

'I'll see what I can do.' I make a note of his number and promise to call him back.

'Who's that?' asks Kate.

'The Crown Prince of Saudi.'

'Really?' asks Kate, looking a little puzzled.

'Well, you know, one of his assistants.'

'Right,' she nods, suddenly a whole lot less interested.

'I've got to call Garry.'

I get Garry on the phone and make the poor sod open up his office and look at the reservations on the computer. He sounds a little grumpy and possibly a little drunk, very much as if I have woken him up from an afternoon snooze in front of *The Sound of Music*.

'We can't do it,' he yawns.

'Make us do it,' I say.

'Look, mate!' he snaps. 'There is just no fucking way. We're full and that's the end of it.'

'But I just can't bear bumping them on to the One and Only, or the Four Seasons,' I sigh.

'There's always the Oberoi.'

'They're all a bunch of cunts. I hate the lot of them.'

'I know,' he agrees. 'But, you know, think who you could curry favour with.'

'Think of the tips,' I moan.

'And the watches.'

'All that lovely lost revenue. Are you sure you can't squeeze them in?'

'It's quite hard to squeeze in a big group like that. Can't he ditch some?'

'He's got about thirty wives and about thirty-five children, he's not the sort of bloke to travel lightly,' I say.

'Well then, there's nothing.'

'I know, but . . .'

'But nothing,' he insists. 'The sooner you accept that is is not going to happen, the sooner I can get back to y tinny and a video and you can carry on drinking ur expensive wine.'

'How did you know I was drinking expensive wine?'

'You always do, mate. It's a Sunday evening and u're always on a nice bit of wine.'

'Am I that predictable?'

'We're all creatures of habit, mate.'

'Which is why we want the crown prince here, cause it means he'll come back.'

'The answer's no. Piss off and don't call me again. I n relaxing, watching a film.'

'Which one?'

'*Chicago*.'

'Damn it. I had you down to be watching *The Sound Music*.'

'I am a queen, mate, not a teenage girl. And you can ll your sheikh mate the answer's no.'

'He's a king.'

'I am hanging up now,' says Garry, and he does.

I call the crown prince's assistant's assistant and tell m the sad news. He asks whether if the crown prince anges his dates a bit, I might be able to fit him in. And ell him the answer is still no. This weekend is full. He

asks me to suggest an alternative, and I find myse
choking on the words 'Four Seasons'.

'The what?' the man asks again.

'Obviously there is nowhere nearly as good as here
I hear myself saying.

'I know that,' he replies. 'That is why we called yo
first. But other than you? It would be good to suggest
few places.'

In the end I tell them to go to the Four Seasons, as
know they would bump on to us if they were in th
same position, and they did give us a nice dinne
the other day. I don't have a relationship with ar
of the managers at the One and Only or at the Oberc
I then make a quick call to the Four Seasons, just t
make sure they have clocked my generosity. They a
effusive and grateful and tell me how fabulous I ar
and I pour myself another glass of wine.

I am just congratulating myself for being so nice ar
generous to the competition when Ben pokes his hea
around the door.

'It seemed a little stupid to ring the bell,' he say
'when I could just walk straight in.'

'Hi, sorry, lovely to see you,' I say, getting up fro
the computer.

'Looking at cars?' he asks, looking over my shoulde

'Afraid so,' I laugh.

'I imagine the need for motor porn gets quite ba

after a few months on the island,' he says, taking a close look at the Porsche.

'Yup,' I say.

'I tell you what I'm missing,' he says.

'What?'

'Adverts.'

'Really?'

'I am so used to seeing them, it is a little weird. I also can't help thinking that real life is happening elsewhere and I am being left behind.'

'You get over that pretty quickly,' I say. 'Drink?'

'Please,' he nods. 'Whatever you're drinking is fine.'

'Yeah, you get over the real-life idea,' I say. 'Who's to say that working in a city and bustling from A to B is any more real than this?'

'Um, I do,' he says, taking a large sip of his glass of cold white wine. 'This is like Mogadon living – a sleepy life with all the rough edges taken off. It makes it much less exhilarating than living in the Big Smoke. You don't use your adrenalin much. There's not exactly much hunting and gathering to be done between here and the spa, is there? That's why you're looking longingly at fast cars on your day off.'

'Quite possibly,' I say, taking another sip of wine. I am exhausted this evening and not in the mood to start justifying my many complicated life decisions to Ben.

'It's a good place for kids,' says Kate, sitting down on the bed.

'If only either of us had any,' says Ben, walking out through the French windows towards the beach. 'Good view.'

'We like it,' I say.

'It is a fuck of a lot better than mine,' says Ben. 'Honestly,' he adds, turning around to face me, 'you could have warned me that this place is a dive unless you're a manager.'

'You *are* a manager,' says Kate. 'Anyway, your last place can't have been much better.'

'But at least I could leave it at the weekend.'

'You can leave here,' she says.

'And go where?'

'To the mainland? Another island?'

'From one island to another? Please,' he says, knocking back his glass of wine in one.

'Do you want a top-up?' I ask.

'The food's on its way,' says Kate. 'I have asked them to come up with something a little special.'

'What, off menu?' asks Ben.

'Something like that,' she smiles.

'Thank God for that,' he sighs. 'I am bored shitless of eating off that thing and I've only been here a week. Christ knows what you lot must feel.'

'Yeah, I know what you mean,' nods Kate.

Ben flops down on the sunbed and kicks his shoes off in the sand. He pushes his reflector shades up on to the top of his head. The sun is dipping down behind the waves. There are a few small clouds in the sky. It is going to be a stunning sunset.

'What do you miss most, then?' he asks, holding his glass up as I pour him a refill.

'Where to start?' Kate inhales. 'Food-wise it is weird stuff like carrot cake, muesli bars covered in yogurt, nice chocolate, sausages, coconut yogurts, Magnum ice creams, crisps. You know, real food that people have in their homes, not bloody hotel food the whole time. Toast and Vegemite.'

'Ham sandwiches. Really good ham sandwiches with English mustard.' I take a swig of wine. 'A fucking ploughman's!'

'A proper cup of coffee in a shop with a view and magazines,' says Kate. 'Reading a magazine that is not out of date.'

'Going to a football match, a concert, a play,' I laugh. 'And I don't even like the theatre!'

'Shops,' says Kate. 'To be able to go shopping. I feel as if I'm turning into one of the Desperates.'

'To be able to wear something that is not linen,' I say.

'Jeans!' says Kate. 'And heels and a handbag. I don't carry a handbag here. What would I put in it? Money and house keys?'

'And food that is laid out flat on a plate and not piled up in a tower,' I add. 'A pint. From a pub. With a friend.'

'Underwear!' chimes in Kate. 'All my bras and pants are grey and there is nowhere to get sexy underwear. Oh, and I would love to look at a furniture shop.'

'A furniture shop?' says Ben. 'What the fuck is that about?'

'I don't know,' smiles Kate, her feet swinging on the hammock. 'A desire to be like a normal couple. To go furniture shopping at the weekend. You know,' she shrugs. 'Isn't that what people do?'

'They go and shout at each other in Ikea,' says Ben.

'I'd love to have an argument in Ikea,' says Kate wistfully.

'One thing about living out here is that it makes you realize how few things you need,' I say, trying to sound a little less desperate and a little more sanguine.

'Tell that to all the tossers who tip up here with their Louis Vuitton suitcases, private jets, super yachts and designer watches. They are all at the cutting edge of consumerism,' says Ben.

'Yeah, well.' I shrug.

'Who wants some Cristal champagne?' announces Jean-François, popping his head out through the sliding doors of the villa.

'Oh hello!' says Kate, getting up out of the hammock. 'Sorry, we didn't hear you.'

'Don't worry,' he replies. 'Who wants some bubbles?' he asks, waving a magnum of Cristal about in front of him.

'Where did you get that?' I ask, already knowing the answer.

'Our friend Mr Georgi is a very generous man,' smiles Jean-François.

'How very kind of him,' says Kate, draining her glass of wine in preparation for a bubbly refill.

'Isn't he just?' says Ben, doing the same.

Jean-François joins us just as five or six waiters arrive from the restaurant with trays and trays of food for our Lebanese feast. They set the whole thing up towards the shore, laying out carpets and lighting flares and putting out endless little titbits on low flat tables. It is a fantastic-looking spread. Even Ben perks up as they leave and is the first to grab a fistful of pitta and a skewer of grilled chicken.

'Now this is more like it,' he says, flopping down on the carpet in the middle of the beach. 'Some meat, champagne and a good sunset with your mates. It beats a Coke and popcorn at the cinema, don't you think?'

'Well,' I smile, sitting down next to him. 'It depends what time of day and day of the week you are asking me.'

'Now?'

'Then yes. It does. Cristal and a sunset win every

time.' We clink glasses and both take a sip. 'But this job is exhausting,' I say. 'There is no differentiation between home and work. I'm driving the buggy home, it's raining and I come across a pothole – I'm the person who sorts it. I am walking through the village and someone wants to talk to me. I walk into the dining room and the first thing I look at is if any of the light bulbs need changing, and if there are, why haven't they been done? I've got OCD. I drive home, I see a guest walking, I offer to give them a lift. You are always on duty.'

'There are worse jobs,' says Ben, knocking back a bit more fizz. 'Got any cigars?'

'Does Dolly Parton sleep on her back?'

Ben and I are sniffing our way through my extensive cigar collection when the villa phone goes. I try to ignore it above the music, but it refuses to stop.

'What?' I ask, finally picking the thing up.

'There's a fight in the village. I think you need to come,' says Bernard.

'Are you sure?'

'Quite sure,' he says. 'Six of the locals have been beating the shit out of each other.'

By the time I get myself to the staff village, things have quietened down a bit, but I can see that Bernard was not joking. There are patches of glutinous blood on the ground, there are smashed-up chairs, a couple of broken windows – it has been some fight. Bernard and Mohammed have the culprits in my office. They are a sorry, sweaty-looking bunch with cuts to their faces and hands. Some of them have ripped clothes, others just look like someone's tap-danced on their face. All six of them are being terminated tonight and will be ferried off the island just as soon as I get the paperwork sorted.

It takes me a couple of hours to rubber-stamp everything. I am sure if I was totally sober things might be a little bit speedier, but you know, it is Sunday night.

So it is eleven o'clock by the time everyone is gathered on the jetty. The giant floodlights are on and all the fired employees are lined up in a row with their hands behind their backs. The situation looks quite bizarre, like we are about to perform some sort of prisoner exchange in a Cold War movie. The engine on the staff ferry is churning over, spewing fumes into the air, as the disgraced waiters and one gardener shuffle on board. There is quite a crowd on the jetty. Some are there to witness the mass firing, others are there to say goodbye to Yoshiji and Angela.

Once the sacked locals have made their woeful exit on to the staff ferry, Yoshiji appears from the shadows. He has a kit bag on his back and is high-fiving and glad-handing his mates as he walks through the applauding crowd. He seems to be on his own. Then just as he stands by the ferry, giving everyone a final wave, Angela bursts weeping and wailing through the crowd.

'Don't leave me! Don't leave me!' she says, throwing herself at him, clasping his knees. 'Please don't leave me behind!'

'What happened there?' I ask Garry, who is standing next to me and is as reliable as Popbitch.

'He's realized that you can't take relationships off the island, so he chucked her this afternoon and is moving on to bigger and better things.'

'And she?'

'She is obviously a little pissed off about this.'

'Right.'

'And will probably weep for a day or two before getting drunk at the staff bar and sleeping with someone else ... possibly him.' He points to Ben, who appears to be walking towards me through the bright searchlights, holding his suitcases. 'Or maybe not,' says Garry, noticing the cases at the same time as I do.

'I'm sorry, mate,' says Ben, shaking his head. 'I'm going. I'm taking the boat outta here. Thanks for the opportunity.' He shakes my hand. 'But I can't stick it here. I can't last another week, let alone a whole fucking two years. It'll drive me mad. I'll end up swimming for it. It is Alcatraz, mate, and you're welcome to it,' he says, giving me a final wave as he walks along the gang-plank.

Bastard, I think, as I squint at him through the glare of the bright floods. Tomorrow I've got to find myself a bloody new deputy manager. Still, I've got a super-model, an Oscar-winning actress, a Greek shipping tycoon and the best tennis player in the world all turning up next week. And another nice chilled bottle of Dom sitting in my fridge. I can think of worse ways to start yet another shitty week in paradise.

HOTEL BABYLON
By Imogen Edwards-Jones & Anonymous

'Something strange occurs to guests as soon as they check in. Even if in real life they are perfectly well-mannered, decent people with proper balanced relationships, as soon as they spin through the revolving hotel doors the normal rules of behaviour no longer seem to apply.'

All of the following is true. Only the names have been changed to protect the guilty. All the anecdotes, the stories, the characters, the situations, the highs, the low, the scams, the drugs, the misery, the love, the death and the insanity are exactly as was told by Anonymous – someone who has spent his whole career working in hotels at the heart of London's luxury hotel industry. However, for legal reasons, the stories now take place in a fictitious hotel known as Hotel Babylon. More than a decade is compressed into twenty-four hours. Everything else is as it should be. The rich spend money, the hotel makes money and the chambermaids still fight the bellboys over a two-pound coin. It's just another twenty-four hours in an expensive London hotel.

'Informative, disgusting and utterly fascinating'
Closer

'Reading *Hotel Babylon* is like mainlining Popbitch'
Metro

'Makes shock revelation after shock revelation'
Daily Mail

'An eye-opener . . . with plenty of tips for the frequent traveller'
The Economist

'Five stars for excess' 'Amusing and appalling'
Sunday Telegraph

9780552151467

CORGI BOOKS

AIR BABYLON
By Imogen Edwards-Jones & Anonymous

'A fascinating exposé of life in the sky'
Marie Claire

Do you know the best place to have sex on a plane?
Do you know that one drink in the air equals three on
the ground? Do you know who is checking you in?
Who is checking you out? Do you know what happens
to your luggage once it leaves your sight? Is it secure?
Are you safe? Do you really know anything about the
industry to which you entrust your life
several times a year?

Air Babylon is a trawl through the highs, the
lows and the rapid descents of air travel. It catalogues
the births, the deaths, the drunken brawls, the sexual
antics and the debauchery behind the scenes of the
ultimate service industry – where the world is
divided into those who wear the uniform
and those who don't . . .

'A shocking but fantastic book'
OK! magazine

'Juicy stuff'
Heat

'Some readers may find a stomach-distress
bag essential'
Sunday Telegraph

9780552153058

CORGI BOOKS

FASHION BABYLON
By Imogen Edwards-Jones & Anonymous

'Jaw-dropping stuff . . . A real must read for anyone
interested in fashion or obsessed by celebrity'
Heat

What is fashion? Who decides what's in and what's
out? Is the catwalk really that catty? Is everyone high
on drugs and full of champagne? What makes a
supermodel so super?

Exquisitely cut and gorgeously detailed, *Fashion Babylon*
takes you through six months in a designer's life. It explains
how the fashion business works – the mark-ups and the
come-downs, the fabulous extremes and the shoddy
short-cuts. Find out who goes to the shows, where they
sit and whose backside they have to kiss to get there.

Whether you just like a bit of shopping or you're a
hardcore fashionista. *Fashion Babylon* will change the
way you sashay into Topshop, flick through the pages
of *Vogue* and worship at the temple of
Harvey Nichols for ever!

'Witty and naughty, it is a must read for every fashionista'
Daily Mail

'The revelations spill out in a succession of bitchy
exchanges that leave you rubbing your hands with glee'
Daily Telegraph

9780552154437

CORGI BOOKS